Complete Guide
to Open Source Big
Data Stack

Michael Frampton

Complete Guide to Open Source Big Data Stack

Michael Frampton
Paraparaumu, New Zealand

ISBN-13 (pbk): 978-1-4842-2148-8   ISBN-13 (electronic): 978-1-4842-2149-5
https://doi.org/10.1007/978-1-4842-2149-5

Library of Congress Control Number: 2018930257

Cover image by Freepik (www.freepik.com)

Managing Director: Welmoed Spahr
Editorial Director: Todd Green
Acquisitions Editor: Susan McDermott
Development Editor: Laura Berendson
Technical Reviewer: Olav Jodens
Coordinating Editor: Rita Fernando
Copy Editor: Deanna Hegle

Distributed to the book trade worldwide by Springer Science+Business Media New York, 233 Spring Street, 6th Floor, New York, NY 10013. Phone 1-800-SPRINGER, fax (201) 348-4505, e-mail orders-ny@springer-sbm.com, or visit www.springeronline.com. Apress Media, LLC is a California LLC and the sole member (owner) is Springer Science + Business Media Finance Inc (SSBM Finance Inc). SSBM Finance Inc is a **Delaware** corporation.

For information on translations, please e-mail rights@apress.com, or visit http://www.apress.com/rights-permissions.

Apress titles may be purchased in bulk for academic, corporate, or promotional use. eBook versions and licenses are also available for most titles. For more information, reference our Print and eBook Bulk Sales web page at http://www.apress.com/bulk-sales.

Any source code or other supplementary material referenced by the author in this book is available to readers on GitHub via the book's product page, located at www.apress.com/9781484221488. For more detailed information, please visit http://www.apress.com/source-code.

Printed on acid-free paper

I would like to dedicate this book to my wife and son whose support has enabled me to complete this project.

Table of Contents

About the Author

Michael Frampton has been in the IT (information technology) industry since 1990, working in a variety of roles (tester, developer, support, quality assurance), and in many sectors (telecoms, banking, energy, insurance). He has also worked for major corporations and banks as a contractor and a permanent member of the staff, including Agilent, BT, IBM, HP, Reuters, and JP Morgan Chase. The owner of Semtech Solutions, an IT/Big Data consultancy, Mike Frampton currently lives by the beach in Paraparaumu, New Zealand, with his wife and son. Mike has a keen interest in new IT-based technologies and the way that technologies integrate. Being married to a Thai national, Mike divides his time between Paraparaumu or Wellington in New Zealand and their house in Roi Et, Thailand.

About the Technical Reviewer

**Olav Jordens** is the technical lead in the big data space at a data-driven telco in New Zealand. His experience in big data has branched out from a decade working in advanced mathematical modelling in investment banking, to applying NoSQL systems in health care informatics, to his current role centered on the Hadoop ecosystems integrated into the core data center of the telco.

Acknowledgments

I would like to thank my wife and son without whose support I don't think a writing project like this would be possible. I would also like to thank the Apress publishing team (Rita Fernando, Laura Berendson, Susan McDermott) and the reviewers (Olav Jordens, Sumit Pal) for their help in developing this book. Finally, I would like to thank all of the people who gave their time to answer my questions and assist me.

Although I was already aware of the importance of Apache Mesos as a cluster manager for Apache Spark, I would also like to thank some of the staff at Basho.com. In the time that this book has taken to develop, Basho ran out of funding and was placed into receivership. However, I would like to thank former Basho staff members Pavel Hardak and Stephen Condon. It was while working with them on MARQS (the Mesos/Riak-based big data stack) that I was inspired to write this book.

Introduction

I have developed this book to investigate Mesos-based cluster development and integration. I found that data center operating system (DCOS; and it's command-line interface [CLI]) was a natural progression from basic Mesos; so you will find that the later chapters of this book concentrate on that. Within the limits of the funding and time available to me, I have investigated each element of a Mesos-based big data stack, starting with a local cloud on Apache CloudStack followed by Apache Brooklyn for release management. Chapters are topic specific covering Mesos-based resource management, storage, processing, and queueing. I examine application frameworks like Akka and Netty; and finally, I cover visualisation.

As with previous book projects, I have taken an integration-based approach, investigating how to make systems work together. I found that it was quite a challenge to create a viable and reliable DCOS-based cluster, but the result was worth the effort. DCOS provides a functionally rich and robust system once the learning curve is mastered.

This book is aimed at anyone who is interested in big data stacks based on Apache Mesos and Spark. It would be useful to have some basic knowledge of Centos Linux and Scala. But don't be deterred if you don't; I believe that if you are interested in these topics and willing to learn, you will succeed. Most chapters contain examples that you can follow to gain a better understanding. I would advise completing the practical examples yourself to increase confidence.

This book covers each topic to the extent that time and resources have allowed. Having completed the book, I am aware that there are many other topics that I would have liked to have examined such as DCOS framework development, Mesos framework intercommunication, and Brooklyn releases to DCOS. I hope that I will be able to address these topics at some point in the future.

In the first chapter, I will provide a fuller introduction to the book architecture and chapter contents. I will describe the big data stack structure as well as extended topics such as scaling and "cloud or cluster."

Contact the Author

As with previous books, I am happy for people to contact me, although I don't guarantee that I will have the time or resources to investigate your problems. Details about my books can be found on my author page on Amazon by following this link:

amazon.com/Michael-Frampton/e/B00NIQDOOM/

I can also be contacted via the LinkedIn web site at the following address:

nz.linkedin.com/pub/mike-frampton/20/630/385

I am happy for you to connect with me there. I also maintain a series of big-data based, easy to understand presentations here:

slideshare.net/mikejf12/presentations

Feel free to take a look and even suggest subjects that you might like to see covered. Finally, you can contact me via my web site (semtech-solutions.co.nz) or email at

info@semtech-solutions.co.nz

I am always interested in new technology, new opportunities, and any type of big data integration. We all have to earn a living, so if you have any projects that you need help with, by all means contact me.

Remember that if you encounter problems, try to find your own solution, keep trying possible solutions, and keep moving. Try joining groups and mailing lists related to the system that you are having the problem with. Join the community and ask for help as well as try to help others. By solving your own problems and just "keeping at it," you will become a more confident person. If you have a question, try to present it with a number of possible solutions.

## CHAPTER 1

The Big Data Stack Overview

This is my third big data book, and readers who have read my previous efforts will know that I am interested in open source systems integration. I am interested because this is a constantly changing field; and being open source, the systems are easy to obtain and use. Each Apache project that I will introduce in this book will have a community that supports it and helps it to evolve. I will concentrate on Apache systems (apache.com) and systems that are released under an Apache license.

To attempt the exercises used in this book, it would help if you had some understanding of CentOS Linux (`www.centos.org`). It would also help if you have some knowledge of the Java (java.com) and Scala (scala-lang.org) languages. Don't let these prerequisites put you off, as all examples will be aimed at the beginner. Commands will be explained so that the beginner can grasp their meaning. There will also be enough meaningful content so that the intermediate reader will learn new concepts.

So what is an open source big data stack? It is an integrated stack of big data components, each of which serves a specific function like storage, resource management, or queuing. Each component will have a big data heritage and community to support it. It will support big data in that it will be able to scale, it will be a distributed system, and it will be robust.

It would also contain some kind of distributed storage, which might be Hadoop or a NoSQL (non-relational Structured Query Language) database system such as HBase, Cassandra, or perhaps Riak. A distributed processing system would be required, which in this case would be Apache Spark because it is highly scalable, widely supported, and contains a great deal of functionality for in-memory parallel processing. A queuing system will be required to potentially queue vast amounts of data and communicate with a wide range of data providers and consumers. Next, some kind of framework will be required to create big data applications containing the necessary functionality for a distributed system.

© Michael Frampton 2018

M. Frampton, *Complete Guide to Open Source Big Data Stack*, https://doi.org/10.1007/978-1-4842-2149-5_1

Given that this stack will reside on a distributed cluster or cloud, some kind of resource management system will be required that can manage cluster-based resources, scale up as well as down, and be able to maximize the use of cluster resources. Data visualisation will also be very important; data will need to be presentable both as reports and dashboards. This will be needed for data investigation, collaborative troubleshooting, and final presentation to the customer.

A stack and big data application release mechanism will be required, which needs to be cloud and cluster agnostic. It must "understand" the applications used within the stack as well as multiple cloud release scenarios so that the stack and the systems developed on top of it can be released in multiple ways. There must also be the possibility to monitor the released stack components.

I think it is worth reiterating what "big data" is in generic terms, and in the next section, I will examine what major factors affect big data and how they relate to each other.

What Is Big Data?

Big data can be described by its characteristics in terms of volume, velocity, variety, and potentially veracity as Figure 1-1 shows in the four V's of big data.

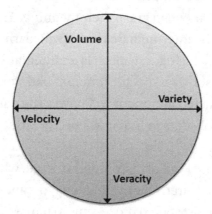

Figure 1-1. The four V's of big data

Data volume indicates the overall volume of data being processed; and in big data, terms should be in the high terabytes and above. Velocity indicates the rate at which data is arriving or moving via system ETL (extract, transform, and load) jobs. Variety indicates the range of data types being processed and integrated from flat text to web logs, images, sound, and sensor data. The point being that over time, these first three V's will continue to grow.

If the data volume is created by or caused by the Internet of things (IoT), potentially sensor data, then the fourth V needs to be considered: veracity. The idea being that whereas the first three V's (volume, velocity, and variety) increase, the fourth V (veracity) decreases. Quality of data can decrease due to data lag and degradation, and so confidence declines.

While the attributes of big data have just been discussed in terms of the 4 V's, Figure 1-2 examines the problems that scaling brings to the big data stack.

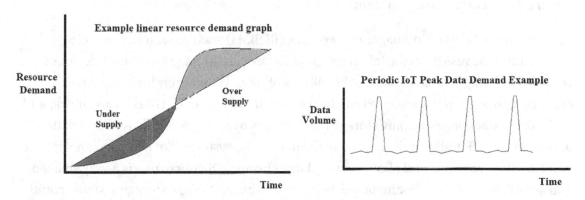

Figure 1-2. *Data scaling*

The figure on the left shows a straight line system resource graph over time with resource undersupply shown in dark grey and resource oversupply shown in light grey. It is true the diagram is very generic, but you get the idea: resource undersupply is bad while oversupply and underuse is wasteful.

The diagram on the right relates to the IoT and sensor data and expresses the idea that for IoT data over time, order of magnitude resource spikes over the average are possible.

These two graphs relate to auto scaling and show that a big data system stack must be able to auto scale (up as well as down). This scaling must be event driven, reactive, and follow the demand curve closely.

3

Where do relational databases, NoSQL databases, and the Hadoop big data system sit on the data scale? Well if you image data volume as a horizontal line with zero data on the left most side and big data on the far right, then Figure 1-3 shows the relationship.

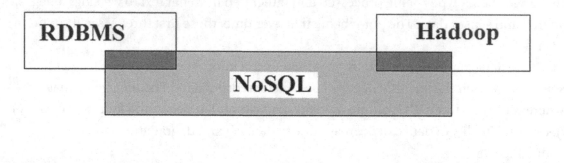

Data Volume

Figure 1-3. *Data storage systems*

Relational database management systems (RDBMs) such as Oracle, Sybase, SQL Server, and DB2 reside on the left of the graph. They can manage relatively large data volumes and single table sizes into the billions of rows. When their functionality is exceeded, then NoSQL databases can be used such as Sybase IQ, HBase, Cassandra, and Riak. These databases simplify storage mechanisms by using, for instance, key/value data structures. Finally, at the far end of the data scale, systems like Hadoop can support petabyte data volumes and above on very large clusters. Of course this is a very stylized and simplified diagram. For instance, large cluster-based NoSQL storage systems could extend into the Hadoop range.

Limitations of Approach

I wanted to briefly mention the limitations that I encounter as an author when trying to write a book like this. I do not have funds to pay for cloud-based resources or cluster time; although a publisher on accepting a book idea will pay an advance, they will not pay these fees. When I wrote my second book on Apache Spark, I paid a great deal in AWS (Amazon Web Services) EC2 (Elastic Compute Cloud) fees to use Databricks. I am hoping to avoid that with this book by using a private cloud and so releasing to my own multiple rack private cluster.

If I had the funds and/or corporate sponsorship, I would use a range of cloud-based resources from AWS, SoftLayer, CloudStack, and Azure. Given that I have limited funds, I will create a local private cloud on my local cluster and release to that. You the reader can then take the ideas presented in this book and extend them to other cloud scenarios.

I will also use small-data volumes, as in my previous books, to present big data ideas. All of the open source software that I demonstrate will scale to big data volumes. By presenting them by example with small data, the audience for this book grows because ordinary people outside of this industry who are interested to learn will find that this technology is within their reach.

Why a Stack?

You might ask the question why am I concentrating on big data stacks for my third book? The reason is that an integrated big data stack is needed for the big data industry. Just as the Cloudera Distribution Including Apache Hadoop (CDH) stack benefits from the integration testing work carried out by the BigTop project, so too would stack users benefit from preintegration stack test reliability.

Without precreated and tested stacks, each customer has to create their own and solve the same problems time and again, and yes, there will be different requirements for storage load vs. analytics as well as time series (IoT) data vs. traditional non-IoT data. Therefore, a few standard stacks might be needed or a single tested stack with guidance provided on how and when to swap stack components.

A pretested and delivered stack would provide all of the big data functionality that a project would need as well as example code, documentation, and a user community (being open source). It would allow user projects to work on application code and allow the stack to provide functionality for storage, processing, resource management, queues, visualisation, monitoring, and release. It may not be as simple as that, but I think that you understand the idea! Preintegrate, pretest, and standardize.

Given that the stack examined in this book will be based on Hadoop and NoSQL databases, I think it would be useful to examine some example instances of NoSQLs. In the next section, I will provide a selection of NoSQL database examples providing details of type, URL, and license.

NoSQL Overview

As this book will concentrate on Hadoop and NoSQL for big data stack storage, I thought it would be useful to consider what the term NoSQL means in terms of storage and provide some examples of possible types. A NoSQL database is non-relational; it provides a storage mechanism that has been simplified when compared to RDBMs like Oracle. Table 1-1 lists a selection of NoSQL databases and their types.

Table 1-1. *NoSQL Databases and Their Types*

Name	Type	URL	License
Accumulo	column	accumulo.apache.org	Apache V2
Cassandra	column	cassandra.apache.org	Apache V2
CouchDB	document	couchdb.apache.org	Apache V2
Hbase	column	hbase.apache.org	Apache V2
MongoDB	document	mongodb.org	Dual GNU
Neo4j	graph	neo4j.com	Dual GPLv3
OrientDB	key/value	orientdb.com	Apache V2
Riak TS	key/value	basho.com	Apache V2
Titan	graph	titan.thinkaurelius.com	Apache V2

More information can be found by following the URLs listed in this table. The point I wanted to make by listing these example NoSQL databases is that there are many types available. As Table 1-1 shows, there are column, document, key/value, and graph databases among others. Each database type processes a different datatype and so uses a specific format. In this book, I will concentrate on column and key/value databases, but you can investigate other databases as you see fit.

Having examined what the term NoSQL means and what types of NoSQL database are available, it will be useful to examine some existing development stacks. Why were they created and what components do they use? In the next section, I will provide details of some historic development and big data stacks.

Development Stacks

This section will not be a definitive guide to development stacks but will provide some examples of existing stacks and explain their components.

LAMP Stack

The LAMP stack is a web development stack that uses **L**inux, **A**pache web server, **M**ySQL database, and the **P**HP programming language. It allows web-based applications and web sites with pages derived from database content to be created. Although LAMP uses all open-source components, the WAMP stack is also available, which uses MS **W**indows as an operating system.

MEAN Stack

The MEAN stack uses the **M**ongoDB NoSQL database for storage; it also uses **E**xpress. js as a web application framework. It uses **A**ngular.js as a model view controller (MVC) framework for running scripts in web browser Javascript engines; and finally, this stack uses **N**ode.js as an execution environment. The MEAN stack can be used for building web-based sites and applications using Javascript.

SMACK Stack

The SMACK stack uses Apache **S**park, **M**esos, **A**kka, **C**assandra, and **K**afka. Apache Spark is the in-memory parallel processing engine, while Mesos is used to manage resource sharing across the cluster. Akka.io is used as the application framework, whereas Apache Cassandra is used as a linearly scalable, distributed storage option. Finally, Apache Kafka is used for queueing, as it is widely scalable and supports distributed queueing.

MARQS Stack

The last stack that I will mention in this section is Basho's MARQS big data stack that will be based on their Riak NoSQL database. I mention it because Riak is available in both KV (Key Value) and TS (Time Series) variants. Given that the data load from the IoT is just around the corner, it would seem sensible to base a big data stack on a TS-based database, Riak TS. This stack uses the components **M**esos, **A**kka, **R**iak, Kafka for **Q**ueueing, and Apache **S**park as a processing engine.

In the next section, I will examine this book's contents chapter by chapter so that you will know what to expect and where to find it.

Book Approach

Having given some background up to this point, I think it is now time to describe the approach that will be taken in this book to examine the big data stack. I always take a practical approach to examples; if I cannot get an install or code-based example to work, it will not make it into the book. I will try to keep the code examples small and simple so that they will be easy to understand and repeat. A download package will also be available with this book containing all code.

The local private cluster that I will use for this book will be based on CentOS Linux 6.5 and will contain two racks of 64-bit machines. Figure 1-4 shows the system architecture; for those of you who have read my previous books, you will recognize the server naming standard.

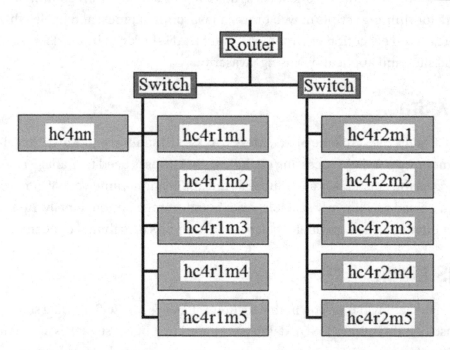

Figure 1-4. *Cluster architecture*

Because I expect to be using Hadoop at some point (as well as NoSQLs) for storage in this book, I have used this server naming standard. The string "hc4" in the server name means Hadoop cluster 4; the r value is followed by the rack number, and you will see that there are two racks. The "m" value is followed by the machine number so the server hc4r2m4 is machine 4 in rack 2 of cluster 4.

The server hc4nn is the name node server for cluster 4; it is the server that I will use as an edge node. It will contain master servers for Hadoop, Mesos, Spark, and so forth. It will be the server that hosts Brooklyn for code release.

In the rest of this book, I will present a real example of the generic big data stack shown in Figure 1-5. I will start by creating a private cloud and then move on to installing and examining Apache Brooklyn. After that, I will use each chapter to introduce one piece of the big data stack, and I will show how to source the software and install it. I will then show how it works by simple example. Step by step and chapter by chapter, I will create a real big data stack.

I won't consider Chapter 1, but it would be useful I think to consider what will be examined in each chapter so that you will know what to expect.

Chapter 2 – Cloud Storage

This chapter will involve installing a private cloud onto the local cluster using Apache CloudStack. As already mentioned, this approach would not be used if there were greater funds available. I would be installing onto AWS, Azure, or perhaps SoftLayer. But given the funding available for this book, I think that a local install of Apache CloudStack is acceptable.

Chapter 3 – Release Management – Brooklyn

With the local cloud installed, the next step will be to source and install Apache Brooklyn. Brooklyn is a release management tool that uses a model, deploy, and monitor approach. It contains a library of well-known components that can be added to the install script. The install is built as a Blueprint; if you read and worked through the Titan examples in my second book, you will be familiar with Blueprints. Brooklyn also understands multiple release options and therefore release locations for clouds such as SoftLayer, AWS, Google, and so forth. So by installing Brooklyn now, in following chapters when software is needed, Brooklyn can be used for the install.

This is somewhat different from the way in which Hadoop was installed for the previous two books. Previously, I had used CDH cluster manager to install and monitor a Hadoop-based cluster. Now that Brooklyn has install and monitoring capability, I wonder, how will it be integrated into cluster managers like CDH?

Chapter 4 – Resource Management

For resource management, I will use Mesos (mesos.apache.org) and will examine the reasons why it is used as well as how to source and install it. I will then examine mesosphere.com and see how Mesos has been extended to include DNS (domain name system) and Marathon for process management. There is an overlap of functionality here because Mesos can be used for release purposes as well as Brooklyn, so I will examine both and compare. Also, Mesosphere data center operating system (DCOS) provides a command-line interface (CLI). This will be installed and examined for controlling cluster-based resources.

Chapter 5 – Storage

I intend to use a number of storage options including Hadoop, Cassandra, and Riak. I want to show how Brooklyn can be used to install them and also examine how data can be moved. For instance, in a SMACK (Spark/Mesos/Application Framework/Cassandra/Kafka) architecture, it might be necessary to use two Cassandra clusters. The first would be for ETL-based data storage, while the second would be for the analytics work load. This would imply that data needs to be replicated between clusters. I would like to examine how this can be done.

Chapter 6 – Processing

For big data stack data processing, I am going to use Apache Spark; I think it is maturing and very widely supported. It contains a great deal of functionality and can connect (using third-party connectors) to a wide range of data storage options.

Chapter 7 – Streaming

I am going to initially concentrate on Apache Kafka as a big data distributed queueing mechanism. I will show how it can be sourced, installed, and configured. I will then examine how such an architecture might be altered for time series data. The IoT is just around the corner, and it will be interesting to see how time series data queueing could be achieved.

Chapter 8 – Frameworks

In terms of application frameworks, I will concentrate on spring.io and akka.io, source and install the code, examine it, and then provide some simple examples.

Chapter 9 – Data Visualisation

For those of you who read the Databricks chapters in my second Spark-based book, this chapter will be familiar. I will source and install Apache Zeppelin, the big data visualsation system. It uses a very similar code base to databricks.com and can be used to create collaborative reports and dashboards.

Chapter 10 – The Big Data Stack

Finally, I will close the book by examining the fully built, big data stack created by the previous chapters. I will create and execute some stack-based application code examples.

The Full Stack

Having described the components that will be examined in the chapters of this book, Figure 1-5 shows an example big data stack with system names in white boxes.

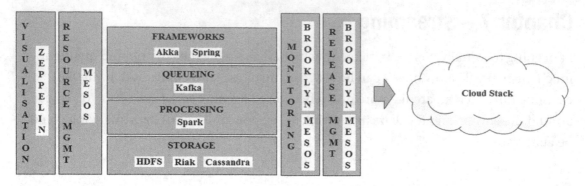

Figure 1-5. *The big data stack*

These are the big data systems that will be examined in this book to make an example of a big data stack reality. Of course there are many other components that could be used, and it will depend on the needs of your project and new projects that are created by the ever-changing world of apache.org.

In terms of storage, I have suggested HDFS (Hadoop Distributed File System), Riak, Cassandra, and Hbase as examples. I suggest these because I know that Apache Spark connectors are available for the NoSQL databases. I also know that examples of Cassandra data replication are easily available. Finally, I know that Basho are positioning their Riak TS database to handle time series data and so will be well positioned for the IoT.

I have suggested Spark for data processing and Kafka for queuing as well as Akka and Spring as potential frameworks. I know that Brooklyn and Mesos have both release and monitoring functionality. However, Mesos is becoming the standard for big data resource management and sharing, so that is why I have suggested it.

I have suggested Apache Zeppelin for data visualisation because it is open source and I was impressed by databricks.com. It will allow collaborative, notebook-based data investigation leading to reports and dashboards.

Finally, for the cloud, I will use Apache CloudStack; but as I said, there are many other options. The intent in using Brooklyn is obviously to make the install cloud agnostic. It is only my lack of funds that force me to use a limited local private cloud.

Cloud or Cluster

The use of Apache Brooklyn as a release and monitoring system provides many release opportunities in terms of supported cloud release options as well as local clusters. However, this built-in functionality, although being very beneficial, causes the question of "cloud vs. cluster" to require an immediate answer. Should I install to a local cluster or a cloud provider? And if so, what are the criteria that I should use to make the choice? I tried to begin to answer this in a presentation I created under my SlideShare space.

slideshare.net/mikejf12/cloud-versus-physical-cluster

What factors should be used to make the choice between a cloud-based system, a physical cluster, or a hybrid system that may combine the two? The factor options might be the following:

- Cost

- Security

- Data volumes/velocity

- Data peaks/scaling

- Other?

There should be no surprise here that most of the time it will be cost factors that cause the decision to be made. However, in some instances, the need for a very high level of security might cause the need for an isolated physical cluster.

As already explained in the previous section, which describes big data where there is a periodic need to scale capacity widely, it might be necessary to use a cloud-based service. If periodic peaks in resource demand exist, then it makes sense to use a cloud provider, as you can just use the extra resource when you need it.

If you have a very large resource demand in terms of either physical data volume or data arriving (velocity), it might make sense to use a cloud provider. This avoids the need to purchase physical cluster-based hardware. However, depending on the actual size, this might not be the saving that it appears to be. For very large volumes, many cloud providers require that you contract for a fixed period, potentially over a number of years.

I have added an "Other" option in the preceding list because there may be other considerations that will affect your choice of service. For instance, you might choose the SoftLayer cloud provider because you need physical, cloud-based, "bare metal" rather than virtual servers to squeeze that extra bit of performance from your Spark cluster.

If cost is your main priority, as it probably will be, make sure that you completely understand **all** of the costs involved for each option. Remember to add in the costs to move off of a physical cluster as well as a cloud-based system into your calculations. Remember that most cloud-based providers will charge you to move your data off of their systems. This cost could be considerable depending on the volume involved.

Try also to research what your competitor and brother companies are doing when making this choice. If they have moved to the cloud only to later move back to a co-located/shared physical cluster, investigate why they made the choice so that you can avoid making a costly mistake.

So in closing this section, I will say that you should do some thorough research before making a choice. If you are concentrating on cost, and you likely will be, then try to make a list of items to consider for each option you look at, such as the following:

- Costs to move data

- Costs to mothball system

- Costs associated with location

- Taxes/tax benefits

- Any vendor lock in involved?

- Cost of hardware

- Cost of hardware failures

- Energy and rental

- Personnel costs

- Data transmission

- Networking

- Other?

There will always be other costs, so try to build your lists and from there your multiyear spreadsheets to compare your options. Do the work to compare the choice of cloud vs. cluster so that you can logically support your choice from the data that you have accumulated.

The Future

The aim of this book is to show how a big data stack might be created and what components might be used. It attempts to do this with currently available Apache full and incubating systems. The aim is to introduce these components by example and show how they might work together. I think that in the very near future, some of the biggest participants in the big data scene will take this kind of approach to make an investigation like this a reality. They will create open-sourced big data stacks for IoT and analytics that will be thoroughly tested and can be trusted. They will enrich the basic components by providing extra example code and documentation. Finally, their approach will make sense and be adopted because user projects will save money through reuse and reduced configuration and coding.

Although I may not be able to create a fully integrated and tested big data stack in the short time available, they will create stacks for big data time series and analytics. I think that technologies such as Mesos, Spark, Kafka, and Zeppelin as well as NoSQL are important and will be used in such a stack.

CHAPTER 2

Cloud Storage

In this chapter, I will source and install Apache CloudStack onto my physical cluster. Remember I am not suggesting that this is the best choice for cloud-based processing; it is just because my resources are limited, and I want to examine cloud-based installs using Apache Brooklyn as well as physical cluster-based installs.

I have included the big data stack diagram from Chapter 1 here to remind the reader where Apache CloudStack fits into the architecture (see Figure 2-1). It provides a cloud installed on physical servers, and Apache Brooklyn can then be used for system component release to that cloud.

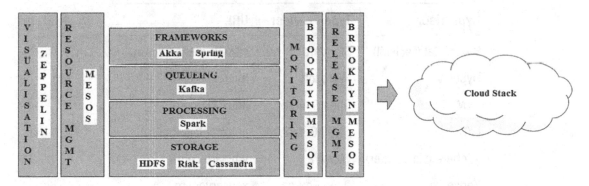

Figure 2-1. *The big data stack*

Although this chapter involves the install of Apache CloudStack, it should not be considered to be an in-depth reference. In this chapter, I will show how to source and install CloudStack as well as examine it's functionality to understand it and keep it running. The primary purpose here is to create a cheap and highly functional cloud that can be used locally and let the rest of the book progress. For those people who want more detail on CloudStack, please check the Apache-based project web site at

cloudstack.apache.org

© Michael Frampton 2018
M. Frampton, *Complete Guide to Open Source Big Data Stack*, https://doi.org/10.1007/978-1-4842-2149-5_2

This will provide further documentation as well as connect you with the project community so that you can investigate and ask questions. Before diving straight into Linux server preparation, I thought it might be useful to examine some of the concepts on which Apache CloudStack is based. The next section will cover this briefly; for further information, examine the CloudStack web site.

CloudStack Overview

Apache CloudStack is an enterprise-level, open-source system for setting up highly scalable infrastructure as a service (IaaS) systems. CloudStack can scale to many thousands of servers and support geographically distributed data centers. CloudStack uses hypervisor software on each server to support virtualisation. At the time of this writing, the current version of CloudStack is 4.10.0.0, and the supported hypervisors are as shown in Table 2-1.

Table 2-1. *CloudStack Supported Hypervisors*

Hypervisor	Type/Provider	URL
BareMetal (via IPMI)	Standard	various implementors
Hyper-V	Microsoft	microsoft.com
KVM	Open Source	linux-kvm.org
LXC	GNU LGPLv2.1+	linuxcontainers.org
vSphere (via vCenter)	VMware	vmware.com
Xenserver	Open Source	xenserver.org
Xen Project	Open Source	xenproject.org

To give an overview of CloudStack, its architecture, and terms, I will use an architectural diagram based on the docs.cloudstack.apache.org web page as shown in Figure 2-2.

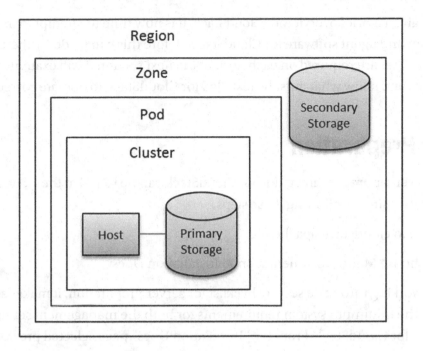

Figure 2-2. *CloudStack architecture*

The CloudStack IaaS system is described in terms of regions, zones, pods, clusters, hosts, and primary/secondary storage. Regions are the largest organisational unit within CloudStack and a means of providing fault tolerance and disaster recovery. A region is a grouping of zones in the same geographical area. A zone can be considered to be a data center and may contain one or more pods as well as secondary storage. Secondary storage can be shared by all of the pods within the zone. Zones can be public or private, with public zones being visible to all users.

Pods are equivalent to racks and are contained within zones; all hosts within the pod are on the same subnet. Pods contain one or more clusters and one or more primary storage servers. A cluster within CloudStack provides a means to group hosts. For instance, there might be multiple types of hypervisor used, so there would be a group of KVM (Kernel-based Virtual Machine) hosts as well as a XenServer server pool.

A host is the smallest organisational unit within CloudStack and represents a single server that will have hypervisor software like KVM installed. Hosts provide resources to support virtual machines. While hosts may be from different manufacturers and in different locations, all of the hosts in a single cluster must have the same resource features, that is, CPU, RAM, and so forth.

Having given a brief overview of CloudStack, it is now time to attempt to install the management and agent software for CloudStack. Before this can be done, there are prerequisites that are required on each host. In the next section, I will examine these prerequisites and show what must be installed for CloudStack to operate correctly.

Server Preparation

The current server preparation guide for CloudStack can be found at the cloudstack. apache.org web site by following these steps:

- Go to cloudstack.apache.org

- Choose Menu Documentation ➤ Installation Docs

Before working through a server checklist for server preparation, it makes sense to consider the minimum system requirements for both the management servers and cluster hosts for CloudStack. From the "Installation Docs" page selected previously, it is possible to select the option "Minimum System Requirements" under "General Installation." The next section will consider these requirements.

Minimum System Requirements

This section will cover the requirements for both the management server and the hypervisor host servers.

Management Server Requirements

The requirements for a management server for CloudStack are as follows:

- Operating System

  - CentOS/RHEL 6.3+ or Ubuntu 14.04(.2)

  - I will be using CentOS Linux 6.8

- Server type and cores

  - 64-bit x86 CPU (more cores results in better performance)

- Memory

  - 4 GB minimum

- Storage

  - 250 GB minimum, 500 GB recommended

- Network

  - At least one network interface controller (NIC)

- IP (Internet protocol) addressing

  - Must be statically allocated

- Hostname

  - Must use fully qualified domain name (FQDN)

Hypervisor Host Requirements

The requirements for a hypervisor server for CloudStack are as follows:

- Must support HVM (hardware virtual machine; Intel-VT or AMD-V enabled)

  - Enable in BIOS (basic input/output system) under processor menu

- Server type and cores

  - 64-bit x86 CPU (more cores results in better performance)

- Memory

  - 4 GB minimum

- Storage

  - 36 GB minimum

- Network

  - At least one NIC

All hypervisor hot fixes must have been applied to the server, and there must be no virtual machines running when CloudStack is installed. Also, recall from the overview that all servers within a CloudStack cluster must be homogeneous. This means that they must all have the same characteristics—that is, the same CPU, hard disk size, memory, and so forth.

Having worked through these lists and checked that the servers are ready for CloudStack, it is time to do some server preparation prior to software installs. The documentation for this can be found on the CloudStack site as follows:

1. Go to cloudstack.apache.org

2. Choose Menu Documentation ➤ Installation Docs

3. Left Hand Menu ➤ Quick Installation Guide for CentOS 6

The following sections describe the server preparation checklist options.

Check CentOS Install

Given that I am using CentOS Linux for this project, there is a minimum requirement of CentOS version 6.3. I can check this from the server hc4nn using the cat command to list the contents of the /etc/centos-release file.

```
[hadoop@hc4nn ~]$ cat /etc/centos-release
CentOS release 6.8 (Final)
```

Secure Shell (SSH) Access

During CloudStack installation, it is necessary to be able to SSH between servers as root. This option should be disabled when a system moves into production. The following commands show how this is checked:

```
[hadoop@hc4nn ~]$ su -
Password:
[root@hc4nn ~]# ssh hc4r1m1
Last login: Sat May  7 15:19:48 2016 from 192.168.1.103
[root@hc4r1m1 ~]# exit
logout
Connection to hc4r1m1 closed.
```

I have used the Linux su (switch user) command to switch the user from the Hadoop account to root. Then I have accessed the server hc4r1m1 via an SSH session as root. Having done this successfully, I have received a session prompt on that server. I have used the exit command to exit the remote server SSH session. Passwordless SSH login can be set up using the SSH-based commands ssh-keygen and ssh-copy-id. The ssh-keygen command will create a set of cryptographic keys, whereas the ssh-copy-id command can be used to copy those keys to a remote server. Check Red Hat Enterprise Linux (RHEL)/CentOS sites for the steps to configure passwordless SSH login.

Configure Network

I generally configure the network interface for my servers from the machine console; so to meet the minimum network interface option, I know that I have eth0 (Ethernet instance 0) available. I can check this using the Linux ifconfig command as shown here.

```
[root@hc4nn sysconfig]# ifconfig

eth0      Link encap:Ethernet  HWaddr D4:85:64:14:0E:30
          inet addr:192.168.1.109  Bcast:192.168.1.255  Mask:255.255.255.0
          UP BROADCAST RUNNING MULTICAST  MTU:1500  Metric:1
          RX packets:816 errors:0 dropped:0 overruns:0 frame:0
          TX packets:417 errors:0 dropped:0 overruns:0 carrier:0
          collisions:0 txqueuelen:1000
          RX bytes:84458 (82.4 KiB)  TX bytes:64590 (63.0 KiB)
          Interrupt:19 Memory:f0500000-f0520000
```

As the root user on host hc4nn, I have used the ifconfig command to ensure that the eth0 NIC exists and is running.

Check Hostname FQDN

Many systems require not just a server name to be defined but an associated domain name as well. When preparing my servers, I set this up by default.

```
[root@hc4nn sysconfig]# grep hc4nn  /etc/hosts
192.168.1.109   hc4nn.semtech-solutions.co.nz      hc4nn

[root@hc4nn sysconfig]# hostname --fqdn
hc4nn.semtech-solutions.co.nz
```

The Linux grep (global regular expression print) command here shows how the entry for hc4nn has been defined in the file /etc/hosts, IP address followed by long name then a short name. The Linux hostname command with a --fqdn switch ensures that the fully qualified domain name is defined.

Configure SELinux

To install CloudStack, SELinux (Security Enhanced Linux) needs to be in permissive mode, so some changes need to be made to the file /etc/selinux/config.

```
[root@hc4nn ~]# cd /etc/selinux; cat config

# This file controls the state of SELinux on the system.
# SELINUX= can take one of these three values:
#       enforcing - SELinux security policy is enforced.
#       permissive - SELinux prints warnings instead of enforcing.
#       disabled - SELinux is fully disabled.
SELINUX=permissive
# SELINUXTYPE= type of policy in use. Possible values are:
#       targeted - Only targeted network daemons are protected.
#       strict - Full SELinux protection.
SELINUXTYPE=targeted
```

To make SELinux change to permissive mode in the current session, use the setenforce (set enforcement) command (shown following) if SELinux is not disabled.

```
[root@hc4nn selinux]# setenforce 0
```

Otherwise these changes will take effect when the server is rebooted.

Configure NTP

The NTP (Network Time Protocol) service needs to be installed so that all cloud server clocks can be synchronized. This service is installed using the yum (Yellowdog updater, modified) command using the root account as follows. The -y switch avoids the need for confirmation during the install:

```
[root@hc4nn selinux]# yum -y install ntp
```

I won't paste the yum command output here—as long as the command finishes with the "Complete!" line, then you have succeeded. Now ensure that the NTP service starts when the server starts by using the chkconfig command with the service name "ntpd" and the on switch. Finally, start the service using the service command with the start switch.

```
[root@hc4nn selinux]# chkconfig ntpd on
[root@hc4nn selinux]# service ntpd start
Starting ntpd:                                              [  OK  ]
```

Configure CloudStack Package Repository

To install CloudStack using the Linux yum command, it is necessary to provide a configuration file for yum so that it knows how to source the install. The following command shows the file cloudstack.repo being created under /etc/yum.repos.d using the vi command:

```
[root@hc4nn ~]# vi /etc/yum.repos.d/cloudstack.repo

[cloudstack]
name=cloudstack
baseurl=http://cloudstack.apt-get.eu/centos/6/4.9/
enabled=1
gpgcheck=0
```

The contents of the file indicate the remote server to use when sourcing software using yum as well as the system name and version to source.

Configure NFS (Network File System)

I am following the Apache CloudStack quick install guide, which advises to set up primary and secondary file system mounts for storage purposes. I plan to create these file systems on the server hc4nn, which I will reserve as the cloud master host. All of the servers from rack one of my cluster will then be added to the cloud as hypervisor host resources. The primary and secondary storage directories from the cloud master host will be mounted onto those hosts. To set this up and test it, the network file system utilities package must be installed using yum as follows:

```
[root@hc4nn ~]# yum -y install nfs-utils
```

Two directories are created under the root partition for CloudStack primary and secondary storage using the Linux mkdir command on the server hc4nn as follows. The -p switch causes mkdir to create all parent directories as needed:

```
[root@hc4nn ~]# mkdir -p /export/primary
[root@hc4nn ~]# mkdir    /export/secondary
```

The /etc/exports file is then modified by adding the following lines to make sure that these directories are available as mounts:

```
vi /etc/exports
/export/secondary *(rw,async,no_root_squash,no_subtree_check)
/export/primary *(rw,async,no_root_squash,no_subtree_check)
```

(Consult the RHEL/CentOS documentation for the various options.)

Now export the /exports directory using the exportfs command in the current session.

```
[root@hc4nn ~]# exportfs -a
```

NFS V4 on CentOS 6.x needs the client domain setting to be the same on all servers. Edit the file /etc/idmapd.conf and set the domain setting to be the server domain name as follows. (Change this value to match your server domain name.) Do this on the management server hc4nn and the hypervisor hosts:

```
vi /etc/idmapd.conf
Domain = semtech-solutions.co.nz
```

Now edit the NFS file /etc/sysconfig/nfs and uncomment the following lines used to define port values:

```
vi /etc/sysconfig/nfs
LOCKD_TCPPORT=32803
LOCKD_UDPPORT=32769
MOUNTD_PORT=892
RQUOTAD_PORT=875
STATD_PORT=662
STATD_OUTGOING_PORT=2020
```

To ensure that the Linux server firewall will accept these changes, modify the file /etc/sysconfig/iptables and add the following lines at the end of the file. Make sure that the "COMMIT" line in this file terminates the file. Normally during a non-production server install, I would switch off the iptables firewall. However, to function correctly during the install, iptables must be enabled:

```
vi /etc/sysconfig/iptables
```

```
# Add entries for Apache Cloudstack4.9
-A INPUT -s 192.168.1.0/24 -m state --state NEW -p udp --dport 111 -j ACCEPT
-A INPUT -s 192.168.1.0/24 -m state --state NEW -p tcp --dport 111 -j ACCEPT
-A INPUT -s 192.168.1.0/24 -m state --state NEW -p tcp --dport 2049 -j ACCEPT
-A INPUT -s 192.168.1.0/24 -m state --state NEW -p tcp --dport 32803 -j ACCEPT
-A INPUT -s 192.168.1.0/24 -m state --state NEW -p udp --dport 32769 -j ACCEPT
-A INPUT -s 192.168.1.0/24 -m state --state NEW -p tcp --dport 892 -j ACCEPT
-A INPUT -s 192.168.1.0/24 -m state --state NEW -p udp --dport 892 -j ACCEPT
-A INPUT -s 192.168.1.0/24 -m state --state NEW -p tcp --dport 875 -j ACCEPT
-A INPUT -s 192.168.1.0/24 -m state --state NEW -p udp --dport 875 -j ACCEPT
-A INPUT -s 192.168.1.0/24 -m state --state NEW -p tcp --dport 662 -j ACCEPT
-A INPUT -s 192.168.1.0/24 -m state --state NEW -p udp --dport 662 -j ACCEPT
```

Make sure that you change the preceding IP address to match your servers. Now the firewall service iptables can be restarted to pick up these changes using the Linux service command as root:

```
[root@hc4nn ~]# service iptables restart; chkconfig iptables on
```

The rpc and nfs services also need to be started in the same way, and then the server must be rebooted. Do this on the hypervisor host and the master on which the manager file systems will be mounted.

```
[root@hc4nn ~]# service rpcbind restart; service nfs restart
[root@hc4nn ~]# chkconfig rpcbind on; chkconfig nfs on
[root@hc4nn ~]# reboot
```

After the reboot, the primary and secondary file systems must be mounted (and then unmounted) on the hypervisor host to test that the configuration is good. It is important to carry out this section correctly and ensure that the mounts work to avoid many storage-related problems later.

```
[root@hc4nn ~]# mkdir /primary
[root@hc4nn ~]# mount -t nfs4 hc4nn:/export/primary /primary

[root@hc4nn ~]# df -kh
Filesystem              Size   Used Avail Use% Mounted on
/export/primary         186G   917M  176G   1% /primary

[root@hc4nn ~] umount /primary

[root@hc4nn ~] mkdir /secondary
[root@hc4nn ~] mount -t nfs4 hc4nn:/export/secondary  /secondary

[root@hc4nn ~]# df -kh
Filesystem              Size   Used Avail Use% Mounted on
/export/secondary       186G   917M  176G   1% /secondary

[root@hc4nn ~] umount /secondary
```

This test is most useful when adding a new host to the cluster; it tests that the storage mounts on the storage server can be mounted on the new host. With these prerequisites taken care of, the CloudStack management server can be installed. This will be attempted in the next section.

CloudStack Server Install

To maintain server metadata, the CloudStack management server uses a MySQL instance. So before the management server is installed, MySQL will be installed and configured. These steps will be carried out on the management server hc4nn.

MySQL Server Install

MySQL will be installed using the Linux yum command as root:

```
[root@hc4nn ~]# yum -y install mysql-server
```

A successful install finishes with the "Complete!" line, and it is now time to configure the install. I will use the same settings as defined on the CloudStack quick install guide. The file my.cnf under /etc needs to be changed as following via the root account using vi:

```
[root@hc4nn ~]# vi /etc/my.cnf
```

The file section called "mysqld" needs to be extended with the following options

```
innodb_rollback_on_timeout=1
innodb_lock_wait_timeout=600
max_connections=350
log-bin=mysql-bin
binlog-format = 'ROW'
```

The chkconfig command is then used to ensure the MySQL server mysqld starts on server reboot using the "on" switch. The server is then started using the Linux service command with the start option.

```
[root@hc4nn ~]# chkconfig mysqld on
[root@hc4nn ~]# service mysqld start
Starting mysqld:                                    [  OK  ]
```

MySQL Connector Installation

Now the MySQL python connector needs to be installed. Create a repository configuration file called mysql.repo using the vi command as shown here:

```
vi /etc/yum.repos.d/mysql.repo
```

```
[mysql-connectors-community]
name=MySQL Community connectors
baseurl=http://repo.mysql.com/yum/mysql-connectors-community/
el/$releasever/$basearch/
enabled=1
gpgcheck=1
```

Note that gpgcheck has been enabled for the mysql connector in the preceding file (gpgcheck=1), so a gpg (GNU Privacy Guard) key needs to be imported. Import the public GPG key from the MySQL repository to enable the install to be verified.

```
rpm --import http://repo.mysql.com/RPM-GPG-KEY-mysql
```

Then install the python MySQL connector using the yum command with a "-y" switch:

```
yum -y install mysql-connector-python
```

Now that MySQL is installed, the CloudStack management server that uses it can be installed.

Management Server Installation

The management server will be installed using the yum command as the root user; the install will refer to the repo configuration file that was created earlier.

```
[root@hc4nn ~]# yum -y install cloudstack-management
```

With the Apache CloudStack Manager software installed, the Manager MySQL database can be set up using the following command:

```
[root@hc4nn ~]# cloudstack-setup-databases cloud:password@localhost
--deploy-as=root
```

You should see a success line that states that the database has been set up and that identifies the db.properties file as following:

```
CloudStack has successfully initialized database, you can check your
database configuration in
```

```
/etc/cloudstack/management/db.properties
```

The CloudStack management server installation can now be finalized by using the following script as root:

```
[root@hc4nn ~]# cloudstack-setup-management
```

If this script runs successfully, you should see the line

```
CloudStack Management Server setup is Done!
```

Given that the Apache CloudStack management server is now installed, thought must be given to system template installation. This will be examined next.

System Template Setup

The CloudStack quick start guide now advises that system templates need to be downloaded to support various hypervisors. These will be downloaded with the following command:

```
[root@hc4nn ~]# cd /usr/share/cloudstack-common/scripts/storage/secondary/
```

```
[root@hc4nn ~]# ./cloud-install-sys-tmplt\
 -m /export/secondary\
```

```
-u http://cloudstack.apt-get.eu/systemvm/4.6/systemvm64template-4.6.0-kvm.
qcow2.bz2\
-h kvm -F
```

The backslash characters that terminate the preceding command lines just allow the command to be split across multiple lines and make it easier to comprehend. The resulting templates are stored to the directory /export/secondary/template on the local server.

That concludes the Apache CloudStack server install. Now it is time to install a KVM hypervisor to support virtual instances. In the next section, I will show how this can be done.

KVM Setup and Installation

Apache CloudStack supports many types of hypervisors, as previously mentioned, to enable virtual machines to be created and run on cloud hosts. In this example of a hypervisor install, I will use KVM; as we are on a CentOS 6.x Linux host, it seems appropriate. KVM means Kernel-based Virtual Machine, and it is available as part of the CentOS 6.x install. The steps provided in this section must be carried out on the hosts that will be added to the cloud that we create. I will execute these commands on the server hc4nn.

Again, I will follow the CloudStack KVM Hypervisor quick install steps to complete this KVM install. There are a number of points to be considered, and they are discussed in the following sections.

Prerequisites

The prerequisites for this host have already been met, but if the KVM hypervisor is installed on other cloud hosts, then the following points must be considered. Use the "Minimum System Requirements" section to make the necessary changes.

- The network must be configured.

- The hostname must be defined in FQDN format.

- SELinux must be configured as permissive.

- NTP must be installed.

- The CloudStack package repository file must be installed.

31

Create Repository File

The CloudStack repository file must be created on the hypervisor host so that the CloudStack agent can be installed:

```
[root@hc4nn ~]# vi /etc/yum.repos.d/cloudstack.repo
```

```
[cloudstack]
name=cloudstack
baseurl=http://cloudstack.apt-get.eu/centos/6/4.9/
enabled=1
gpgcheck=0
```

KVM Installation

The KVM hypervisor agent can be installed as root using yum with the following command:

```
[root@hc4nn ~]# yum -y install cloudstack-agent
```

With the agent installed, KVM now needs to be configured, and there are a few parts to this.

KVM QEMU (Quick Emulator) Configuration

KVM uses the Linux libvirt (library virtualisation) library to support virtualisation, and it is the qemu hypervisor driver within the libvirt library that needs to be configured. The file /etc/libvirt/qemu.conf needs to be modified so that the following line exists and is not commented out. Make sure that the double quotes shown here exist:

```
[root@hc4nn ~]# vi /etc/libvirt/qemu.conf
vnc_listen="0.0.0.0"
```

Libvirt Configuration

The libvirt, installed as part of the agent install, now needs to be configured to listen for unsecured tcp (Transmission Control Protocol) connections. This is possible by making the following changes to the libvirt deamon file /etc/libvirt/libvirtd.conf:

```
[root@hc4nn ~]# vi /etc/libvirt/libvirtd.conf

listen_tls = 0
listen_tcp = 1
tcp_port = "16059"
auth_tcp = "none"
mdns_adv = 0
```

The parameters sent to the libvirt deamon also need to be changed in the file /etc/sysconfig/libvirtd. The following line needs to be uncommented:

```
[root@hc4nn ~]# vi /etc/sysconfig/libvirtd
LIBVIRTD_ARGS="--listen"
```

Finally, the libvirtd service needs to be restarted to pick up these changes as root as follows:

```
[root@hc4nn ~]# chkconfig libvirtd on; service libvirtd restart

Stopping libvirtd daemon:                              [  OK  ]
Starting libvirtd daemon:                              [  OK  ]
```

Check KVM Running

Now it is possible to check that the KVM hypervisor is running using the Linux lsmod command and grepping the output for the string "kvm." As shown here, all seems to be working:

```
[root@hcnn secondary]# lsmod | grep kvm
kvm_intel               55464  0
kvm                    345038  1 kvm_intel
```

To add a server to an Apache CloudStack cluster, the KVM installation section needs to be completed (assuming the hypervisor is KVM). This starts with the installation of the CloudStack agent software.

Host Naming

It is also necessary to ensure that the host is named correctly and has an entry in the /etc/hosts file that includes its fully qualified domain name. See the entries following from my server hc4nn:

```
[root@hc4nn ~]# cat /etc/hosts
127.0.0.1    localhost localhost.localdomain localhost4 localhost4.localdomain4
::1          localhost localhost.localdomain localhost6 localhost6.localdomain6

192.168.1.109    hc4nn.semtech-solutions.co.nz      hc4nn

192.168.1.113    hc4r1m1.semtech-solutions.co.nz    hc4r1m1
192.168.1.114    hc4r1m2.semtech-solutions.co.nz    hc4r1m2
192.168.1.115    hc4r1m3.semtech-solutions.co.nz    hc4r1m3
192.168.1.116    hc4r1m4.semtech-solutions.co.nz    hc4r1m4
192.168.1.117    hc4r1m5.semtech-solutions.co.nz    hc4r1m5

192.168.1.118    hc4r2m1.semtech-solutions.co.nz    hc4r2m1
192.168.1.119    hc4r2m2.semtech-solutions.co.nz    hc4r2m2
192.168.1.120    hc4r2m3.semtech-solutions.co.nz    hc4r2m3
192.168.1.121    hc4r2m4.semtech-solutions.co.nz    hc4r2m4
192.168.1.122    hc4r2m5.semtech-solutions.co.nz    hc4r2m5
```

I have ensured that the server hostnames contain the domain name as well; this means that it is the FQDN that appears when the hosts are added to CloudStack.

```
[root@hc4nn ~]# cat /etc/sysconfig/network

NETWORKING=yes
HOSTNAME=hc4nn.semtech-solutions.co.nz
```

Given that the CloudStack manager and agent software has been installed, and the steps to add a host to a CloudStack cluster have been examined, it is now time to access the CloudStack system. In the next section, I will examine the creation of a CloudStack cluster using the web-based CloudStack user interface.

CloudStack Cluster Configuration

Now that the CloudStack manager has been installed on the CentOS 6.x server hc4nn, and the CloudStack agent is running on that host, the CloudStack user interface can be accessed to finish the install. It is available at

`http://hc4nn:8080/client/`

The default account is called "admin" with a preset password value of "password." Once logged in, choose the "Continue With Basic Install" option. You will then be prompted to enter and reenter a new password for the admin account. Enter new values, and then choose "Save and Continue."

Next click OK to add a zone; I have called my zone "Zone1" and specified DNS (domain name system) addresses supplied by Google as shown in Figure 2-3.

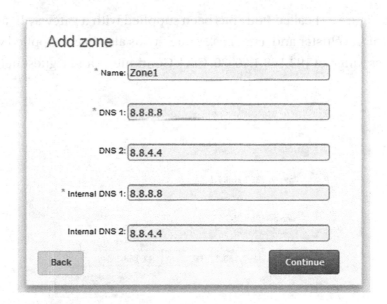

Figure 2-3. *CloudStack Add zone*

Click Continue, followed by OK to add a Pod; remember that a zone can be considered to be equivalent to a data center, and a pod could be considered to be a rack cabinet within that data center. When creating a pod, an IP address range must be supplied for the cluster-based hosts that will exist in the Pod (see Figure 2-4).

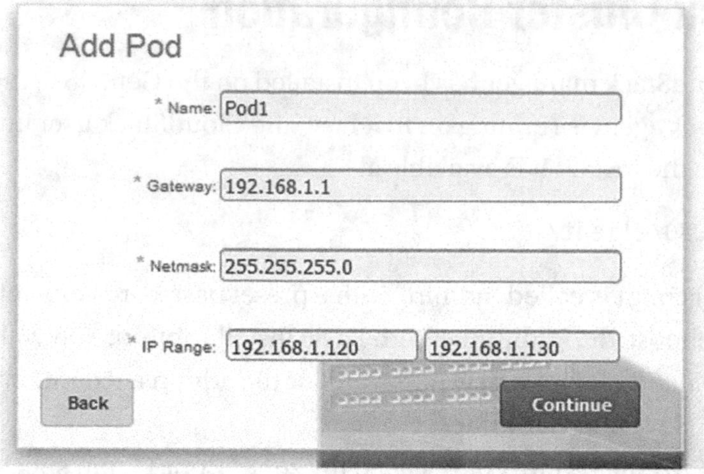

Figure 2-4. *CloudStack Add Pod*

The pod in Figure 2-4 called Pod1 has been supplied with a gateway IP address to access the rest of the cluster and a netmask value. It has also been supplied with an initial IP address range of 192.168.1.20–30. Click Continue to add a guest network (see Figure 2-5).

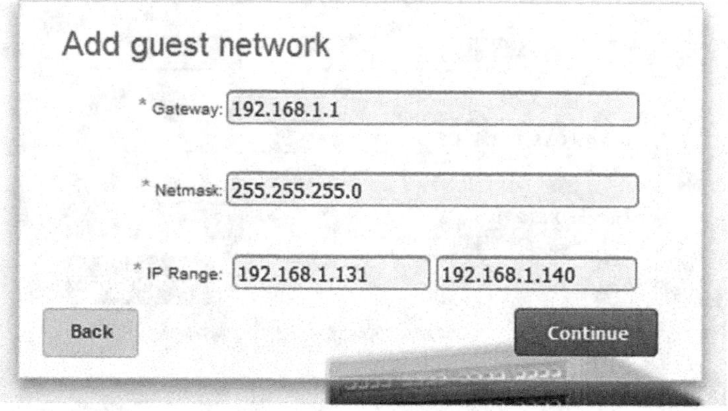

Figure 2-5. *CloudStack Add guest network*

The guest network that has been created in the Figure 2-5 has the same gateway and netmask IP addresses used during pod creation. The guest network IP address range has been set to be 192.168.1.131–140. These are the IP addresses that will be used when creating virtual instances later. Click Continue to progress, followed by OK to add a cluster. Remember that within a pod, a cluster is a group of hosts that will use the same hypervisor. Given that the OS being used in this project will be CentOS minimal installs, then the hypervisor to be used will be KVM. This happens naturally, as KVM is supplied with CentOS. A KVM-based cluster called Cluster1 has been created in Figure 2-6.

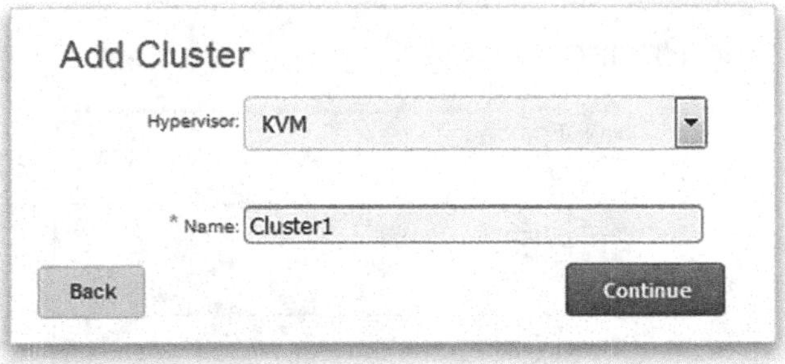

Figure 2-6. *CloudStack Add Cluster*

Click Continue followed by OK to add a host to the KVM-based cluster that was just created. Remember that the CloudStack agent and KVM steps must be followed to add extra hosts. Also, the /etc/hosts file must be set up, and the hostname should be defined as an FQDN value in /etc/sysconfig/network.

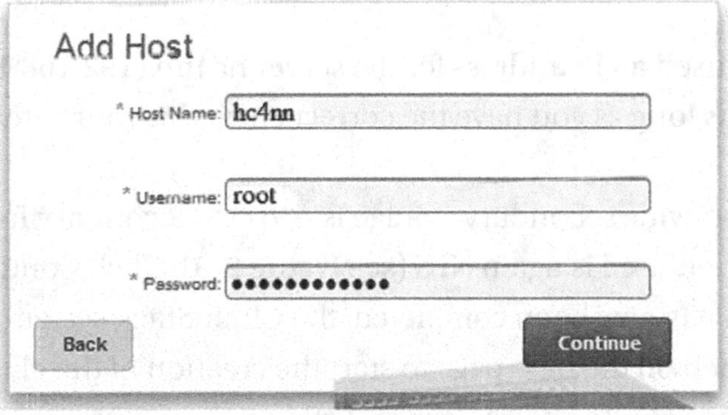

Figure 2-7. *CloudStack Add Host*

Figure 2-7 shows the host hc4nn being added to the cluster Cluster1; by default, it is a KVM-based host, as that is the type defined by the cluster. Root access has been used to add the host to the cluster. Click Continue, followed by OK, to add primary storage. Remember that primary storage is used by hosts, whereas secondary storage is available at the zone level. It is a place to store needed data like templates and ISOs for host instance creation.

Figure 2-8 shows primary storage being added to the cluster from server hc4nn using the path /export/primary. The protocol used is NFS; click Continue to progress, followed by OK to add secondary storage.

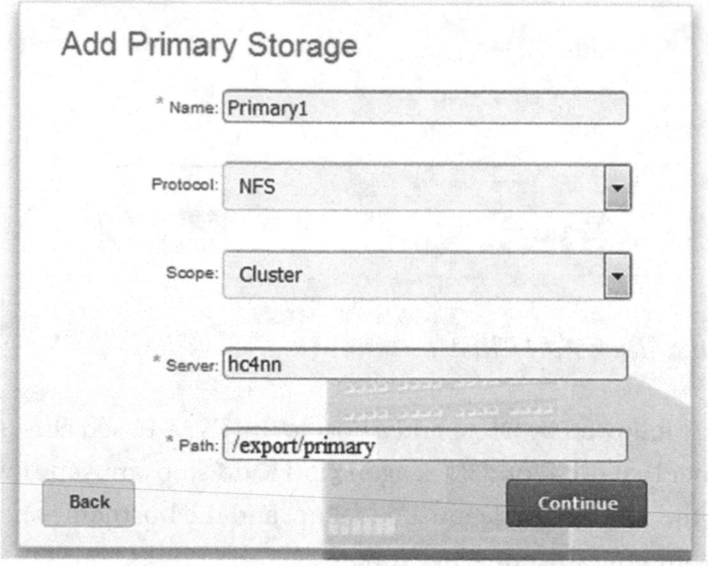

Figure 2-8. *CloudStack Add Primary Storage*

Note that I have used an IP address for the server hc4nn (192.168.1.109) to add secondary storage. As long as you have the correct entries in your /etc/hosts, you could use either method.

The path for zone-wide secondary storage is /export/secondary from the server hc4nn, and the method used is again NFS (see Figure 2-9). Click Continue to progress. As the configuration has now been completed, the CloudStack system is ready to be launched. Click launch on the next page to start the creation of the cluster; if any errors occur, then use the back button to go back and change your cluster options. Some typical errors that may occur are

- Incorrect naming of hosts to be added
- Incorrect IP address ranges
- Pod and guest network IP address ranges overlapping (they should not)

- Failure to set up /etc/hosts files correctly

- Failure to ensure that CloudStack agent is running on hypervisor hosts

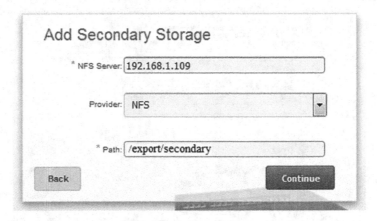

Figure 2-9. *CloudStack Add Secondary Storage*

If all goes well, you should see a screen like Figure 2-10, followed by a screen that indicates "Cloud Setup Successful." Choose the launch option to access the cloud instance user interface.

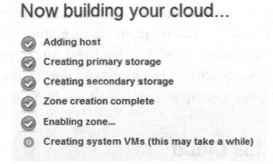

Figure 2-10. *CloudStack launch cloud*

Now the cloud that has been created, it may be examined and managed in the Apache CloudStack cloud user interface shown in Figure 2-11.

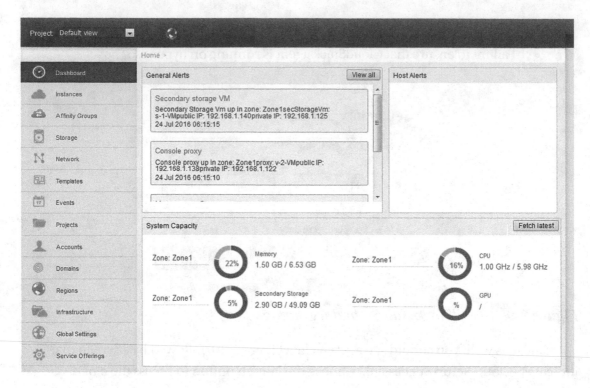

Figure 2-11. *CloudStack cloud user interface*

A dashboard is displayed on entry that shows command options on the left, alerts on the top of the screen, and system capacity graphs on the bottom of the screen.

When adding a host to a cluster in Apache CloudStack, the steps in the section "KVM Setup and Installation" must be followed. In the next section, I will show how to install hosts into the cloud using this section to prepare the hosts that will be added to the cloud.

Adding Hosts to the Cloud

Following the previous discussion, a private Apache CloudStack cloud has now been created as a target location for software installs later in the book using Apache Brooklyn. However, a cloud with a single host for storage purposes will not suffice, and so more hosts will need to be added. In this section, I will expand the cloud by adding more hosts to it.

As stated at the end of the last section, to add hosts to the cloud, each server must be prepared by ensuring that KVM is available and that the Apache CloudStack agent is installed. Follow the steps in the "KVM Setup and Installation" section, and then proceed from here.

To add a host to the cloud, select the "Infrastructure" menu option on the left of the CloudStack manager user interface, and then select "View All" under hosts (see Figure 2-12). Finally, click the "+ Add Host" button on the top right of the screen. An add host window will appear.

Figure 2-12. CloudStack Add Host

I have added this host to Zone1 ➤ Pod1 ➤ Cluster1; and given that I am creating a small cloud for demonstration purposes, I will add all of the hosts to a single, KVM-based cluster (see Figure 2-13). If a real production cloud was being created, there would potentially be multiple regions and zones (data centers) containing multiple pods (racks) that would contain multiple clusters of various types of hypervisor (KVM, Xen, HyperV).

For now, I will repeat this process to add all of the hosts in a rack of my servers to the KVM-based cluster, Cluster1.

Name	Zone	Pod	Cluster	State		Quickview
hc4r1m5.semtech-solutions.co.nz	Zone1	Pod1	Cluster1	⚪	Up	✚
hc4r1m4.semtech-solutions.co.nz	Zone1	Pod1	Cluster1	⚪	Up	✚
hc4r1m3.semtech-solutions.co.nz	Zone1	Pod1	Cluster1	⚪	Up	✚
hc4r1m2.semtech-solutions.co.nz	Zone1	Pod1	Cluster1	⚪	Up	✚
hc4r1m1.semtech-solutions.co.nz	Zone1	Pod1	Cluster1	⚪	Up	✚
hc4nn.semtech-solutions.co.nz	Zone1	Pod1	Cluster1	⚪	Up	✚

Figure 2-13. *CloudStack Cluster1 completed*

As you can see, I now have servers hc4nn and hc4r1m1 to hc4r1m5 added to a KVM-based, Apache CloudStack cluster, Cluster1. You can see from the preceding host list that it is possible to determine both the host state and cluster location from the host list details. The full server names on the left of the list are taken from the hostname defined in the file /etc/sysconfig/network on each server.

By clicking on the Quick View plus (+) icon on the right of each list server, it is possible to gain both some extra information about each server and manage each server in the list.

Figure 2-14. *CloudStack host quick view*

The details in Figure 2-14 give me the internal cloud ID of each host as well as details like its state. It also gives me some command options; for instance, I could disable the host and place it in maintenance mode if, say, a disk was failing.

Before moving on, I will mention a final point about the host list. Next to the "+ Add Host" button above the list, there is a Metrics button. Clicking that button provides the host details shown in Figure 2-15.

Resources				CPU Usage				Mem Usage			Network Usage		
Name	State	Instances	Cores	Total	Used	Allocated	Total	Used	Allocated	Read	Write	Quickview
hc4r1m5.semtech-solutions.co.nz		0 / 0	2	5.98 Ghz (x1)	0.01 Ghz	0.00 Ghz	2.58 GB (x1)	0.29 GB	0.00 GB	0.00 GB	0.00 GB	+
hc4r1m4.semtech-solutions.co.nz		0 / 0	2	5.98 Ghz (x1)	0.01 Ghz	0.00 Ghz	2.58 GB (x1)	0.29 GB	0.00 GB	0.00 GB	0.00 GB	+
hc4r1m3.semtech-solutions.co.nz		0 / 0	2	5.98 Ghz (x1)	0.01 Ghz	0.00 Ghz	2.58 GB (x1)	0.29 GB	0.00 GB	0.00 GB	0.00 GB	+
hc4r1m2.semtech-solutions.co.nz		0 / 0	2	5.98 Ghz (x1)	0.01 Ghz	0.00 Ghz	2.58 GB (x1)	0.29 GB	0.00 GB	0.00 GB	0.00 GB	+
hc4r1m1.semtech-solutions.co.nz		0 / 0	2	5.98 Ghz (x1)	0.02 Ghz	0.00 Ghz	6.53 GB (x1)	0.32 GB	0.00 GB	0.00 GB	0.00 GB	+
hc4nn.semtech-solutions.co.nz		0 / 0	2	5.98 Ghz (x1)	0.24 Ghz	1.50 Ghz	6.53 GB (x1)	2.37 GB	1.75 GB	0.00 GB	0.01 GB	+

Figure 2-15. *CloudStack host metrics*

As you can see from the list in this figure, the performance metrics are comprehensive in terms of CPU, memory, and network. This form alone could be useful when trying to monitor or track a resource issue in the cloud. Notice that the instances column lists zero for each host; no virtual KVM-based guest instances have been created on the cloud yet. That will be tackled in the next section.

Adding an Instance to the Cloud

Now that a KVM-based cloud has been created and hosts have been added to it to provide the resource necessary to support it, virtual instances need to be created that will be used for software installs within the cloud by external systems like Apache Brooklyn. This section will tackle a single creation of an instance that can then be repeated to add as many instances as the cloud can support. Use the metrics refers to Figure 2-15 host metrics as instances are added to determine the load on the hosts and the free resources available to support the addition of further instances.

Registering an ISO with CloudStack

New instances can be created from existing templates within Apache CloudStack or from ISO images. Given that I want to create instances using a 6.x minimal version of CentOS, I will register an ISO. From the Apache CloudStack interface, choose the left menu option "Templates." At the top of the screen, change the "Selected View" menu to "ISO." On the right of the screen select the "+ Register ISO" button. This brings up the Register ISO form shown in Figure 2-16, which I have already completed.

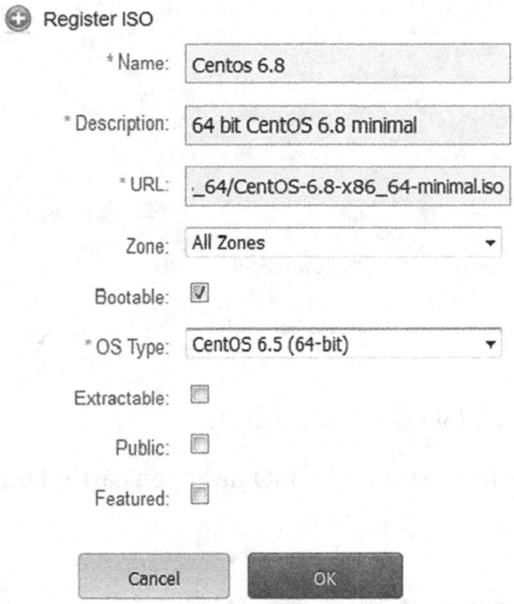

⊕ Register ISO

* Name:	Centos 6.8
* Description:	64 bit CentOS 6.8 minimal
* URL:	_64/CentOS-6.8-x86_64-minimal.iso
Zone:	All Zones ▾
Bootable:	☑
* OS Type:	CentOS 6.5 (64-bit) ▾
Extractable:	☐
Public:	☐
Featured:	☐

Cancel   OK

Figure 2-16. *CloudStack Register ISO form*

Note that this is a CentOS 6.8 minimal install ISO to be available to all zones in the cloud, which will be bootable. It will be downloaded via URL from

```
http://vault.centos.org/6.8/isos/x86_64/CentOS-6.8-x86_64-minimal.iso
```

Due to the length of time taken to write this book CentOS 6 has been deprecated in favour of CentOS 7. Hence the CentOS 6 ISO suggested above is now sourced from `vault.centos.org`.

```
http://mirror.xnet.co.nz/pub/centos/7/isos/x86_64/
```

The ISO has been given an OS Type of CentOS 6.5 because that was the latest version available within CloudStack. By clicking OK, CloudStack will download the ISO, store it, and therefore it will be available for creating new KVM based instances.

Once an ISO-based template has been created, CloudStack needs to download the ISO file for it to be used in instance creation. By selecting the ISO in the ISO templates list and clicking on the Zones tab, you can see the download state for that ISO. Figure 2-17 shows a compounded view of an ISO being downloaded in Zone1; and for another, the download is complete, and the ISO is in ready state.

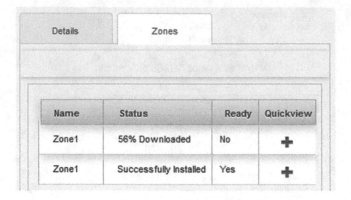

Figure 2-17. *CloudStack ISO download state*

Now that the process to download an ISO has been carried out, a virtual instance can be created using that ISO.

Creating an Instance from an ISO

To create a KVM-based virtual instance on this private cloud, the CloudStack manager menu option "Instances" can be used on the user interface. On the top right side of this page, there is an option button "+ Add Instance" to add an instance to the cloud. Click that and a wizard is started, which is shown in Figure 2-18.

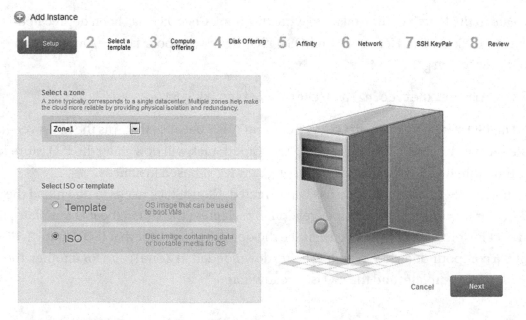

Figure 2-18. *CloudStack Add instance*

Section (1) of this wizard will lead you through the selection of the zone, Zone1, and the choice of either a template or ISO install. In this case, we will choose ISO to match the centOS 6.8 ISO that was just downloaded. Click Next to continue.

Section (2) of this wizard controls the selection of the install template to be used; select the "My ISO's" tab and select the centOS 6.8 ISO that was just created. Click Next to continue.

Section (3) of this wizard controls the selection of compute offerings in terms of the instance size; I selected small instances. Click Next to continue.

Section (4) of this wizard controls the selection of instance disk offerings, which allows the size of the virtual disk that the instance will have. Either select 5, 20, or 100 GB or set a custom value. Click Next to continue.

Section (5) of this wizard controls affinity groups; as I have no affinity groups, click Next to continue.

Section (6) of this wizard controls the instance network; I chose the default network. Click Next to continue.

Section (7) of this wizard controls instance SSH or secure shell; I have none. Click Next to continue.

Section (8) of this wizard allows a review of the instance configuration: the possibility to edit options and set the keyboard. When you are sure that all options are correct, you can click "Launch VM" to create and start the virtual guest instance on your private cloud. The result is shown in Figure 2-19.

	Name	Internal name	Display Name	IP Address	Zone Name	State	Quickview
☐	centOS-6-8-instance-1	i-2-3-VM	centOS-6-8-instance-1		Zone1	Running	+

Figure 2-19. CloudStack instance list

Note that the instance is running and has a name, a display name, an associated zone, but no IP address yet. There is a quick view option for the instance on the right of the list in Figure 2-19. The command options available depend on the state of the instance, that is, Running or Stopped. Figure 2-20 shows the options to control the instance for both states.

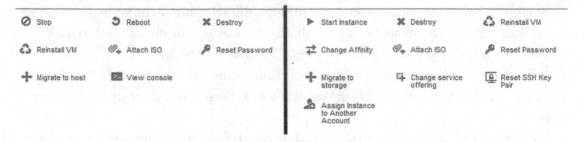

Figure 2-20. *CloudStack instance quick view options*

The options on the left of Figure 2-20 are for a started instance, while those on the right are for a stopped instance. Those that are of immediate use are the options to start and stop the instance as well as connect to the console so that the CentOS Linux install within the instance can be managed.

Note that Figure 2-20 shows the option to connect an ISO. When an instance is created, it has an ISO file connected to it, and this is used for the instance install. When you first connect to the instance via the console, a CentOS 6.8 install must be carried out. I won't display that here, as it is fairly standard. However, some points should be noted.

- When the instance install is completed, the instance should be shut down using the preceding options; and the ISO should be disconnected from the instance. Otherwise, the instance will try to reinstall again. Once this is done, restart the instance.

- Set the instance name in /etc/sysconfig/network so that it can be referenced externally.

- The network for the instance for Ethernet configuration eth0 needs to be configured. It will have been installed to use DHCP (Dynamic Host Configuration Protocol)—this will be examined following.

- The instance /etc/hosts file will need to be configured to represent the instance hostname and IP address. Again, this will be examined following.

- A static IP address will need to be assigned to the instance within the cloud so that the instance can be accessed externally from the cloud.

The single, cloud-based instance, centOS-6-8-instance-1, that has been created so far has automatically been assigned an IP address because its Ethernet configuration has been set up to use DHCP. If I open the instance console and examine the Ethernet configuration in the file

/etc/sysconfig/network-scripts/ifcfg-eth0,

I can see, as shown in Figure 2-21, the network configuration for eth0. I can see that it will be started at boot (ONBOOT=yes), that it is network manager controlled (NM_CONTROLLED=yes), and that an IP address will be automatically assigned (BOOTPROTO=dhcp).

It is important to consider this network configuration because this instance will automatically be assigned the first IP address available. That does not mean that it will always keep the same IP address when restarted or rebooted. The changing of an instance's IP address would be a problem, as I need to build a cloud-based cluster where each machine within the cloud and externally are able to address each other. So each virtual cluster instance member needs to have a static and unchanging IP address.

```
DEVICE=eth0
HWADDR=06:B2:18:00:00:11
TYPE=Ethernet
UUID=bb68ce7b-4128-4e0d-b0c8-7b86b0058087
ONBOOT=yes
NM_CONTROLLED=yes
BOOTPROTO=dhcp
```

Figure 2-21. *CloudStack instance Ethernet configuration*

I can determine this instance's IP address by using the Linux command "ifconfig -a" to show all of the instance's configured network interface information. Figure 2-22 shows the output and indicates that the instance's IP address is 192.168.1.136.

```
[root@centos-6-8-instance-1 ~]# ifconfig -a eth0
eth0      Link encap:Ethernet  HWaddr 06:B2:18:00:00:11
          inet addr:192.168.1.136  Bcast:192.168.1.255  Mask:255.255.255.0
          inet6 addr: fe80::4b2:18ff:fe00:11/64 Scope:Link
          UP BROADCAST RUNNING MULTICAST  MTU:1500  Metric:1
          RX packets:9 errors:0 dropped:0 overruns:0 frame:0
          TX packets:9 errors:0 dropped:0 overruns:0 carrier:0
          collisions:0 txqueuelen:1000
          RX bytes:1192 (1.1 KiB)  TX bytes:866 (866.0 b)

[root@centos-6-8-instance-1 ~]# _
```

Figure 2-22. *CloudStack instance Ethernet configuration*

What I need to do is ensure that the instance's IP address is defined as a static value so that other virtual instances within the cloud and servers external to the cloud can always reach it as the same address. This is important because many big data systems are clustered, and nodes within each system-based cluster need to be static. This is achieved by changing the instance's Ethernet configuration for eth0 as shown in Figure 2-23.

```
DEVICE=eth0
BOOTPROTO=static
ONBOOT=yes
NETMASK=255.255.255.0
IPADDR=192.168.1.136
NAME="System eth0"
GATEWAY=192.168.1.1
NM_CONTROLLED=yes
DNS1=8.8.8.8
DNS2=8.8.4.4
HWADDR=06:9E:D4:00:00:11
TYPE=Ethernet
UUID=edd13a79-38e0-4b5d-92bc-89976729edbd
```

Figure 2-23. *CloudStack instance static Ethernet configuration*

You can see that the instance's network configuration has now been changed to static (BOOTPROTO=static) and that a static IP address has been assigned (IPADDR=192.168.1.136). Also, values have been assigned for the netmask, gateway, and DNS servers. I can now follow this same process to statically assign IP addresses to KVM-based instances as they are created. What I have done is allocate the same IP address that was dynamically assigned to the instance from the range of values available.

So now that the process to create and configure an instance has been shown to work, the instance's position in a hybrid network must be considered. I mean that there will be servers within the cloud as well as outside of it. Can the instance "see" an external server and can an external server "see" the instance? I will use the Linux ping command to test this. I will test the server hc4r2m5, which is outside the cloud, and see whether it can ping the instance. I will then try to ping this server from the instance. Figures 2-24 and 2-25 show the results.

```
[root@centos-6-8-instance-1 ~]# ping 192.168.1.122
PING 192.168.1.122 (192.168.1.122) 56(84) bytes of data.
64 bytes from 192.168.1.122: icmp_seq=1 ttl=64 time=0.691 ms
64 bytes from 192.168.1.122: icmp_seq=2 ttl=64 time=0.609 ms
64 bytes from 192.168.1.122: icmp_seq=3 ttl=64 time=0.652 ms
64 bytes from 192.168.1.122: icmp_seq=4 ttl=64 time=0.586 ms
64 bytes from 192.168.1.122: icmp_seq=5 ttl=64 time=0.650 ms
```

Figure 2-24. *CloudStack instance ping hc4r2m5*

```
[root@hc4r2m5 ~]# ping 192.168.1.136
PING 192.168.1.136 (192.168.1.136) 56(84) bytes of data.
64 bytes from 192.168.1.136: icmp_seq=1 ttl=64 time=1.55 ms
64 bytes from 192.168.1.136: icmp_seq=2 ttl=64 time=0.261 ms
64 bytes from 192.168.1.136: icmp_seq=3 ttl=64 time=0.514 ms
64 bytes from 192.168.1.136: icmp_seq=4 ttl=64 time=0.525 ms
64 bytes from 192.168.1.136: icmp_seq=5 ttl=64 time=0.502 ms
```

Figure 2-25. *CloudStack hc4r2m5 ping instance*

From the ping commands shown here it can be seen that the instance centos-6-6-instance-1 can reach the external server because data is returned when the instance pings hc4r2m5. Also, the host hc4r2m5 being outside the cloud can see the instance; when it pings, the instance data is returned.

We have now seen how to create a basic zone within CloudStack and add hosts to a KVM cluster. The method for creating ISO template-based instances has been used to create virtual KVM-based CentOS 6.x guest instances within a cluster. It has also been shown that the instances that are created are visible from within and external to the cloud. Using these techniques, the cloud-based cluster can be expanded by adding more hosts to the cloud and more instances to create as large a virtual cluster as desired.

You may have noticed that when creating Zone1, the basic option for creation was selected in the form-based wizard. In the next section, I would like to briefly examine an advanced zone creation.

Advanced Zone Creation

An advanced zone creation provides greater control of the options used to create the zone. For instance, extra modules can be added when creating network interfaces. Many of the steps carried out to create a new zone have already been covered, so I will just mention them and fully examine the new steps.

On the left-hand CloudStack menu, choose Infrastructure; and on the Zones icon on the right-hand display, click "View All." On the top right of the page, click the "+ Add Zone" button. As Figure 2-26 shows, select the Advanced install option. Click Next.

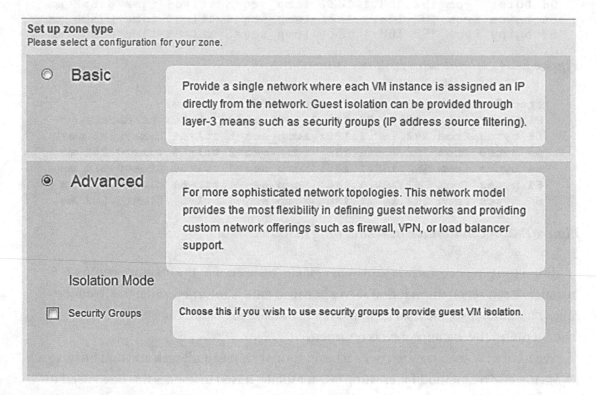

Set up zone type
Please select a configuration for your zone.

○ **Basic**
Provide a single network where each VM instance is assigned an IP directly from the network. Guest isolation can be provided through layer-3 means such as security groups (IP address source filtering).

◉ **Advanced**
For more sophisticated network topologies. This network model provides the most flexibility in defining guest networks and providing custom network offerings such as firewall, VPN, or load balancer support.

Isolation Mode

☐ Security Groups
Choose this if you wish to use security groups to provide guest VM isolation.

Figure 2-26. *CloudStack advanced zone install*

The zone form will be filled out as per Figure 2-3, only this time the zone will be called Zone2. The hypervisor will again be KVM. Set the DNS values to 8.8.8.8 and 8.8.4.4, and then click Next. The next step is new: Step 3 involves a physical network set up as shown in Figure 2-27.

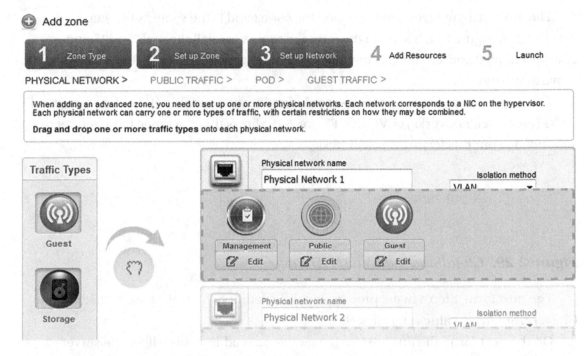

Figure 2-27. *CloudStack physical network setup*

I haven't changed any of the options here; the important part is that there is a public component to the physical network that has been set up. Click Next to assign an IP address range to the network as per Figure 2-28. Enter form details as per Figure 2-28, click add, and then next to move to the next form.

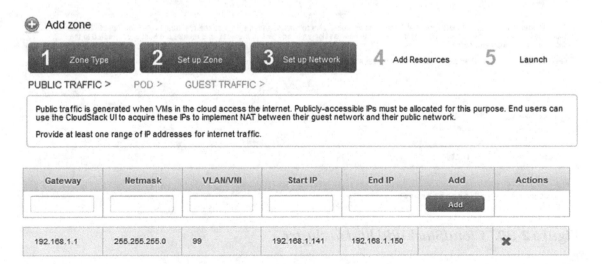

Figure 2-28. *CloudStack add IP address range*

The next form involves defining a pod for Zone2 and is the same as the step described by Figure 2-4. Just fill in the form the same way, call the pod "Pod2," and choose a new IP address range. I have chosen the range 192.168.1.151–160. Click Next to move to the next form.

The next form defines the integer-based identification number (ID) range for virtual LANs (local area networks) or VLANs. Figure 2-29 shows that the range has been set to 100–199. Fill out this form and select Next.

VLAN/VNI Range:	100	199

Figure 2-29. *CloudStack add VLAN ID range*

The next form, Step 4 in the process, involves defining the KVM-based cluster name Cluster2. Set these values and click Next.

On the next form, the first host for the new zone is added; this will be the server hc4r1m1 that was used for the NFS mount testing previously. Figure 2-30 shows the details; click Next to continue.

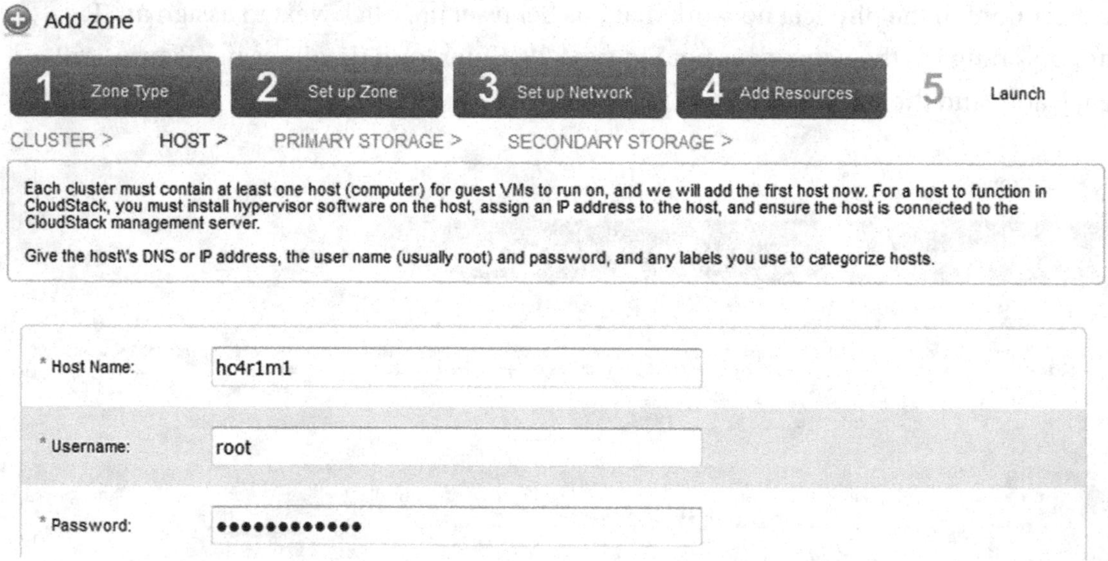

Figure 2-30. *CloudStack add host to cluster*

Primary and secondary storage are added to this zone as per Figures 2-8 and 2-9, the only difference being that the names have changed to Primary2 and Secondary2. Click Next to continue from each form.

You will now see a cloud ready to launch; follow the same steps as previously to launch the new zone-based architecture.

Before going any further, make sure that the system VMs start correctly; this is why so much attention and care was taken with storage and NFS mounts. Go to

Infrastructure ➤ System VMs

Make sure that the system VMs are in the started state as per Figure 2-31. Make sure that the VM names do not change. Constantly incrementing names would imply a storage problem.

Name	Type	Zone	VM state	Agent State	Quickview
v-1-VM	Console Proxy VM	Zone2	Running	Up	+
s-2-VM	Secondary Storage VM	Zone2	Running	Up	+

Figure 2-31. *CloudStack system VMs*

Now extra hosts can be added to Zone2 as per Figure 2-12; install template ISOs can be added to the zone as per Figure 2-16; and instances can be created in the new zone as per Figure 2-17 onward.

Having shown how virtual clusters can be created within CloudStack, I thought it would be useful to examine problem solving next.

Problem-Solving

Apache CloudStack has a characteristic of silently failing when problems occur, and so some skills are needed to be able to investigate issues that might exist. This section will provide you with some tools and techniques to enable you to examine your problems. Some indications that problems exist will be

- System VM instances will not start.

- System VM instances will constantly change state and name, the number in the name incrementing.

- Downloaded ISO files are not in ready state.

- Downloaded ISO files are not available for instance creation.

- System VM and instance consoles are not accessible.

To tackle some of these problems, the first area to check should be the CloudStack user interface events list. However, if there is no detail there, the CloudStack log files should be checked.

CloudStack Log Files

The log files available on a CloudStack host will depend on the components installed on that host. Remember that CloudStack is a master- and agent-based system with agents installed on each cloud host. The pwd (print working directory) and ls (list segments) commands following show that the logs are available under the directory /var/log/ cloudstack. They also show that the management and ipallocator logs are only available on the management server hc4nn. This should be your first area to check in case of a problem. Check log file contents for errors and java core dumps.

```
[root@hc4r1m1 cloudstack]# pwd ; ls
/var/log/cloudstack
agent

[root@hc4nn cloudstack]# pwd ; ls
/var/log/cloudstack
agent   ipallocator   management
```

CloudStack Storage

Remember that secondary storage is allocated at the zone level, while primary storage is allocated at the host level. If there is a problem with ISO-based template downloads, it could be due to a storage-based issue. When CloudStack agents start, they mount storage from the NFS-based service. The listing following is an example of this.

```
[root@hc4r1m1 cloudstack]# df -kh
Filesystem              Size  Used Avail Use% Mounted on
192.168.1.109:/export/primary
        186G  6.7G  170G   4% /mnt/f219b84d-3491-3c1b-bb50-7729622e2888
```

Within Cloudstack storage an internal ID is given, in this case "/f219b84d-3491-3c1b-bb50-7729622e2888." The preceding listing using the Linux df (disk free) command shows primary storage from hc4nn mounted onto the server hc4r1m1. It is worth manually checking that these host-based mounts exist in case of a problem.

Also, secondary storage is generally not allowed to be provided internally within the cluster. A machine outside of the cluster should be used. As I have a limited number of machines to use, I have used the machine hc4nn within the cluster for storage. To do this, I need to change the global settings value secstorage.allowed.internal.sites. This value can be found by selecting the left menu global settings option. Then search for the option value. I set it as follows:

```
secstorage.allowed.internal.sites     192.168.1.109
```

That is the IP address of the name node server hc4nn.

CloudStack System VMs

Generally, CloudStack system VMs can be accessed using the quick view "view console" option available in both instance and VM lists. The root account can be used with a password of either "password" or the value that was set when creating the cloud.

Figure 2-32 shows the secondary storage mounted on the VM s-2-VM from the management server hc4nn. In the case of a VM-based problem, it is worth checking that these mounts exist.

```
192.168.1.109:/export/secondary                    186G   6.7 G   170 G   4% /m
nt/SecStorage/b204baef-0d0a-3c0a-9786-fb28b4721d94
root@s-2-VM:~# exit_
```

Figure 2-32. *CloudStack system VMs secondary storage*

CloudStack Firewall Issues

It is also a good idea to check that firewalls are configured correctly. Try pinging between hosts and virtual instances. A badly configured host firewall can cause many of the issues described previously.

Conclusion

I have shown in this chapter how Apache CloudStack can be sourced as well as installed. I have also examined the prerequisites for cloud management as well as host cloud members. I have examined basic as well as advanced zone creation as well as the architecture of the cloud.

The aim of this chapter was to provide enough detail about Apache CloudStack to enable a cloud-based cluster to be created, and that has been achieved. Some techniques have also been introduced for problem-solving. If you encounter issues, make the Apache CloudStack web site at cloudstack.apache.org your first point of reference. Check the install documentation thoroughly, and register with the mailing lists.

The next chapter will examine Apache Brooklyn and will show how Brooklyn uses a blueprint-based process to install components to the cloud that has just been created.

CHAPTER 3

Apache Brooklyn

In this chapter, I will examine the Apache Brooklyn project, which is a system for modelling, installing, and monitoring applications based on YAML (Yet Another Markup Language) blueprint configurations. I will start by giving an overview of the Brooklyn product and then provide some detail about blueprints. Then I will source and install Apache Brooklyn, and I will also show how the user interface can be remotely accessed. The user interface will be examined to explain how Brooklyn supports the process of modelling, deployment, and monitoring. Finally, some applications will be installed to both cloud and server locations by modelling them using blueprints.

To investigate Brooklyn, I will first need to install it; the next section will show how that is done.

Brooklyn Install

In this section, I will source and install the Apache Brooklyn system on the CentOS 6.x server hc4r2m1. I will concentrate on downloading and installing the Brooklyn binaries as well as the client cli (command-line interface) application. I will use the Linux-based wget (web get) command to source the Brooklyn binaries. Because I am using a CentOS minimal install, many commands like wget are not installed with the operating system. The following command shows how the wget command can be installed using the Linux yum command. The "-y" flag just means that it is not necessary to confirm the install.

```
[root@hc4r2m1 ~]# yum -y install wget
```

I will download the Brooklyn binaries to a temporary directory /tmp/brooklyn, which can be created as follows:

```
[root@hc4r2m1 ~]# cd /tmp; mkdir brooklyn; cd brooklyn
```

© Michael Frampton 2018
M. Frampton, *Complete Guide to Open Source Big Data Stack*, https://doi.org/10.1007/978-1-4842-2149-5_3

Then both the Apache Brooklyn binaries and the cli package can be downloaded using wget as follows. These commands are sourcing Brooklyn version 0.9, the most stable version at the time of this writing. The Brooklyn source code and a vagrant-based install can also be sourced from the same location on this server.

```
[root@hc4r2m1 brooklyn]# wget http://www-eu.apache.org/dist/brooklyn/
apache-brooklyn-0.9.0/apache-brooklyn-0.9.0-bin.tar.gz
```

```
[root@hc4r2m1 brooklyn]# wget http://www-eu.apache.org/dist/brooklyn/
apache-brooklyn-0.9.0/apache-brooklyn-0.9.0-client-cli-linux.tar.gz
```

These packages are gzipped (GNU zipped) compressed tar (Tape ARchive) files, so they need to be unpacked. The downloaded files are shown here; the Linux gunzip command is then used to uncompress the files to create .tar files.

```
[root@hc4r2m1 brooklyn]# ls -l
total 57692
-rw-r--r--. 1 root root 57152333 Apr 12 23:39 apache-brooklyn-0.9.0-bin.
tar.gz
-rw-r--r--. 1 root root  1919346 Apr 12 23:39 apache-brooklyn-0.9.0-client-
cli-linux.tar.gz
[root@hc4r2m1 brooklyn]# gunzip  *.gz
[root@hc4r2m1 brooklyn]# ls -l
total 81204
-rw-r--r--. 1 root root 77834240 Apr 12 23:39 apache-brooklyn-0.9.0-bin.tar
-rw-r--r--. 1 root root  5314560 Apr 12 23:39 apache-brooklyn-0.9.0-client-
cli-linux.tar
```

Next the Linux tar command is used to unpack the two tar archives; the options passed to the tar command are x (extract), v (verbose), and f (file). The long file listing using the ls command then shows that the tar archives still exist as well as the two unpacked directory structures.

```
[root@hc4r2m1 brooklyn]# tar xvf apache-brooklyn-0.9.0-bin.tar
[root@hc4r2m1 brooklyn]# tar xvf apache-brooklyn-0.9.0-client-cli-linux.tar

[root@hc4r2m1 brooklyn]# ls -l
total 81212
drwxr-xr-x. 5 1000 1000     4096 Apr  8 21:48 apache-brooklyn-0.9.0-bin
```

```
-rw-r--r--. 1 root root 77834240 Apr 12 23:39 apache-brooklyn-0.9.0-bin.tar
drwxrwxr-x. 2 1000 1000     4096 Apr  9 00:07 apache-brooklyn-0.9.0-client-
cli-linux
-rw-r--r--. 1 root root  5314560 Apr 12 23:39 apache-brooklyn-0.9.0-client-
cli-linux.tar
```

These Brooklyn binary directory trees currently reside under the /tmp temporary directory. They need to be moved to a better, more permanent location. That is what the next commands do. The Linux mv or move command is used to move the new software directories to the /opt file system. The Linux ln command is then used to create symbolic links to those software directories so that the final paths to reach them are simplified.

```
[root@hc4r2m1 brooklyn]# mv apache-brooklyn-0.9.0-bin /opt
[root@hc4r2m1 brooklyn]# mv apache-brooklyn-0.9.0-client-cli-linux /opt
[root@hc4r2m1 brooklyn]# cd /opt

[root@hc4r2m1 opt]# ln -s apache-brooklyn-0.9.0-bin brooklyn
[root@hc4r2m1 opt]# ln -s apache-brooklyn-0.9.0-client-cli-linux brooklyn-cli
```

Now that Brooklyn is installed I will check that the server is working by running the "brooklyn" binary with the help option. The binary is found in the bin directory as follows. If all is well, the output should appear as follows. Usage information is displayed as well as some common command options:

```
[root@hc4r2m1 opt]# cd brooklyn/bin; ./brooklyn help

OpenJDK 64-Bit Server VM warning: ignoring option MaxPermSize=256m; support
was removed in 8.0
usage: brooklyn [(-v | --verbose)] [(-q | --quiet)] [-D <defines1>...]
<command>
        [<args>]
```

The most commonly used brooklyn commands are:

```
cloud-blobstore     Access blobstore details of a given cloud
cloud-compute       Access compute details of a given cloud
copy-state          Retrieves persisted state
generate-password   Generates a hashed web-console password
help                Display help for available commands
```

```
info                Display information about brooklyn
launch              Starts a server, optionally with applications
list-objects        List Brooklyn objects (Entities, Policies,
                    Enrichers and Locations)
```

See 'brooklyn help <command>' for more information on a specific command.

That looks fine, so now I will start the Brooklyn binary by using the launch command as follows. The & or ampersand character at the end of the line just runs the command in the background and frees up the terminal session later for other commands:

```
[root@hc4r2m1 bin]# ./brooklyn launch    &
```

The logged output in the session window is minimal but should be examined, as it tells the user how to access the Brooklyn user interface. Look for the line that contains the text "Started Brooklyn console at"; this shows that the console can be accessed on the local server at http://127.0.0.1:8081/.

```
OpenJDK 64-Bit Server VM warning: ignoring option MaxPermSize=256m; support
was removed in 8.0
```

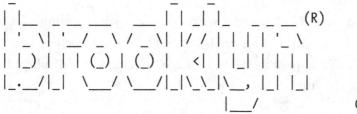

```
                                                  0.9.0
```

```
2016-09-17 15:20:05,733 INFO  No security provider options specified.
Define a security provider or users to prevent a random password being
created and logged.
2016-09-17 15:20:05,733 INFO  Starting Brooklyn web-console with
passwordless access on localhost and protected access from any other
interfaces (no bind address specified)
2016-09-17 15:20:05,734 INFO  Allowing access to web console from localhost
or with brooklyn:XHZfyuNpqf
2016-09-17 15:20:07,847 INFO  Started Brooklyn console at
http://127.0.0.1:8081/, running classpath://brooklyn.war@
2016-09-17 15:20:07,870 INFO  Persistence disabled
```

```
2016-09-17 15:20:07,870 INFO  High availability disabled
2016-09-17 15:20:11,843 INFO  Launched Brooklyn; will now block until
shutdown command received via GUI/API (recommended) or process interrupt.
```

The line in the preceding output that contains the text "Allowing access to web console" provides a username and password for accessing this Brooklyn session. The Apache Brooklyn log files are also available under the install directory within the bin subdirectory as the Linux ls command following shows. These logs should be examined, as if, like me, you want to know how to access Brooklyn across a network; you will need a username and password to gain access:

```
[root@hc4r2m1 bin]# pwd
/opt/brooklyn/bin

[root@hc4r2m1 bin]# ls
brooklyn        brooklyn-client-cli   brooklyn.info.log
brooklyn.bat    brooklyn.debug.log    brooklyn.ps1
```

If you access the preceding Brooklyn URL on the local machine, then you will not be prompted for a username and password. However, if, like me, you access Brooklyn across a network, as I suspect most people will, then you must look for the following line in the log files:

```
brooklyn.info.log:2016-09-17 15:36:24,717 INFOo.a.b.r.s.p.BrooklynUserWith
RandomPasswordSecurityProvider [main]: Allowing access toweb console from
localhost or with brooklyn: XHZfyuNpqf
```

This provides you with the necessary access details to access the user interface; the password will be randomly generated with each restart of the Brooklyn server. Once you have logged in, you will be presented with the user interface home page shown in Figure 3-1.

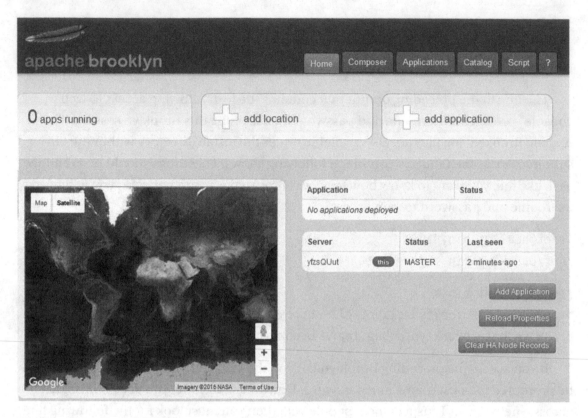

Figure 3-1. *Brooklyn home page*

There are options here to add locations and applications: both items can be defined in terms of blueprints, which we will examine later. Locations define where applications will be installed, while application definitions define what will be installed. The home page also provides a list of currently running applications. Finally, it shows the status of the Brooklyn server.

By choosing to add a location, you can either add a cloud-based location, BYON (bring your own node), to specify an existing server or specify an advanced option. Locations must be created so that they can be used in the blueprints that will be created in this chapter. Applications and the policies necessary to install and control them can then be created. Figure 3-2 shows the form that is displayed when creating a location.

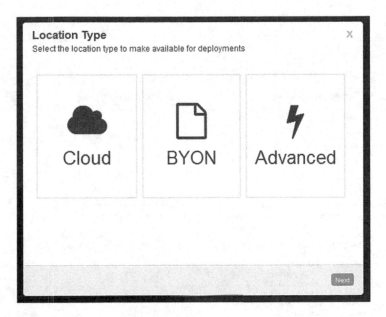

Figure 3-2. *Brooklyn add a location*

By choosing to add an application from the user interface, I am prompted with a number of template options. These options are taken from the catalog applications template list (see Figure 3-3). Select a template—I will choose the simplest one—and select the YAML composer button to move to the composer window (see Figure 3-4).

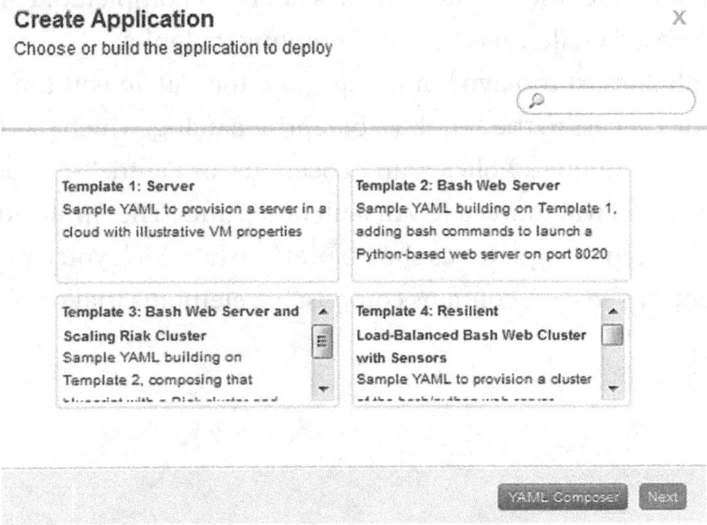

Create Application
Choose or build the application to deploy

Template 1: Server
Sample YAML to provision a server in a cloud with illustrative VM properties

Template 2: Bash Web Server
Sample YAML building on Template 1, adding bash commands to launch a Python-based web server on port 8020

Template 3: Bash Web Server and Scaling Riak Cluster
Sample YAML building on Template 2, composing that

Template 4: Resilient Load-Balanced Bash Web Cluster with Sensors
Sample YAML to provision a cluster

YAML Composer   Next

Figure 3-3. *Brooklyn add an application*

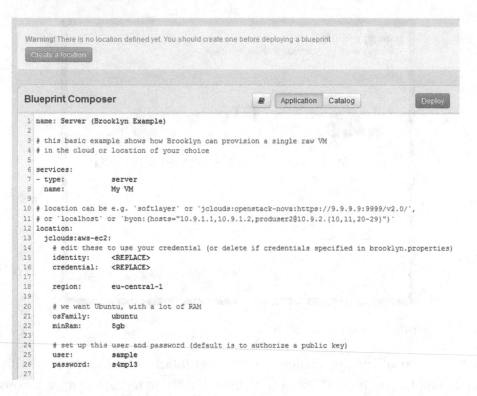

```
Warning! There is no location defined yet. You should create one before deploying a blueprint

Create a location
```

```
Blueprint Composer                          [icon]  Application  Catalog                    Deploy

 1  name: Server (Brooklyn Example)
 2
 3  # this basic example shows how Brooklyn can provision a single raw VM
 4  # in the cloud or location of your choice
 5
 6  services:
 7  - type:          server
 8    name:          My VM
 9
10  # location can be e.g. `softlayer` or `jclouds:openstack-nova:https://9.9.9.9:9999/v2.0/`,
11  # or `localhost` or `byon:(hosts="10.9.1.1,10.9.1.2,produser2@10.9.2.{10,11,20-29}")`
12  location:
13    jclouds:aws-ec2:
14      # edit these to use your credential (or delete if credentials specified in brooklyn.properties)
15      identity:      <REPLACE>
16      credential:    <REPLACE>
17
18      region:        eu-central-1
19
20      # we want Ubuntu, with a lot of RAM
21      osFamily:      ubuntu
22      minRam:        8gb
23
24      # set up this user and password (default is to authorize a public key)
25      user:          sample
26      password:      s4mpl3
27
```

Figure 3-4. *Brooklyn complete a template*

Notice that you can deploy the blueprint from the composer but that there is a warning here that indicates that the location has not been completed. Fill in the missing details and cloud-based credentials before attempting to deploy.

The Catalog tab on the Brooklyn home page (and the Catalog button in the Composer) provides access to the Brooklyn blueprint catalog, which has four main sections: Applications, Entities, Policies, and Locations, as Figure 3-5 shows. The catalog after install is populated with quite a few default blueprints. The Applications section contains application-type templates as shown previously, which you can use to write blueprints. The Entities section contains composable elements that can be added to your blueprints.

The Policies section contains some default policies that can be added to your blueprints to manage failure, scaling, and connection management. You will need to write further policies, and a link was provided above the default policies to suggest how this might be carried out in Java.

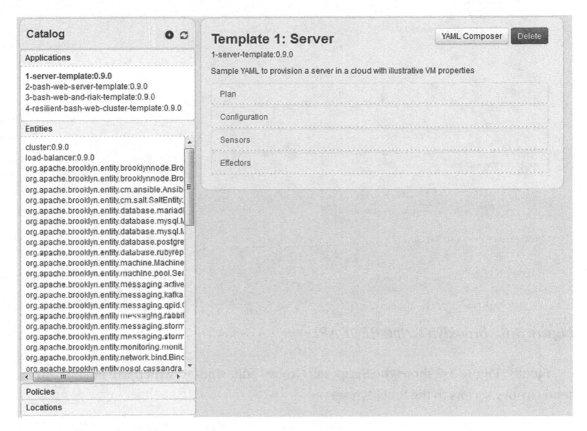

Figure 3-5. *Brooklyn: the catalog*

The Locations section in Figure 3-5 is empty by default but can be added to. Also, there are many example blueprints, which include ideas for location values in the GitHub-based links following:

```
https://github.com/brooklyncentral/blueprint-library
https://github.com/apache/incubator-brooklyn
```

The Script tab on the Brooklyn user interface describes the REST (representational state transfer) based user interface or allows the user to create Groovy-based scripts to be run against the Brooklyn server. This provides part of the operations interface that was mentioned earlier.

Figure 3-6 shows the Script REST interface description expanded for the /access REST API (application programming interface) function.

Figure 3-6. *Brooklyn script: REST API*

Finally, Figure 3-7 shows the Script tab Groovy edit window, which will enable you to send Groovy scripts to the Brooklyn server.

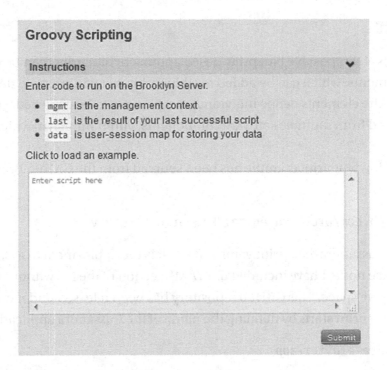

Figure 3-7. Brooklyn script: Groovy

I will close this section here because the rest of this chapter will provide more detail about the use of Brooklyn. In the next section, I will give a Brooklyn overview to give a wider perspective. After that, I will move on to creating a blueprint and using the user interface to deploy it.

Brooklyn Overview

Apache Brooklyn (brooklyn.apache.org) is an open sourced deployment and monitoring system that uses blueprints to model applications that are then released using those blueprints. It offers a model, deploy, and monitor application life cycle, which supports the OASIS CAMP (Cloud Application Management Platforms; see www.oasis-open.org/committees/tc_home.php?wg_abbrev=camp) standard.

Blueprints

Brooklyn offers a composable blueprint-based approach; blueprints can be defined as repository elements, which can be added to a blueprint that you create to deploy your system. While the elements define individual components to be deployed, your system will be modelled from multiple software components within Brooklyn, which could be clustered.

The following blueprint example has been sourced from the GitHub Brooklyn central project at

`https://github.com/brooklyncentral/blueprint-library.`

It is called cassandra-blueprint.yaml and models the deployment of a Cassandra NoSQL database node. I have included the YAML section of the file without the comments to save space. This GitHub repository has been released under an Apache 2.0 license. The blueprint starts by defining the name of the Cassandra application:

```
name: cassandra-cluster-app
```

Then it defines the services that this deployment will provide; the type is defined as a Cassandra cluster. The initial cluster size is defined as five nodes, while the quorum size is defined as three nodes. Those familiar with ZooKeeper will understand that the quorum size is the minimum number of nodes needed for voting and reaching an agreement. There is also a section that determines the provisioning in terms of minimum properties:

```
services:
- type: brooklyn.entity.nosql.cassandra.CassandraCluster
  name: Cassandra Cluster
  brooklyn.config:
    cluster.initial.size: 5
    cluster.initial.quorumSize: 3
    provisioning.properties:
      minCores: 4
      minRam: 8192
```

Finally, the location is defined as Amazon AWS cloud; in this case, EC2 will be used with the zone being eu-west-1. The EC2 service provides dynamically allocated, cloud-based hosts.

```
location: aws-ec2:eu-west-1
```

It is also important to note that blueprints are composable: one blueprint can refer to another that is already in the Brooklyn repository. For instance, the blueprint snippet following refers to the CouchbaseCluster entity in the Brooklyn repository:

```
Services:
-type: brooklyn.entity.nosql.couchbase.CouchbaseCluster
      initialSize   5
```

REST API

The Brooklyn user interface is composed of REST interface elements built using Swagger. Many of the paths that you see generated as you navigate around the user interface can be used as a pure REST API to extract information from Brooklyn. For instance, the Brooklyn URL for listing my applications is

```
http://192.168.1.118:8081/#v1/applications,
```

while the REST-based Brooklyn equivalent is as follows:

```
http://192.168.1.118:8081/v1/applications,
```

which would currently return nothing, as no applications exist yet. To examine the Brooklyn catalogue entity load-balancer, the URL would be

```
http://192.168.1.118:8081/#v1/catalog/entities/load-balancer:0.9.0.
```

And the Brooklyn REST equivalent, which returns JSON (JavaScript Object Notation) based data for the load balancer would be

```
http://192.168.1.118:8081/v1/catalog/entities/load-balancer:0.9.0.
```

So you could use the Brooklyn REST interface to extract information without using the Brooklyn user interface if you needed to.

Policy Management

Brooklyn has a number of built-in policies that can be added to blueprints, and these can be found from the user interface. Select the catalog tab and choose the Catalog Policies section. The predefined polices are as follows:

```
org.apache.brooklyn.policy.autoscaling.AutoScalerPolicy:0.9.0
org.apache.brooklyn.policy.ha.ConnectionFailureDetector:0.9.0
org.apache.brooklyn.policy.ha.ServiceReplacer:0.9.0
org.apache.brooklyn.policy.ha.ServiceRestarter:0.9.0
org.apache.brooklyn.policy.ha.SshMachineFailureDetector:0.9.0
```

So there are predefined policies here to auto scale and detect failures in connections and services. There are also policies to replace and restart services. I can determine a little more information about these services if I use the REST interface. For instance, if I look at the auto scaler using the following path

```
/v1/catalog/policies/org.apache.brooklyn.policy.autoscaling.
AutoScalerPolicy:0.9.0
```

I get the following JSON output giving more details about the policy:

```
{
  "symbolicName": "org.apache.brooklyn.policy.autoscaling.AutoScalerPolicy",
  "version": "0.9.0",
  "name": "Auto-scaler",
  "javaType": null,
  "planYaml": "brooklyn.policies: [{ type: org.apache.brooklyn.policy.
  autoscaling.AutoScalerPolicy }]",
  "description": "Policy that is attached to a Resizable entity and
  dynamically adjusts its size in response to either keep a metric within a
  given range, or in response to POOL_COLD and POOL_HOT events",
  "deprecated": false,
  "links": {
    "self": "\/v1\/catalog\/policies\/org.apache.brooklyn.policy.
    autoscaling.AutoScalerPolicy:0.9.0\/0.9.0"
  },
```

```
    "id": "org.apache.brooklyn.policy.autoscaling.AutoScalerPolicy:0.9.0",
    "type": "org.apache.brooklyn.policy.autoscaling.AutoScalerPolicy"
}
```

Monitoring

The Brooklyn model involves a cycle of model in blueprints, deploy, and monitor, but how does the monitoring occur? Well, blueprints can contain policies, as already described previously, and it is the policies that connect to "sensors" in the entities. You can either use predefined policies or write your own in Java as the link following advises:

`https://brooklyn.apache.org/v/latest/java/policy.html`

For instance, later in this chapter, a blueprint will be created to deploy Mule ESB (enterprise service bus), the ETL tool, to a server. The deployed Mule runtime will then be monitored along with the Mule application deployed within the runtime using Mule's JMX (Java Management Extensions) interface. Then the operations that are defined both within the blueprint and its entities will be used for both application monitoring and management.

Operations

So in practice, how can Brooklyn be used for operations or for creating and controlling the systems that the blueprints describe? The following list is taken from the Brooklyn web site, and I have expanded it to provide more detail:

- The User Interface

  The user interface either as a GUI (graphical user interface) or the REST interface can be used for system deployment and management. Blueprints can be composed of existing objects or new blueprints can be developed/pasted into the catalog.

- High Availability

    I would include persistence in this topic as well. If I build an entity cluster and use Brooklyn to monitor it and ensure it is available, then Brooklyn becomes a single point of failure. However, Brooklyn can persist its state to storage so that when it restarts, it can pick up from the point of failure.

    Also for clustered apps and master/slave clustered systems, Brooklyn supports policies for standby nodes and promotes to master in case of a master failure.

To this point, I have shown you how to install Apache Brooklyn, and I have examined the user interface and given an overview of its functionality. Now it is time to carry out a practical example of blueprint development. Brooklyn bases its management life cycle on blueprints, so I think that the bulk of this chapter should concentrate on blueprint development. The next section will involve an example of server-based (BYON) and cloud-based blueprint location development and deployment.

Modelling With Blueprints

This section will concentrate on some real examples allowing for blueprint development as well as providing a chance to examine Java JVM (Java virtual machine) code, which will support Brooklyn deployments.

Application Installs

Cluster-based storage mechanisms such as Hadoop, Cassandra, and Riak all need data delivery mechanisms to be populated. Mule ESB from Mulesoft is a popular option because it has an open-source community version available. This means that small organisations can use the Mule open-source version before migrating to an enterprise option later. The first development example following attempts to deploy Mule using blueprints.

Server-Based Install

I thought that a deployment of Mule ESB (mulesoft.com) would be a good example of a server-based Brooklyn install. To deploy an instance of Mule, I will need a YAML file to model the release and a JVM, which will provide functionality to support the deployment. Luckily the guys at Ricston (ricston.com) have already tackled this problem and provided sample code. With their permission, I will reproduce their work here. The original link is

```
www.ricston.com/blog/mule-brooklyn/
```

They have modified the brooklyn.entity.webapp.tomcat.TomcatServer entity and saved the code to GitHub at the following URL:

```
github.com/ricston-git/brooklyn-mule-entity
```

The Ricston Brooklyn Mule code is stored in a github.com repository. To access it, I will need to install a Linux GitHub client. I will do that using the Linux yum install command. The following git command then shows that the install worked and that version 1.7.1 of the git client is installed:

```
[root@hc4r2m1 bin]# yum -y install git
Complete!

[root@hc4r2m1 bin]# git --version
git version 1.7.1
```

I will now use the git client to clone or copy the Ricton Mule repository to the local machine and store the resulting code to the directory /opt/mule/ricston.

```
[root@hc4r2m1 ricston]# git clone https://github.com/ricston-git/brooklyn-
mule-entity
```

If the clone is successful, the repository called brooklyn-mule-entity will have been copied to the preceding ricston directory. As the Linux ls command following shows, the repository now exists, and a src directory structure exists, which contains the code that will be used in this section:

```
[root@hc4r2m1 ricston]# ls
brooklyn-mule-entity
```

```
[root@hc4r2m1 ricston]# cd brooklyn-mule-entity/
[root@hc4r2m1 brooklyn-mule-entity]# ls
blueprints  pom.xml  README.md  src  TODO.md
```

The existence of a file called pom.xml indicates that this source directory structure will need to be built using Maven. To do that, I will need to install Maven onto the local server. The commands following show that I have sourced a Maven repo (repository configuration file) from the server repos.fedorapeople.org using wget. This allows me to use the yum command to install Maven, as yum now knows, using the repo file, where to find the package. The final command following shows that Version 3.3.9 of Maven has been installed:

```
[root@hc4r2m1 brooklyn-mule-entity]# wget http://repos.fedorapeople.org/
repos/dchen/apache-maven/epel-apache-maven.repo -O /etc/yum.repos.d/epel-
apache-maven.repo
```

```
[root@hc4r2m1 brooklyn-mule-entity]# yum -y install apache-maven
```

```
[root@hc4r2m1 brooklyn-mule-entity]# mvn --version
Apache Maven 3.3.9 (bb52d8502b132ec0a5a3f4c09453c07478323dc5; 2015-11-
11T05:41:47+13:00)
```

Now it is possible to build the Ricston Mule, JVM-based source code using the Maven mvn command. A clean of the source tree is carried out at the same time to ensure that all objects are recompiled.

```
[root@hc4r2m1 brooklyn-mule-entity]#  mvn clean assembly:assembly

[INFO] ------------------------------------------------------------------
[INFO] BUILD SUCCESS
[INFO] ------------------------------------------------------------------
[INFO] Total time: 04:28 min
[INFO] Finished at: 2016-09-27T19:39:37+13:00
[INFO] Final Memory: 49M/620M
[INFO] ------------------------------------------------------------------
```

Now that the source tree has been built, I can navigate to the target directory from which I can launch the Brooklyn and Mule applications.

```
[root@hc4r2m1 brooklyn-mule-entity]# cd ./target/brooklyn-mule-entity-
0.0.1-SNAPSHOT-dist/
[root@hc4r2m1 brooklyn-mule-entity]# cd brooklyn-mule-entity-0.0.1-
SNAPSHOT/
```

The Linux ls command following shows the contents of the snapshot directory. Brooklyn will be launched using the start.sh script, which will call Mule-based functionality in the jar (Java ARchive) file:

```
[root@hc4r2m1 brooklyn-mule-entity-0.0.1-SNAPSHOT]# ls
brooklyn-mule-entity-0.0.1-SNAPSHOT.jar  conf     start.sh
brooklyn-mule-entity.debug.log           lib
brooklyn-mule-entity.info.log            README.txt
```

Before starting Brooklyn, I thought it might be useful to show how the start.sh script launches Brooklyn by setting up the class path to access conf, patch, and lib directories. It also calls the class brooklyn.entity.mule.main.BrooklynMuleMain from the preceding jar file. It passes all arguments to the start.sh bash script to the Java-based command via the "$@" option.

```
$JAVA -Xms256m -Xmx1024m -XX:MaxPermSize=1024m\
    -classpath "conf/:patch/*:*:lib/*"\
    brooklyn.entity.mule.main.BrooklynMuleMain\
    "$@"
```

The command following executed from the source tree snapshot directory uses the start.sh script to start Brooklyn by passing it the launch parameter. The "&" character means that the command is executed as a background process, and so the terminal session is freed for further commands:

```
[root@hc4r2m1 brooklyn-mule-entity-0.0.1-SNAPSHOT]# ./start.sh   launch  &
```

For Brooklyn-based deployment to work on the local server and potentially other servers, passwordless ssh (secure shell) access must be set up. I will set it up on the local server by first issuing the ssh-keygen command and accepting all default options.

This creates a .ssh directory under $HOME as shown following. Public and private RSA (Rivest, Adi Shamir) based keys are created:

```
[root@hc4r2m1 mule]# ssh-keygen
[root@hc4r2m1 mule]# ls $HOME/.ssh
authorized_keys  id_rsa  id_rsa.pub
```

Next I will use the ssh-copy-id command to allow the root user passwordless ssh access to the local server. This may seem counterintuitive, but Brooklyn creates an ssh session on the local server when deploying (as do many clustered systems) and so needs to be able to SSH to the local server for installs on localhost. I also test the ssh connection and exit from the new session that I have successfully created.

```
[root@hc4r2m1 mule]# ssh-copy-id root@hc4r2m1
[root@hc4r2m1 mule]# ssh hc4r2m1
Last login: Sat Oct  1 14:41:31 2016 from 192.168.1.4
[root@hc4r2m1 ~]# exit
logout
```

Having logged into the Brooklyn user interface at http://192.168.1.118:8081 using the username and password supplied in the session output as shown earlier, it can now be seen that the MuleServerApp class supplied in the Ricston GitHub code exists in the Brooklyn catalog as shown in Figure 3-8.

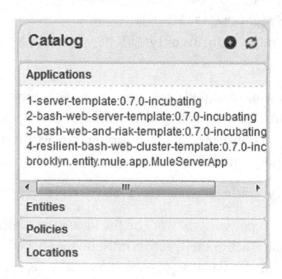

Figure 3-8. *Brooklyn Catalog: Mule class*

Now a YAML file can be used to call this class and so install a version of Mule. The YAML-based blueprint that I will use is based on the Ricston example, but it installs a later version of Mule, Version 3.8.1.

```
name: Simple Mule blueprint
location: localhost
services:
- type: brooklyn.entity.mule.app.MuleServerApp
  name: Simple Mule blueprint
  period: 5000ms
  brooklyn.config:
    install.dir: /opt/mule/runtime/
    run.dir: /opt/mule/runtime/mule-standalone-3.8.1
version: 3.8.1
```

The preceding blueprint is a simple example; it names the application to be deployed as "Simple Mule blueprint." It specifies a single install location as localhost. It specifies the install via a service with the type specified as the catalog-based MuleServerApp. The configuration is specified in terms of an install and run directory under/opt. Finally, the version of Mule to be installed is defined as 3.8.1, a current version.

I also needed to change the following code in the Ricston repository to make Version 3.8.1 the default value to get this to work. The pwd command following shows the location in the source tree. The vi commands show the two Java files that I changed. The source code beneath each vi command shows the changes that I made. I also specified the default install path to be under/opt:

```
[root@hc4r2m1 mule]# pwd
/opt/mule/ricston/brooklyn-mule-entity/src/main/java/brooklyn/entity/mule

[root@hc4r2m1 mule]#  vi MuleServer.java

    ConfigKey<String> SUGGESTED_VERSION = ConfigKeys.newConfigKeyWithDefault
(SoftwareProcess.SUGGESTED_VERSION, "3.8.1");

[root@hc4r2m1 mule]#  vi app/MuleServerApp.java

        addChild(EntitySpec.create(MuleServer.class).
        configure(SoftwareProcess.INSTALL_DIR, "/opt/mule/runtime/")
                .configure(SoftwareProcess.RUN_DIR, "/opt/mule/runtime/
                mule-standalone-3.8.1")
```

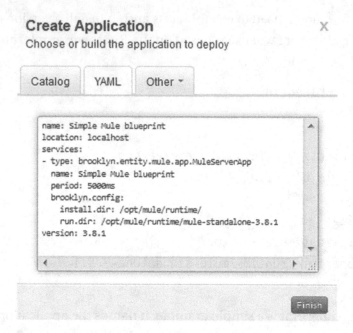

Figure 3-9. Brooklyn: Execute the YAML blueprint

Figure 3-9 shows the YAML blueprint being executed. To reach this form, select the Applications tab. Then select the black plus button in the Applications section. Then select the YAML tab on the pop-up form. Selecting the Finish button now causes Brooklyn to attempt to deploy the Mule application. Brooklyn will source Mule from the following path, as this is embedded with the Ricston source:

```
repository-master.mulesoft.org/nexus/content/repositories/releases/org/
mule/distributions/mule-standalone/3.8.1/mule-standalone-3.8.1.tar.gz
```

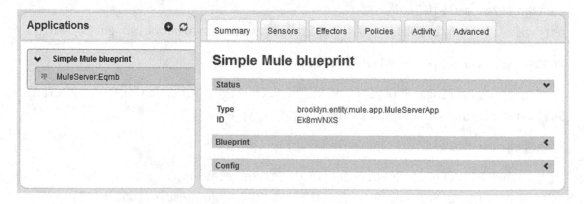

Figure 3-10. Brooklyn: Mule install

Figure 3-10 shows the Mule-based application being installed by Brooklyn; you can tell it is installing because the icon next to the MuleServer.Eqmb text under Applications consists of revolving green dots.

After a successful install, the icons related to the application will change to a solid green as shown in the Figure 3-11. Also, the application will have a RUNNING state. The pwd and ls Linux commands following show that Mule 3.8.1 has been installed under/opt:

```
[root@hc4r2m1 runtime]# pwd
/opt/mule/runtime

[root@hc4r2m1 runtime]# ls
BROOKLYN  mule-standalone-3.8.1  mule-standalone-3.8.1.tar.gz

[root@hc4r2m1 runtime]# ls mule-standalone-3.8.1
apps                                              docs        logs
bin                                               domains     MIGRATION.txt
brooklyn-jmxmp-agent-shaded-0.7.0-incubating.jar  examples    README.txt
conf                                              lib         src
console.log                                       LICENSE.txt
```

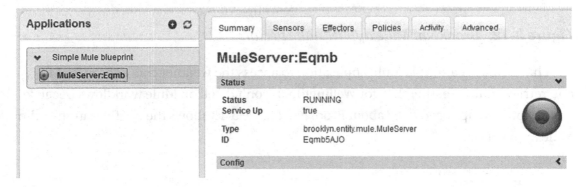

Figure 3-11. *Brooklyn: Mule successful install*

Apache Brooklyn has installed and executed Mule for use as the (filtered) Linux ps (process status) command output following shows:

```
[root@hc4r2m1 runtime]# ps -ef | grep mule
root      5157  5104  0 17:24?         00:00:00 /bin/sh /opt/mule/runtime/
mule-standalone-3.8.1/./bin/mule console
```

A single Mule runtime server is of little use without some applications running within it to collect data. Figure 3-12 shows the Brooklyn application-based effectors that can be used to manage the Mule runtime. There are options to start and stop the runtime as well as deploy and undeploy Mule applications within it.

Figure 3-12. *Brooklyn: Mule application effectors*

I have created a simple Mule application to access the weather.com site via its API and retrieve daily weather data for Wellington. I won't dwell on Mule workflows because this chapter is supposed to be about Brooklyn. Figure 3-13 shows the configuration of the Mule application.

```
 1 http.req.host=api.wunderground.com
 2 http.req.port=80
 3 http.req.basepath=/
 4 http.req.timeout=90000
 5 http.key=57330
 6 http.country=New_Zealand
 7 http.city=Wellington
 8 http.date=#[server.dateTime.format('yyyyMMdd')]
 9 http.req.path=api/${http.key}/history_${http.date}/q/${http.country}/${http.city}.xml
10 http.req.protocol=HTTP
11
12 poll.freq.days=1
13
14 file.path=/opt/mule/data/weather/
15 file.name=Wellington.#[server.dateTime.format('yyyyMMddhhmmss')].xml
```

Figure 3-13. *Brooklyn: Mule application configuration*

The Mule application flow shown in Figure 3-14 uses an HTTP requestor to access weather.com. It polls this site and retrieves data daily. It then converts the data to a string, logs the attempt, and writes the data to the file system.

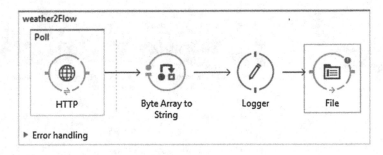

Figure 3-14. *Brooklyn: Mule application flow*

I have exported this flow to a zip file called weather2.zip and saved it to my web site at the URL following. I will now use the Brooklyn deploy effector for the Mule runtime class to deploy this Mule-based flow to the Brooklyn-based Mule runtime.

`http://www.semtech-solutions.co.nz/mule/weather2.zip`

Figure 3-15 shows the pop-up window that appears when the Brooklyn Mule runtime application deploy effector is selected. It takes two parameters: the URL to the zipped Mule application and the target name of the application. As shown in Figure 3-15, fill in these options and select the red Invoke button.

MuleServer:Eqmb deploy   ×

Deploys the given packaged Mule app from a source URL. Uses targetName as app name in $MULE_HOME/apps

Name	Value
url	http://www.semtech-solutions.co.nz/mule/weather2.zip
targetName	weather2

Cancel   Invoke

Figure 3-15. *Brooklyn: Mule application deploy*

As shown in Figure 3-16, a successful Brooklyn application Mule deploy causes a completed state with a green icon. The times to start and finish are also shown, as well as an ID and the action name.

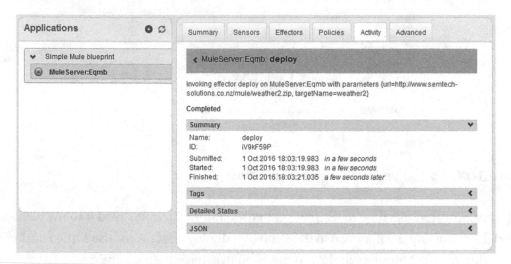

Figure 3-16. *Brooklyn: Successful mule application deploy*

The Mule-based application deployment can also be checked on the local server because Mule applications are deployed to the runtime apps directory. As the Linux listing shows following, the weather2 Mule flow exists and has been unpacked by the Mule runtime:

```
[root@hc4r2m1 mule-standalone-3.8.1]# pwd
/opt/mule/runtime/mule-standalone-3.8.1

[root@hc4r2m1 mule-standalone-3.8.1]# ls apps
default   default-anchor.txt   weather2   weather2-anchor.txt
```

Also, the first thing this flow will try to do is access the weather.com site API and try to download some data. The data will be stored in xml format under the /opt/mule/ data/weather directory. As the Linux pwd and ls commands following show, all is working, as data has been retrieved.

```
[root@hc4r2m1 weather]# pwd
/opt/mule/data/weather
```

```
[root@hc4r2m1 weather]# ls -l
total 60
-rw-r--r--. 1 root root 58582 Oct  1 18:17 Wellington.20161001061716.xml
```

So what conclusion can be drawn from using a Mule deployment as a Brooklyn blueprint-based example? Brooklyn has provided the functionality to simply model and deploy both the Mule runtime as well as Mule-based applications. The process becomes simple, and Brooklyn provides an interface with which to monitor the Mule-based deployment.

This install example has shown how Brooklyn blueprints can be used to install to servers, but what about installs to the cloud? This will be tackled in the next section by deploying Cassandra nodes to cloud-based instances on Apache CloudStack.

Cloud-Based Install

As already mentioned, this section will use CentOS-based virtual instances on Apache CloudStack for blueprint-based Cassandra deployment. The first example will deploy a single Cassandra node; and when that is shown to be successful, then a Cassandra cluster will be created.

Remember that Apache CloudStack is being used as an example of a cloud-based system. Large-scale enterprise customers would probably use a better known cloud-based system such as Azure, Cloudsoft, Amazon AWS, or Google cloud. But this example is still relevant; the idea is that the cloud-based location for deployment becomes generic and part of the deployment.

Figure 3-17 shows three virtual instances that I have created using a CentOS 6 ISO. I won't repeat the details of the instance creation here, as that was covered in the last chapter. The servers are named Server1, Server2, and Server3. Server1 will initially be used for a single Cassandra install, and then a Cassandra Cluster will be created using all of these instances.

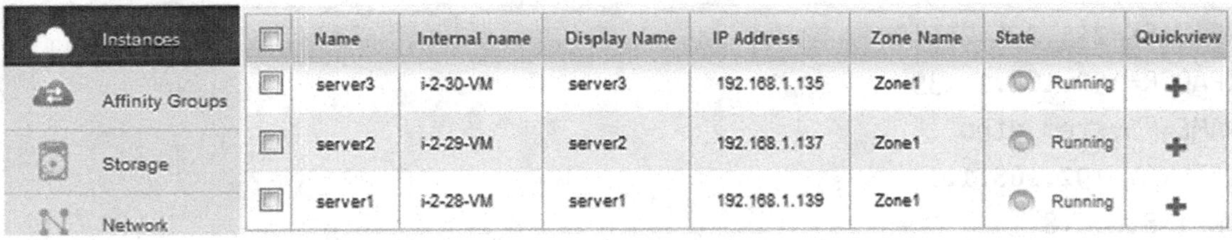

	Name	Internal name	Display Name	IP Address	Zone Name	State	Quickview
Instances	server3	i-2-30-VM	server3	192.168.1.135	Zone1	Running	+
Affinity Groups	server2	i-2-29-VM	server2	192.168.1.137	Zone1	Running	+
Storage / Network	server1	i-2-28-VM	server1	192.168.1.139	Zone1	Running	+

Figure 3-17. *CloudStack instances for deployment*

Remember that instances can always be examined by selecting the left menu Instances option in the CloudStack user interface. Figure 3-17 shows that all instances to be used in this section are running and that they are all associated to Zone1. They all have IP addresses allocated, and they are all accessible from the server on which Apache Brooklyn is running via passwordless ssh.

In this case, Apache Brooklyn is running on the host hc4r2m1; and as shown following, Server1 with IP address 192.168.1.139 is accessible both using ping and ssh. This means that once Cassandra is installed using Brooklyn, I can access each virtual instance and examine the Cassandra-based install and use Cassandra tools to check that the install is working:

```
[root@hc4r2m1 ~]# ping 192.168.1.139
PING 192.168.1.139 (192.168.1.139) 56(84) bytes of data.
64 bytes from 192.168.1.139: icmp_seq=1 ttl=64 time=2001 ms
64 bytes from 192.168.1.139: icmp_seq=2 ttl=64 time=1002 ms

[root@hc4r2m1 ~]# ssh 192.168.1.139
Last login: Sun Nov 27 16:01:11 2016 from 192.168.1.118
[root@server1 ~]#
```

To ensure ssh access from the Brooklyn server to the virtual instances, I had to use the Linux ssh-copy-id command with a parameter of root@192.168.1.139 from the Brooklyn server. I also needed to set up the network on each virtual instance to ensure that it was visible from outside of the cloud. The example following shows how virtual instance Server1 was set up.

```
[root@server1 ~]# cd /etc/sysconfig/network-scripts
[root@server1 network-scripts]# cat ifcfg-eth0
DEVICE=eth0
BOOTPROTO=static

ONBOOT=yes
NETMASK=255.255.255.0
IPADDR=192.168.1.139
NAME="System eth0"
GATEWAY=192.168.1.1
DNS1=8.8.8.8
DNS2=8.8.4.4
```

```
NM_CONTROLLED=yes
TYPE=Ethernet
UUID=ec8800b4-7d03-44a8-b7f6-615ff649170f
```

The important parts to the preceding configuration are the NETMASK, IPADDR (IP address), GATEWAY, and DNS values. They ensure that the instance is visible outside the cloud, and the preceding ping command shows that this is true. When these changes are made, the instance network service needs to be restarted for the changes to take effect. The Linux service command following executed as root on the instance shows how this is done:

```
[root@server1  service network restart
```

Given that the instances have been created, are running, and are visible on the network, a Cassandra-based cloud install can now be attempted using Brooklyn blueprints. Note that static instances are being used in this chapter; it is also possible to use dynamic instances. This means that the blueprints can also be used to create the virtual instances on which they deploy, but it is simpler in CloudStack to introduce cloud-based deployment in this way.

The blueprint that will be used for this deployment is shown following, the application name in Brooklyn will be called "Cassandra Simple Cluster Node." The deployment location is defined as a BYON, server Server1 with IP address 192.168.1.139:

```
name: Cassandra Simple Cluster Node
location:
  byon:
    user: root
    hosts:
    - 192.168.1.139
services:
- type: org.apache.brooklyn.entity.nosql.cassandra.CassandraNode
  start.timeout: 30m
  stopIptables: true
  brookyn.policies:
  - type: org.apache.brooklyn.policy.ha.ServiceRestarter
  brooklyn.enrichers:
  - type: org.apache.brooklyn.policy.ha.ServiceFailureDetector
```

The service that will be deployed will be a single CassandraNode, and I have also included an example policy ServiceRestarter and an enricher ServiceFailureDetector to show that the blueprint can be extended with catalog-based, predefined functionality. Last, two other CassandraNode attributes have been added. A start.timeout value has been defined so that sufficient install time will be allowed, and stopIptables has been defined to ensure that the instance firewall will be down after the install to allow simplified networking.

This simple blueprint is pasted into the composer section of the Apache Brooklyn user interface, and the deploy button is selected.

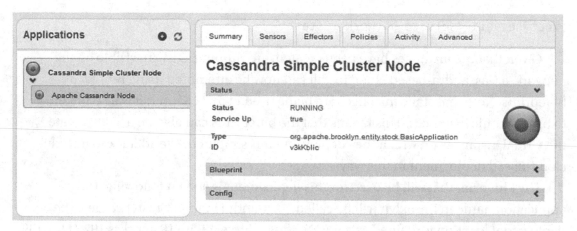

Figure 3-18. *Brooklyn: CloudStack Cassandra Node deploy*

As Figure 3-18 demonstrates, the deployment has been successful, indicated by the green icons for both the application name "Cassandra Simple Cluster Node" and the Apache Cassandra Node. Apache Brooklyn has used passwordless ssh access that was previously set up to the cloud instance to install Cassandra. It should now be possible to examine the install on the virtual instance Server1.

As already shown, I can access the instance Server1 from the Brooklyn server hc4r2m1 using ssh.

```
[root@hc4r2m1 .ssh]# ssh 192.168.1.139
```

The first problem that I face is knowing where Cassandra has been installed. Given that I know that cqlsh is a Cassandra command, I can search for it on the instance using the Linux find command as shown following. I will search all locations under the root file system /.

```
[root@server1 ~]# find / -name cqlsh
```

/root/brooklyn-managed-proc.esses/apps/TMV6HR2u/entities/CassandraNode_
mPtOICvo/bin/cqlsh
/root/brooklyn-managed-processes/apps/v3kKblic/entities/CassandraNode_
aYGMy6Mv/bin/cqlsh
/root/brooklyn-managed-processes/installs/CassandraNode_1.2.16/apache-
cassandra-1.2.16/bin/cqlsh

The resulting output of this command shows multiple Brooklyn apps exist under the Linux file system path.

/root/brooklyn-managed-processes/apps/

This is due to multiple attempted installs of Cassandra. I will use the latest installed application, which is called TMV6HR2u. Following, I have used the Linux cd (change directory) command to move to the Cassandra Node bin directory. The Linux ls command then shows the Cassandra-based commands that are available within the Server1 instance Cassandra application.

```
[root@server1~]# cd /root/brooklyn-managed-processes/apps/
[root@server1~]# cd TMV6HR2u/entities/CassandraNode_mPtOICvo/bin/
[root@server1 bin]# ls
cassandra              cqlsh.bat           sstable2json.bat     sstablesplit
cassandra.bat          debug-cql           sstablekeys          sstablesplit.bat
cassandra-cli          debug-cql.bat       sstablekeys.bat      sstableupgrade
cassandra-cli.bat      json2sstable        sstableloader        sstableupgrade.bat
cassandra.in.sh        json2sstable.bat    sstableloader.bat    stop-server
cassandra-shuffle      nodetool            sstablemetadata.bat
cassandra-shuffle.bat  nodetool.bat        sstablescrub
cqlsh                  sstable2json        sstablescrub.bat
```

Moving up one level in the Cassandra application installation file system shows the subdirectories within the installed application. As expected, there is a Cassandra bin directory as well as conf (configuration), data, lib (library), log files, and a tools directory.

```
[root@server1 CassandraNode_mPtoICvo]# cd .. ; ls
bin                                cassandra.log   interface     tools
brooklyn_commands                  commitlog       lib
brooklyn-jmxmp-agent-shaded-0.9.0.jar  conf        pylib
cassandra-console.log              data            saved_caches
```

To finalize this simple example, I will prove that this Cassandra node is installed and running by using the Cassandra nodetool command available in the preceding bin directory. I know that by default the Cassandra JMX port is 7199, so that will be used to check the Cassandra install. I have used the nodetool command following to obtain the Cassandra node status. I have simplified both the ID and Rack names to ensure that the data fits on the page. The output following shows that the Cassandra node is running with a Normal state on Rack1:

```
[root@server1 CassandraNode_mPtoICvo]# ./bin/nodetool -p 7199 status

Datacenter: datacenter1
========================
Status=Up/Down
|/ State=Normal/Leaving/Joining/Moving
--  Address        Load        Owns    Host      ID        Rack
UN  192.168.1.139  14.03 KB    100.0%  57c0d5f3  3283980   rack1
```

This installed application instance can be removed from the Brooklyn interface simply by selecting the application advanced option expunge. I have expunged this install to tackle a Cassandra cluster install next. It is interesting to install a simple Cassandra node using blueprints, but Cassandra is a distributed application; so to be useful, it would need to operate in a cluster. The next example will show that a whole Cassandra cluster can be created in the same way using a simple blueprint.

I only have three cloud-based instances on which to install my Cassandra cluster, servers Server1 to Server3. That means that my initial Cassandra cluster size will be limited to three nodes. The blueprint following will be used to create the cluster:

```
name: Cassandra Simple Cluster
location:
  byon:
    user: root
```

```
hosts:
- 192.168.1.139
- 192.168.1.135
- 192.168.1.137

services:
- type: org.apache.brooklyn.entity.nosql.cassandra.CassandraDatacenter
  cassandra.cluster.name: 'my cluster'
  cluster.initial.size: 3
  start.timeout: 30m
  stopIptables: true
  brooklyn.policies:
    - type: org.apache.brooklyn.policy.ha.ServiceRestarter
      brooklyn.enrichers:
    - type: org.apache.brooklyn.policy.ha.ServiceFailureDetector
```

Note that the install location is very similar to the last example except that extra locations have been added for the three virtual server instances Server1–Server3. Also, the service to be used this time is called CassandraDataCenter, which is provided by default within the Brooklyn catalog entity list.

This cluster-based entity (CassandraDataCenter) creates a Cassandra cluster by using the CassandraNode entity that was used in the previous blueprint. Given that it uses CassandraNode, we should not be surprised that CassandraNode attributes like start.timeout are used in this blueprint. Also, the policies used in this blueprint remain unchanged, that is, FailureDetection and ServiceRestarter.

Paste this blueprint into the composer window on the Brooklyn interface and select deploy. If all goes well, the deployment-based icons in the Brooklyn interface should display as green tokens as shown in the figure below following. The display has been expanded to show that the Brooklyn-based application is now called "Apache Cassandra Datacenter Cluster." Each of the three Cassandra nodes are shown in the figure below the application. Each node has been assigned a system-generated name.

Brooklyn indicates, as shown in Figure 3-19, that the Cassandra cluster has been installed and is running. This can be tested, as in the last example, by accessing a CloudStack-based virtual instance and using Cassandra-based tools to prove that the Cassandra cluster is running correctly.

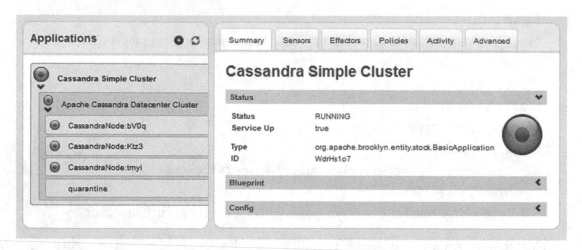

Figure 3-19. *Brooklyn: CloudStack Cassandra cluster deploy*

Using ssh from the Brooklyn server, I have accessed the virtual instance Server3. It is important to note at this point that there may be multiple applications installed on this instance or multiple application instances created through repeated install attempts.

```
[root@hc4r2m1 ~]# ssh 192.168.1.135

[root@server3 ~]# find / -name nodetool
/root/brooklyn-managed-processes/apps/WdrHs1o7/entities/CassandraNode_
bVOqjYtd/bin/nodetool
/root/brooklyn-managed-processes/apps/FPIUKIjY/entities/CassandraNode_
S5pdcs9T/bin/nodetool
/root/brooklyn-managed-processes/apps/wa8XQH4n/entities/CassandraNode_
XoHNOSHK/bin/nodetool
/root/brooklyn-managed-processes/apps/H7Q3CCpJ/entities/CassandraNode_
yDmK6Clp/bin/nodetool
/root/brooklyn-managed-processes/apps/l2QcHnDD/entities/CassandraNode_
bQkNSrFR/bin/nodetool
```

```
/root/brooklyn-managed-processes/apps/dBoE2ktC/entities/CassandraNode_
Z66wLVTU/bin/nodetool
/root/brooklyn-managed-processes/apps/fvqw2TnY/entities/CassandraNode_
RPCxpHhU/bin/nodetool
/root/brooklyn-managed-processes/apps/xOJVT6U5/entities/CassandraNode_
OVBDNFcT/bin/nodetool
/root/brooklyn-managed-processes/installs/CassandraNode_1.2.16/apache-
cassandra-1.2.16/bin/nodetool
```

As this search on the instance Server3 shows when searching for the nodetool command using the Linux-based find command, there are multiple instances of the application CassandraNode installed on this virtual server. Given that I have only created one running CassandraNode install, I know that I will be looking for the latest install.

```
[root@server3 ~]# cd /root/brooklyn-managed-processes/apps/
 [root@server3 apps]# ls -lrt
total 32
drwxr-xr-x. 3 root root 4096 Nov 27 17:46 FPIUKIjY
drwxr-xr-x. 3 root root 4096 Nov 27 18:03 H7Q3CCpJ
drwxr-xr-x. 3 root root 4096 Nov 27 18:19 fvqw2TnY
drwxr-xr-x. 3 root root 4096 Nov 27 18:27 dBoE2ktC
drwxr-xr-x. 3 root root 4096 Nov 27 18:43 wa8XQH4n
drwxr-xr-x. 3 root root 4096 Nov 27 18:50 xOJVT6U5
drwxr-xr-x. 3 root root 4096 Nov 27 18:51 l2QcHnDD
drwxr-xr-x. 3 root root 4096 Nov 27 18:58 WdrHs1o7
```

By moving to the apps directory using the Linux cd command and creating a date based listing of the system assigned CassandraNode application installs, I can see that the latest install is named WdrHs1o7. That is the install that I will be interested in.

```
[root@server3 apps]# cd WdrHs1o7/entities/CassandraNode_bVOqjYtd
[root@server3 CassandraNode_bVOqjYtd]# ls
bin                                     cassandra.log  data       saved_
                                                                  caches
brooklyn_commands                       cassandra.pid  interface  tools
brooklyn-jmxmp-agent-shaded-0.9.0.jar   commitlog      lib
cassandra-console.log                   conf           pylib
```

To move further into the install hierarchy, I used the Linux cd command to change the directory to the installed CassandraNode. As before, there are bin (binary) and conf (configuration) directories, among others. By moving into the bin directory, I can use the CassandraNode installed commands.

```
[root@server3 CassandraNode_bVOqjYtd]# cd bin
[root@server3 bin]# ls
cassandra              cqlsh.bat            sstable2json.bat     sstablesplit
cassandra.bat          debug-cql            sstablekeys          sstablesplit.bat
cassandra-cli          debug-cql.bat        sstablekeys.bat      sstableupgrade
cassandra-cli.bat      json2sstable         sstableloader        sstableupgrade.bat
cassandra.in.sh        json2sstable.bat     sstableloader.bat    stop-server
cassandra-shuffle      nodetool             sstablemetadata.bat
cassandra-shuffle.bat  nodetool.bat         sstablescrub
cqlsh                  sstable2json         sstablescrub.bat
```

The Cassandra nodetool status command following shows that the Cassandra cluster is running and that it has the expected three nodes. Also as expected, they have state normal and exist on Cassandra rack rack1:

```
[root@server3 bin]# ./nodetool -p 7199 status
Datacenter: datacenter1
=======================
Status=Up/Down
|/ State=Normal/Leaving/Joining/Moving
--  Address         Load       Owns    Host ID     Token      Rack
UN  192.168.1.135   14.04 KB   33.3%   6cd06dd5    6808581    rack1
UN  192.168.1.137   10.78 KB   33.3%   6cb57e90    6596671    rack1
UN  192.168.1.139   14.02 KB   33.3%   5101d16a    5489247    rack1
```

As previously, the nodetool status output has been clipped in terms of host and token IDs to make it fit on the page. Finally, the nodetool command has been used with the ring option following to show that the Cassandra three-node cluster is up.

```
[root@server3 bin]# ./nodetool -p 7199 ring

Datacenter: datacenter1
==========
Address          Rack     Status State  Load       Owns     Token
192.168.1.135   rack1    Up     Normal 14.04 KB   33.33%   6808581890
192.168.1.137   rack1    Up     Normal 10.78 KB   33.33%   6596671994
192.168.1.139   rack1    Up     Normal 14.02 KB   33.33%   5489247491
```

The preceding output shows that for datacenter1, each of the three Cassandra cluster nodes has a status of Up and a state of Normal. That's quite powerful; with a simple Cassandra-based blueprint, it has been possible to define, create, and monitor a Cassandra cluster in the cloud. This will save time and money not only in cluster creation but support as well. Obviously there is more work to be done to define cluster attributes via the blueprint, but the potential I hope is obvious.

Conclusion

This chapter has introduced Apache Brooklyn, shown how it can be sourced, and how it can be installed. The Brooklyn user interface has been examined in terms of its components and functionality. The idea that Brooklyn blueprints can be created by choosing building blocks from the catalog has been examined. Also, simple blueprints have been created and executed to show that real-world systems can be modelled, deployed, and monitored easily.

Blueprint-based simple examples have been created for basic servers and cloud-based instances. These have, I think, been useful and practical examples because Mule ESB is used in big data systems as an ETL tool to feed data into clusters. Also, Cassandra clusters are used as a NoSQL storage solution. Being able to model, automatically install, and then monitor these systems using blueprints is both interesting and worthwhile.

In the next chapter, I will examine Mesos-based resource management.

CHAPTER 4

Apache Mesos

In this chapter, I will examine the Apache Mesos project (mesos.apache.org), which is an open-source, distributed, cluster management system that enables multiple systems or frameworks to share a cluster by providing resource isolation and security. It is designed to operate on data center scale clusters and is in use by some of the world's largest organisations, for example, PayPal and eBay.

I will examine the means by which Mesos can be sourced and built from source; I will also show how it can be tested once built. Having reached that point, I will examine the possibility of sourcing Mesos binary releases.

Given that I believe that a chapter like this would not be complete without examining the Mesosphere project (mesosphere.com), I will also source and install that system. Mesosphere is a data center scale operating system (DCOS) providing an integrated environment that is based on Mesos but with added tools and interfaces. It provides cluster management, scheduling, DNS, and a range of tools that make cluster management and support more manageable.

Finally, to close this chapter, I will examine the Apache Myriad project, which is an incubator project that aims to integrate Mesos and Yarn, the Hadoop-based resource negotiator. Currently, it is possible to use Hadoop HDFS with Mesos but not Yarn. If a cluster is going to be managed, which system would manage it, Mesos or Yarn? Which would schedule and actually allocate resources? The Myriad project is attempting to integrate Yarn with Mesos by having Mesos manage Yarn. This will provide greater integration opportunities in the future between existing Hadoop stack providers and Mesos.

The next section will briefly examine the Mesos system architecture in terms of Mesos masters and agents as well as ZooKeeper and Mesos clients.

© Michael Frampton 2018

M. Frampton, *Complete Guide to Open Source Big Data Stack*, https://doi.org/10.1007/978-1-4842-2149-5_4

Mesos Architecture

Figure 4-1 is based on the one on the mesos.apache.org site and is reproduced here to give a general overview of the Mesos architecture. Full details can be found at the following URL:

`http://mesos.apache.org/documentation/latest/architecture/`

Mesos runs master processes, which in turn connect to agent processes running on each node in the cluster. The agents run frameworks (which are containerized) on each agent node in which the workloads run. Client processes connect to the master process to schedule and execute workloads. To enable high availability, it is possible to configure multiple Mesos masters with all but one being in standby mode. A ZooKeeper quorum is then used to manage failover.

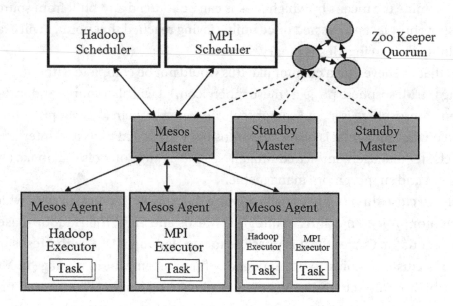

Figure 4-1. *Mesos architecture*

Mesos makes resource offerings to frameworks that they can accept, for instance, if their data locality needs are met. If a resource offer is accepted by a framework, then the client process will schedule the framework-based Mesos task.

The next section will examine a Mesos source system download and build to show how an individual Mesos node can be built.

Mesos Install

In this section, I will provide a brief overview of the big data stack components introduced to date and then show how Mesos can be sourced and built on a single node. I will then examine the possibility of a Mesos binary release.

Overview

Before I delve into the process of sourcing and building the latest Mesos code set, I thought it would be useful to step back and remind the user where Mesos will fit into the big data stack. Figure 4-2 shows the original stack diagram presented in Chapter 1 with the components that have not yet been examined grayed out. In Chapter 2, a local cloud was created and the idea raised that a hybrid cluster could be created from cloud-based instances and local servers. Chapter 3 introduced Apache Brooklyn, a means by which systems that are going to be released to those cloud-based or local servers could be modelled, released, and monitored using blueprints. Now Apache Mesos is being investigated: it will provide a means by which the cluster that is being created can be managed. It will allow multiple frameworks or systems to share the cluster effectively without resource contention.

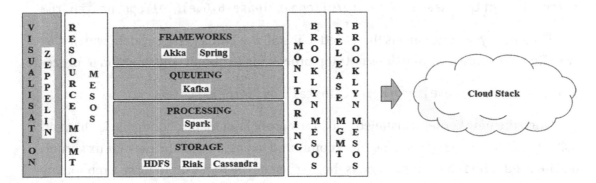

Figure 4-2. *Big data stack architecture*

The next section will source and build Apache Mesos and will conclude with an execution of a test Framework to ensure that the built Mesos node is operating correctly.

Building Mesos

I am using CentOS 6.8 minimal Linux servers to build Mesos, and I am following the suggested Mesos build path from the Apache Mesos web site following:

```
https://mesos.apache.org/getting-started/
```

I know that the guide in the preceding URL suggests that it is supplied for CentOS 6.6; but by following the steps and notes following, Mesos can be sourced, built, installed, and run successfully.

The next section will examine the system requirements that need to be met on a Centos 6.8 Linux server before Mesos can be installed. They originate from the preceding Mesos URL but have been extended to cover any issues that have been encountered.

Mesos System Requirements

The CentOS Linux kernel needs to be updated to support process isolation; RPM (RPM packaged management) based packages need to be sourced from the elrepo.org web site using the Linux rpm commands following:

```
$ rpm --import https://www.elrepo.org/RPM-GPG-KEY-elrepo.org
```

```
$ rpm -Uvh http://www.elrepo.org/elrepo-release-6-6.el6.elrepo.noarch.rpm
```

The Linux yum command is then used to install the Linux kernel update with a -y switch to ensure that yum does not stop processing to obtain confirmation to proceed.

```
$ yum --enablerepo=elrepo-kernel install -y kernel-lt
```

Once the new kernel is installed, the Linux grub, boot loader, config file is changed using the following sed (stream editor) command to ensure that the new Linux kernel will be used. The reboot command is then issued as the root user to force a reboot and so use the new kernel.

```
$ sed -i 's/default=1/default=0/g' /boot/grub/grub.conf
```

```
$ reboot
```

It is now necessary to install some components like tar and wget using the Linux yum command, which this Mesos install will depend on. The update of the nss (name service switch) component will support java bindings, allowing them to build properly. The -y switch used with the yum command will just avoid the need for install confirmation.

```
$ yum -y install tar wget git which nss
```

When using a Mesos release that is greater than 0.21.0, a C++ compiler is needed, which provides full C++11 support. (C++11 is an ISO standard for C++-based development.) This Mesos install will use Mesos 1.1.0, which is the latest available version at this time (December 2016). The GCC (GNU Compiler Collection) compiler will be used with a version number greater than 4.8, which is available in the yum-based component devtoolset-2. To install this, a yum repo file needs to be sourced from the CERN.ch web site. This is what the Linux-based wget command does following. It creates the repo file /etc/yum.repos.d/slc6-devtoolset.repo:

```
$ wget -O /etc/yum.repos.d/slc6-devtoolset.repo \
  http://linuxsoft.cern.ch/cern/devtoolset/slc6-devtoolset.repo
```

Recall that the back slash character (\) in the preceding command just allows me to spread the command over multiple lines and make it more legible. Next, the CERN-based gpg key needs to be imported using the Linux rpm command. This will allow for the devtoolset component to be validated once it is sourced later using yum.

```
$ rpm --import http://linuxsoft.cern.ch/cern/centos/7/os/x86_64/RPM-GPG-
KEY-cern
```

It is now necessary to source a yum Apache Maven repo file to support a Maven install. Maven will be one of the tools used to build Apache Mesos. The Linux wget command following sources the repo file /etc/yum.repos.d/epel-apache-maven.repo.

```
$ wget http://repos.fedorapeople.org/repos/dchen/apache-maven/epel-apache-
maven.repo \
  -O /etc/yum.repos.d/epel-apache-maven.repo
```

When the version of the Mesos system used is greater than 0.21.0 (we are using 1.1.0), then a version of the source code, control system subversion is required with release version greater than 1.8. Also, the development release of subversion is needed.

To support this install, a WANdisco SVN (subversion) repo file must be created as shown following. The file will be created (using a bash here document) as /etc/yum.repos.d/wandisco-svn.repo:

```
$ bash -c 'cat > /etc/yum.repos.d/wandisco-svn.repo <<EOF
[WANdiscoSVN]
name=WANdisco SVN Repo 1.8
enabled=1
baseurl=http://opensource.wandisco.com/centos/6/svn-1.8/RPMS/$basearch/
gpgcheck=1
gpgkey=http://opensource.wandisco.com/RPM-GPG-KEY-WANdisco
EOF'
```

Next, the development tools package is installed using the Linux yum command; this will install many of the essential tools needed to build Mesos and avoid the need to install them individually.

```
$ yum groupinstall -y "Development Tools"
```

It is worth noting at this point that to get this install sequence to work, I executed it many times. During one instance, the SVN WANdisco-based install failed with the following error:

```
Error Downloading Packages:
  subversion-1.8.17-1.x86_64: failure: x86_64/subversion-1.8.17-1.x86_64.
rpm from WANdiscoSVN: [Errno 256] No more mirrors to try.
```

I think that this was an isolated issue, and it only occurred once. I also think it was caused by yum- and gpg-based error checking. The solution was to set gpgcheck=0 in the preceding repo file and reinstall the development tools package.

The version of subversion, the source code control system that has been installed, can now be checked. This is done by calling the Linux svn command with the --version switch. Remember that a version greater than 1.8 is required; and as the output following shows, Version 1.8.17 is installed:

```
$ svn --version
```

```
svn, version 1.8.17 (r1770682)
   compiled Dec  1 2016, 13:36:09 on x86_64-unknown-linux-gnu
```

Next, the yum-based package "devtoolset-2-toolchain" will be installed, which includes the GCC compiler Version 4.8.2 and a number of other needed development packages.

```
$ yum install -y devtoolset-2-toolchain
```

Now a range of yum-based packages will be installed to support the Mesos install; some obvious packages in the list following are Maven, Python, and Java:

```
$ yum install -y apache-maven python-devel java-1.7.0-openjdk-devel
```

```
$ yum install -y zlib-devel libcurl-devel openssl-devel cyrus-sasl-devel
```

```
$ yum install -y cyrus-sasl-md5 apr-devel subversion-devel apr-util-devel
```

Now a shell session is created using the scl (software collections) command, which allows access to the software collection environment. This allows access to the "devtoolset-2" package that was just installed in a Linux bash shell. The g++ command executed following with a --version flag is used to check that the version of g++ installed is greater than 4.8. As you can see, Version 4.8.2 has been installed, so that's fine:

```
$ scl enable devtoolset-2 bash
```

```
$ g++ --version  # Make sure you've got GCC > 4.8!
```

```
g++ (GCC) 4.8.2 20140120 (Red Hat 4.8.2-15)
Copyright (C) 2013 Free Software Foundation, Inc.
```

Process isolation in Mesos uses cgroups that are managed by cgconfig on Linux. The cgconfig service is not started by default on CentOS 6.8 and so needs to be installed, configured, and started, which is what the following commands do.

The default configuration for cgroups in the file /etc/cgconfig.conf does not attach the perf_event subsystem. To set this up, add the line

```
perf_event = /cgroup/perf_event
```

to the file. The full contents of my version of the file is as follows:

```
mount {
        cpuset      = /cgroup/cpuset;
        cpu         = /cgroup/cpu;
        cpuacct     = /cgroup/cpuacct;
        memory      = /cgroup/memory;
```

```
        devices    = /cgroup/devices;
        freezer    = /cgroup/freezer;
        net_cls    = /cgroup/net_cls;
        blkio      = /cgroup/blkio;
        perf_event = /cgroup/perf_event;
}
```

Now the libcgroup module is installed using the Linux yum command with a -y switch to avoid install confirmation.

```
$ yum install -y libcgroup
```

The cgconfig service can then be started using the Linux service command as root with a start option. The output from the command following shows that it has started correctly. I have also issued a chkconfig command with an on switch for the cgconfig service to ensure that it is automatically started if the server reboots.

```
$ service cgconfig start

Starting cgconfig service:                                    [  OK  ]

$ chkconfig cgconfig on
```

Finally, I have disabled the firewall on my server by stopping the iptables service. If you are creating a production install, you will not want to do this; but I just want to simplify the process. I have also issued a chkconfig command to ensure that the iptables service is not started if the server is rebooted.

```
$ service iptables stop

$ chkconfig iptables off
```

With the prerequisites for an Apache Mesos build covered, the Mesos source can now be obtained and a build attempted. This will be examined in the next section.

Mesos Build

I will create a temporary area when sourcing Mesos, extract the code, and then move the extracted code to a good location under /opt. From there I can execute the build, run tests, and install Mesos. The following Linux mkdir (make directory) command creates a directory /tmp/mesos and moves to that location:

```
$ mkdir /tmp/mesos ; cd /tmp/mesos
```

Then version 1.0.0 of the Mesos source is obtained using the following wget command. Mesos is obtained as a gzipped tar package of type .tar.gz:

```
$ wget http://www.apache.org/dist/mesos/1.1.0/mesos-1.1.0.tar.gz
```

The downloaded Mesos source package is then extracted using the Linux tar command with the -zxf switches. The f option specifies the file to extract, the x option means extract, and the z option allows the extraction of the gzipped format.

```
$ tar -zxf mesos-1.1.0.tar.gz
```

Given that the code is now extracted to a subdirectory called mesos-1.1.0, I will move that directory to /opt and then change directory to /opt.

```
$ mv mesos-1.1.0 /opt ; cd /opt
```

To simplify the path that I must use to access the Mesos system in the future, I will create a symbolic link called /opt/mesos that points to the package directory that was just moved /opt/mesos-1.1.0. This link is created using the Linux ln (make link) command with a -s switch. The following listing command ls -l shows that the link has been created:

```
$ ln -s mesos-1.1.0 mesos
$ ls -l

total 8
lrwxrwxrwx. 1 root root     11 Dec 28 20:34 mesos -> mesos-1.1.0
drwxr-xr-x. 9  501 wheel 4096 Nov  5 01:59 mesos-1.1.0
```

We will now use that link to change the directory into the Mesos release directory.

```
$ cd mesos
```

It is possible to build the Mesos code from a git-based repository; I will expand on that later. If you were to do that, you would need to use the bootstrap command to prepare the release. That is,

```
$ ./bootstrap.
```

I won't do that now, as I have downloaded the source, but I thought I would mention the command's use and meaning. To support the release, the JAVA_HOME variable needs to be defined. The following export command defines the variable to match the Java package that was just installed:

```
$ export JAVA_HOME=/usr/lib/jvm/java-1.7.0-openjdk-1.7.0.121.x86_64
```

The Mesos build needs to be able to find $JAVA_HOME/bin/java; otherwise errors like this can occur:

```
checking value of Java system property 'java.home'... /usr/lib/jvm/java-
1.8.0-openjdk-1.8.0.111-0.b15.el6_8.x86_64/jre
configure: error: could not guess JAVA_HOME
```

Next, a build directory /opt/mesos/build is created using the Linux mkdir command to execute the Mesos build. The Linux cd command is then used to change directory into that location.

```
$ mkdir build
```

```
$ cd build
```

From the build directory, the Mesos configure script is then called with a relative path of ../ or the directory above the current location. This script will prepare the build environment and set up make files.

```
$ ../configure
```

I can then use those make files by executing the following make command; the -j option specifies that the build will use two cores, while the V option will silence the build. You may remove the V option if you wish to see more output from the build.

```
$ make -j 2 V=0
```

When the build has completed, you can run the make check command following from the build directory. This will install the test framework commands that are necessary later in this chapter:

```
$ make check
```

You can ensure that the test framework has been created by executing the following commands from the build directory. As shown, the test framework exists, so the make check command has succeeded:

```
$  pwd ; ls -l src/test-framework
/opt/mesos/build
-rwxr-xr-x. 1 root root 7814 Dec 28 22:00 src/test-framework
```

Finally, a make install command will be executed to move Mesos components into standard locations so that they will be automatically found when Mesos is run.

```
$ make install
```

With the Mesos system built, I will examine the top-level directories under the build directory. The pwd command following shows the current location, whereas the ls command shows the content of the build directory. The contents of the bin and src directories will be used shortly:

```
$ pwd
/opt/mesos/build
```

```
$ ls
3rdparty  config.log  config.status  libtool  mesos.pc  src
bin       config.lt   include        Makefile mpi
```

The following ls command shows the contents of the build/bin directory; the mesos-master.sh and mesos-agent.sh scripts will be used later to start a Mesos master and slave agent. The prefixes shown following, gdb and lldb, are used for debugging Mesos, while valgrind is a programming tool for memory debugging.

```
$ ls bin
```

```
gdb-mesos-agent.sh     lldb-mesos-tests.sh     mesos-slave.sh
gdb-mesos-local.sh     mesos-agent-flags.sh    mesos-tests-flags.sh
gdb-mesos-master.sh    mesos-agent.sh          mesos-tests.sh
gdb-mesos-slave.sh     mesos-local-flags.sh    valgrind-mesos-agent.sh
gdb-mesos-tests.sh     mesos-local.sh          valgrind-mesos-local.sh
lldb-mesos-agent.sh    mesos-master-flags.sh   valgrind-mesos-master.sh
lldb-mesos-local.sh    mesos-master.sh         valgrind-mesos-slave.sh
lldb-mesos-master.sh   mesos.sh                valgrind-mesos-tests.sh
lldb-mesos-slave.sh    mesos-slave-flags.sh
```

Before attempting to start Mesos, I will create some system directories for it to support logging and runtime data. The mkdir commands following create Mesos working directories under /var/log and /var/lib:

```
$ mkdir  /var/lib/mesos
```

```
$ mkdir  /var/log/mesos
```

In the next section, I will examine how to start Mesos on a single node and show that it is running.

Starting Mesos

Like many of the distributed big data systems, such as Hadoop and Spark, Mesos is a master/slave-based system. A single master component (or multiple masters if high availability (HA) is used) manage a cluster of Mesos slave or agent components. The commands following show how a single Mesos master and agent can be started:

To launch the master component, the mesos-master.sh script is used in the bin directory. A --ip switch is used to specify the IP address of the host. I have used the server's IP address, as I intend to access Mesos remotely. A --work_dir switch has been used to specify the directory that Mesos should store runtime data. Finally, redirection has been used to store the command's output to a file called master.log.

```
$ ./bin/mesos-master.sh --ip=192.168.56.3 --work_dir=/var/lib/mesos >
./master.log 2>&1  &
```

The agent start command is much the same as the master. The script is now called mesos-agent.sh, and a --master option is used to identify the Mesos master component on the local server at port 5050. The only difference here is that a --launcher option has been used of type posix (portable operating system interface). This tells the agent to look for cgroup information under the directory /cgroup and not /sys/cgroup.

```
$ ./bin/mesos-agent.sh --master=192.168.56.3:5050 --launcher=posix  --work_
dir=/var/lib/mesos > ./agent.log 2>&1  &
```

It is now possible to prove that these scripts are running from the command line using the grep command. The Linux ps -ef command gives a full Linux process listing; the grep commands following then search that content for the Mesos master and agent scripts. As you can see, the master and agent are running with process numbers 1373 and 1397:

```
$ ps -ef | grep mesos-master
root      1373  1358  0 17:09 pts/0     00:00:10 /opt/mesos/build/src/.libs/
lt-mesos-master --ip=192.168.56.3 --work_dir=/var/lib/mesos
root      1483  1358  0 19:19 pts/0     00:00:00 grep mesos-master

$ ps -ef | grep mesos-agent
root      1397  1358  0 17:09 pts/0     00:00:01 /opt/mesos/build/src/.libs/
lt-mesos-agent --master=192.168.56.3:5050 --launcher=posix --work_dir=/var/
lib/mesos
root      1485  1358  0 19:19 pts/0     00:00:00 grep mesos-agent
```

Given that Mesos is now running, its user interface can be accessed from a web browser at port 5050 using the local server's IP address, which is 192.168.56.3:

```
http://192.168.56.3:5050
```

The next section will examine the Mesos web-based user interface.

Mesos User Interface

The main Mesos user interface (Figure 4-3) is accessed by the URL given at the end of the last section on port 5050.

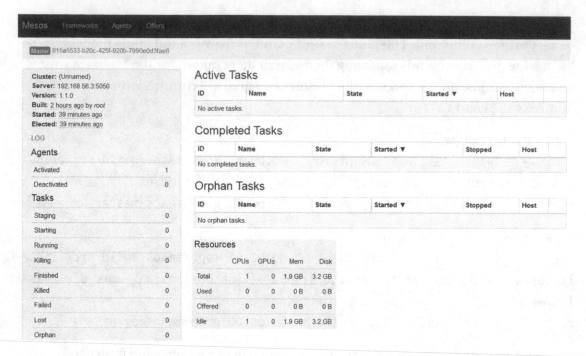

Figure 4-3. *Mesos user interface*

The front page of the Mesos user interface has four main menu options: Mesos, Frameworks, Agents, and Offers. The Mesos option in Figure 4-3 shows active, completed, and orphaned tasks. It also shows all of the states that those tasks may be in, from Staging through to Orphan. It shows the number of activated and deactivated agents as well as some details about the version of the Mesos build. (I have manipulated this image to make it fit the page—the resources section should really be at the bottom of the left-hand menu.) It shows the cluster-based resource details in terms of CPU, GPU (graphics processing unit), memory, and disk.

I will examine frameworks a little later when a test Mesos framework is run. The next Figure 4-4 shows the Mesos Agents menu option; in this case, a single agent is shown running on the local host.

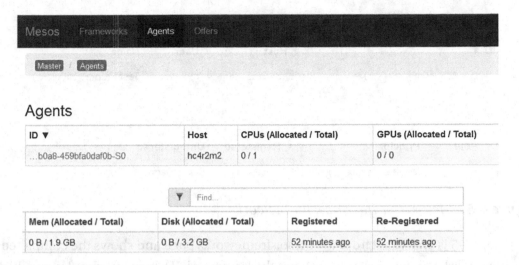

Figure 4-4. *Mesos user interface: Agents*

The Agents page lists the agents in the cluster in terms of their IDs, the hosts that they run on, and the resources allocated to them. It also shows master registration times to give an indication of how long this agent has been running.

Given that Mesos is now running, and its user interface is accessible, it is time to try and run a test framework. The "make check" build command run earlier created the necessary frameworks as part of the build. The Mesos quick start has further details of frameworks to be run. From the /opt/mesos/build/ directory, I will run the following Mesos test framework as root. The example framework following is a C++ framework:

```
$ pwd
/opt/mesos/build/
$ ./src/test-framework --master=192.168.56.3:5050
```

Once run, the Mesos user interface can be used to check the frameworks menu option. This will show the frameworks that have been run on the Mesos cluster; see Figure 4-5 following.

Completed Frameworks

ID ▼	Host	User	Name
...920b-7990e0d3fae6-0000	hc4r2m2	root	Test Framework (C++)

▼ Find...

Role	Principal	Registered	Unregistered
*	test-framework-cpp	5 hours ago	5 hours ago

Figure 4-5. *Mesos user interface: Frameworks*

Figure 4-5 is an extract from the Mesos frameworks page and shows the completed C++ framework that was just run. It shows the framework ID, host, user, and name. It also shows role, principal, as well as registration details.

By selecting the framework ID in Figure 4-5, it is possible to view task details for that framework. Figure 4-6 following shows an example of a completed framework's tasks.

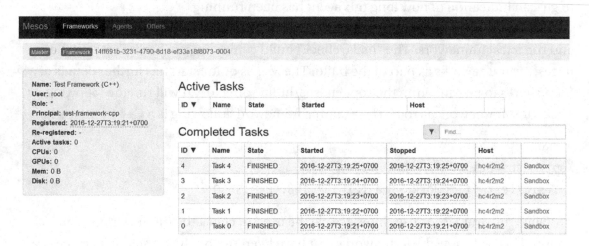

Figure 4-6. *Mesos user interface: Tasks*

Figure 4-6 shows that the C++ framework that was run contained five tasks that completed with a status of FINISHED. Start and stop times are provided as well as the host and environment that they ran in.

I would like to close this section by providing a little more information on the Mesos file system. For instance, when running frameworks, I found the log files associated with a given framework under the following directory:

```
/var/lib/mesos/slaves/14ff691b-3231-4790-8d18-ef33a18f8073-S0/
frameworks/14ff691b-3231-4790-8d18-ef33a18f8073-0004/executors/default/
runs/latest
```

This path shows the logs for the slave or agent b3073deb-533f-46df-a322-a43999d47193-S0. The framework run instance ID is 14ff691b-3231-4790-8d18-ef33a18f8073-0004. Logs for the framework run are found in the latest subdirectory in this path; they are called "stderr" and "stdout." The Linux more commands following show their content. These log files are very useful: if a framework fails, they may show the reason why:

```
$ more stdout

Registered executor on hc4r2m2
Starting task 0
Finishing task 0
Starting task 1
Finishing task 1
Starting task 2
Finishing task 2
Starting task 3
Finishing task 3
Starting task 4
Finishing task 4

$ more stderr

I1227 09:19:21.513962 29638 exec.cpp:162] Version: 1.1.0
I1227 09:19:21.539650 29644 exec.cpp:237] Executor registered on agent
14ff691b-3231-4790-8d18-ef33a18f8073-S0
I1227 09:19:25.647706 29644 exec.cpp:414] Executor asked to shutdown
```

There are also a couple of other test frameworks available that can be run: a Java and a Python framework. The commands to run them are shown following. Just change the IP address to match your server(s):

```
$  ./src/examples/java/test-framework 192.168.56.3:5050
```

```
$  ./src/examples/python/test-framework 192.168.56.3:5050
```

The next section will cover some potential errors that may occur during the build.

Build Errors

I thought it would be useful to provide a section to cover some of the errors that may be encountered when building and using Mesos. The error following occurred because I had not set up an entry in /etc/hosts for my local server:

```
WARNING: Logging before InitGoogleLogging() is written to STDERR
I1224 17:50:34.481420 26356 main.cpp:243] Build: 2016-12-24 16:42:26 by root
I1224 17:50:34.481608 26356 main.cpp:244] Version: 1.1.0
Failed to obtain the IP address for 'hc4r2m2'; the DNS service may not be
able to resolve it: Name or service not known
```

The next error occurred because the Mesos agent when run expected cgroups to be under /sys rather than /cgroups. The solution was to use a "--launcher=posix" switch when starting the agent to indicate that the local host had a posix cgroup format.

```
Failed to create a containerizer: Could not create MesosContainerizer:
Failed to create launcher: Failed to create Linux
```

```
launcher: Failed to mount cgroups hierarchy at '/sys/fs/cgroup/freezer':
Failed to create directory '/sys/fs/cgroup/freezer': No such file or
directory
```

The next section will consider the Mesosphere system, an integrated, Mesos-based cluster management system.

Mesosphere DCOS

When writing a chapter on Mesos, I don't think it would be complete without considering Mesosphere, which is an integrated Mesos-based system for cluster management. It includes tools for long-term and batch scheduling such as Marathon and Chronos. It provides web-based user interfaces for application and cluster management as well as a command line interface (CLI).

DCOS is an acronym for Data Center Operating System. As per Mesos in the previous section, the aim is to allow multiple frameworks to share the resources of a cluster with Mesos managing those resources via a system of resource offers. In this section, I will install DCOS from the site dcos.io and carry out an advanced CLI install. I have chosen this approach because it allows me command line access, and I can also install master servers and agents separately.

The following sections will separate the install into manageable sections such as creating the install server, considering prerequisites, and installing the master and agent nodes. Finally, the resulting interfaces and possible error conditions will be examined.

Overview

I will install DCOS using three machines: an install server (192.168.1.119/hc4r2m2), a master server (192.168.1.120/hc4r2m3), and an agent or slave server (192.168.1.121/hc4r2m4). Of course in a data center install, there could be thousands of servers and multiple master servers, but this minimal install will illustrate the process. The following sections will start by considering the SSH configuration used and the prerequisites needed. Each server will then be installed separately. This install will be carried out on CentOS 7.2 (required by DCOS) 64-bit minimal servers. The details for this install can be found on the dcos.io site at

```
https://dcos.io/docs/1.8/administration/installing/custom/
```

SSH configuration

Given that I have only three servers in use for this mini Mesosphere install, I will enable SSH (secure shell) access between them. This will enable me to move between them easily during the setup. I will enable SSH access from the install server to the master and agent. I will also enable SSH access from the master server to its agent.

On the install server (192.168.1.119/hc4r2m2) as the root user, I execute the following command to generate SSH RSA (Rivest-Shamir-Adleman) based keys:

```
$ ssh-keygen
```

Entering empty responses to prompts creates an RSA-based key that will be used for the install. This creates an SSH configuration under $HOME/.ssh on the local server. Now I copy the newly generated key to all servers (even the local one) using the ssh-copy-id command. The root password must be entered when prompted.

```
$ ssh-copy-id    root@192.168.1.119
$ ssh-copy-id    root@192.168.1.120
$ ssh-copy-id    root@192.168.1.121
```

I test this by trying to access each server using the ssh command. I should not be prompted for a password to gain access. If prompted to accept the server, I type yes.

```
$ ssh hc4r2m2
$ ssh hc4r2m3
$ ssh hc4r2m4
```

To exit each session I type exit to return to the original install server session. SSH access is configured on the master server (192.168.1.120/hc4r2m3) in the same way. An RSA key is created using ssh-keygen. Then the key is copied to both the master and agent servers. Finally, ssh access is tested. You should not be prompted for a password.

```
$ ssh-keygen
```

```
$ ssh-copy-id    root@192.168.1.120
$ ssh-copy-id    root@192.168.1.121
```

```
$ ssh hc4r2m3
$ ssh hc4r2m4
```

Assuming that the SSH access configuration is successful, it is now time to consider the prerequisites for a DCOS install.

Install Prerequisites

In this section, I will cover the prerequisites for the DCOS install; these actions should be carried out on each server (including the install server).

Do not try to minimize the machines used by not using a separate install server. The install server should not be one of the master or agent machines.

I will begin by installing some of the required yum-based packages for the install. I will use the -y switch to avoid the need for install prompts.

```
$ yum -y install tar xz unzip  ipset curl
```

Next I will install Docker, which supports Mesos containerisation. The details for this Docker install can be found on the dcos.io site at the following URL:

```
https://dcos.io/docs/1.7/administration/installing/custom/system-
requirements/install-docker-centos/
```

Before continuing, a yum upgrade will be executed to make sure that all yum-based packages on the server are up to date. This may take quite a while (mine took 30 minutes), so be patient. The -y switch avoids the need for install prompts, and --assumeyes assumes that all responses will be yes. The --tolerant option just makes yum tolerant of command line errors.

```
$ yum -y upgrade --assumeyes --tolerant
```

Before continuing, it is necessary to ensure that the kernel is at least 3.10. Remember that in the Mesos install earlier in this chapter, the kernel had to be updated to support Mesos. The Linux uname command with a -r switch provides kernel release details. Note that we have a 3.10 kernel.

```
$ uname -r
3.10.0-327.el7.x86_64
```

To support Mesos Docker use, a storage overlay must be used. The following command creates a config file called overlay.conf under the directory /etc/modules-load.d/. It contains a single command word, overlay:

```
$  tee /etc/modules-load.d/overlay.conf <<-'EOF'
overlay
EOF
```

This change will take effect on a server reboot, so start the reboot with the Linux reboot command reboot as the root user.

```
$ reboot
```

Log back into the server as root and verify that the overlay change has been effective with the following lsmod (list modules) command. If the output shows an overlay line as in the following, then it has worked:

```
[root@hc4r2m2 ~]# lsmod | grep overlay
overlay                42451  0
```

Now create the yum.repo configuration file for Docker so that the Docker engine can be installed using yum. A file called docker.repo will be created under /etc/yum.repos.d/ using the following command. Note that the baseurl in this repo file supports a CentOS 7 Docker install:

```
$  tee /etc/yum.repos.d/docker.repo <<-'EOF'
[dockerrepo]
name=Docker Repository
baseurl=https://yum.dockerproject.org/repo/main/centos/7/
enabled=1
gpgcheck=1
gpgkey=https://yum.dockerproject.org/gpg
EOF
```

Now configure Docker to use the overlay just created by creating an override.conf file under /etc/systemd/system/docker.service.d/. Note that the original install instructions advise that a virtual device option (-H fd://) should be added to the end of the ExecStart line. I removed this to avoid Docker start errors.

```
$ mkdir -p /etc/systemd/system/docker.service.d
$ tee /etc/systemd/system/docker.service.d/override.conf <<- EOF
[Service]
ExecStart=
ExecStart=/usr/bin/docker daemon --storage-driver=overlay
EOF
```

Also, to avoid Docker install warnings, I precreated the docker directory /var/lib/docker/:

```
$ mkdir /var/lib/docker
```

Next disable SE Linux by changing the file /etc/sysconfig/selinux; set SE Linux disabled as shown following. If this is not done, then Docker will issue errors when installing. Also the DCOS master and agent scripts will fail:

```
$ vi /etc/sysconfig/selinux
SELINUX=disabled
```

To avoid the need to reboot the server to pick up the changes, also set SE Linux to permissive with the following command, which will allow DCOS to work:

```
$ setenforce 0
```

A check of the SE Linux configuration mode using the sestatus (SELinux status) command following shows that in the current session SE Linux is in permissive mode, whereas the configuration file that was just changed is in disabled mode. Either will work for Mesos:

```
$ sestatus | grep -i mode

Current mode:                  permissive
Mode from config file:         disabled
```

Now install the docker engine using the Linux yum command; this will use the repo file that was just created to locate the Docker binaries.

```
$ yum -y install --assumeyes --tolerant docker-engine
```

Enable docker daemon using the systemctl command following so that future reboots of the server will cause Docker to be started. For CentOS 7, systemctl now performs the same function that chkconfig did for CentOS 6:

```
$ systemctl enable docker
```

Now start the Docker daemon to support the support the rest of the DCOS Mesos install.

```
$ systemctl start docker
```

Verify that Docker is installed and running by issuing a docker info command to obtain install configuration information from a running Docker server.

```
$ docker info
```

I won't include the whole output of the docker info command here to save space. As long as you see an info output list like that following, you are OK to proceed:

```
Containers: 1
 Running: 0
 Paused: 0
 Stopped: 1
Images: 2
Server Version: 1.12.6
Storage Driver: overlay
......
Insecure Registries:
 127.0.0.0/8
```

I will also install the network time protocol (NTP) component so that each server synchronizes its system time using ntpd.

```
$ yum -y install ntp
```

Then enable the NTP daemon using the systemctl command so that it starts on reboot and start the service.

```
$ systemctl enable ntpd.service
$ systemctl start ntpd
```

Another prerequisite for the Mesos DCOS master and agent is that a group called nogroup exists in the /etc/group configuration file. To meet this, I have manually added the group using the vi editor as shown following. Then I prove that it exists by using the getent (get entries) command:

```
vi /etc/group
nogroup:x:5000:

$ getent group nogroup
nogroup:x:5000:
```

That completes the list of necessary prerequisites to allow the DCOS master and agent installs to complete. Now the install server (hc4r2m2) can be prepared to progress the DCOS advanced CLI install.

Install Server

As previously mentioned, my install server (192.168.1.119/hc4r2m2) will be used to source the DCOS scripts and prepare for the DCOS CLI advanced install. Each master and agent install will use this server to source install scripts. To progress this install, I will create a temporary directory under /opt/ called dcos_tmp. I will then move to that directory using the cd command. Finally, I will create a directory called genconf that will be used to support the DCOS install.

```
$ mkdir /opt/dcos_tmp/
$ cd /opt/dcos_tmp/
$ mkdir genconf
```

The DCOS install needs a way of detecting the IP address on each server. To do this, a script called ip-detect needs to be created under the genconf directory. Given that all servers being used here are installed with CentOS 7.2, then the command "ip addr" can be used to determine network interfaces. Given that I know from experience that the network interface that I am interested in will start with enp, then I can use the following command to get the enp-based interface name that I want:

```
$ ip addr | grep enp
2: enp0s25: <BROADCAST,MULTICAST,UP,LOWER_UP> mtu 1500 qdisc pfifo_fast
state UP qlen 1000
    inet 192.168.1.119/24 brd 192.168.1.255 scope global enp0s25
```

The preceding output shows that IP address 192.168.1.119 is associated with network interface enp0s25. I need to know that to create an ip-detect script for DCOS.

```
$ cat <<EOF > /opt/dcos_tmp/genconf/ip-detect
#!/usr/bin/env bash
set -o nounset -o errexit
export PATH=/usr/sbin:/usr/bin:$PATH
echo $(ip addr show enp0s25| grep -Eo '[0-9]{1,3}\.[0-9]{1,3}\.[0-9]{1,3}\.
[0-9]{1,3}' | head -1)
EOF

$ chmod 755 ./genconf/ip-detect
```

The preceding cat command creates a file called genconf/ip-detect, which contains a simple bash script to determine the server's IP address. The chmod script just makes the script executable. As you can see in the following, the script works and will be transferred to the other servers as the master and agent are installed.

```
$ ./genconf/ip-detect
192.168.1.119
```

A simple yaml-based configuration file now needs to be created called genconf/config.yaml to support the DCOS install. The cat command following dumps this text to the new file. It defines a bootstrap URL that other servers will use to connect to the install server. It names the cluster and defines which servers are masters. It also defines the names of the DNS servers that will be used.

```
$ cat <<EOF > /opt/dcos_tmp/genconf/config.yaml
---
bootstrap_url: http://192.168.1.119:9000
cluster_name: 'cluster1'
exhibitor_storage_backend: static
ip_detect_filename: /opt/dcos_tmp/genconf/ip-detect
master_discovery: static
master_list:
- 192.168.56.3
```

```
resolvers:
- 8.8.4.4
- 8.8.8.8
EOF
```

Now the curl ("see" URL) command is used to download the script dcos_generate_config.sh from the dcos.io site. This is a big file weighing in at around 550 MB, so it will take some time to download. This script has a lot of embedded data like a DCOS tar file for later installs. Once downloaded, the chmod command is used to make the script executable. The script is then executed using the bash command.

```
$ cd  /opt/dcos_tmp/
$ curl -O https://downloads.dcos.io/dcos/EarlyAccess/commit/14509fe1e7899f4
39527fb39867194c7a425c771/dcos_generate_config.sh

$ chmod 755 dcos_generate_config.sh

$ bash ./dcos_generate_config.sh
```

I have severely limited the output of this script to display a few lines following; the actual output covers many pages. As long as you receive no errors and see the "Generating" line at the end, you should be fine:

```
Extracting image from this script and loading into docker daemon, this step
can take a few minutes
dcos-genconf.14509fe1e7899f4395-3a2b7e03c45cd615da.tar
c56b7dabbc7a: Loading layer 5.041 MB/5.041 MB
cb9346f72a60: Loading layer 22.73 MB/22.73 MB
bc3f3016e472: Loading layer 4.063 MB/4.063 MB
24e0af39909a: Loading layer 129.5 MB/129.5 MB
fd56668380be: Loading layer 2.048 kB/2.048 kB
90755ec2374c: Loading layer 415.4 MB/415.4 MB
58ae10cff6df: Loading layer 4.608 kB/4.608 kB
.....
Package filename: packages/dcos-metadata/dcos-metadata--setup_
baffb473b10beb8312459104d944e4c03222bb6b.tar.xz
Generating Bash configuration files for DC/OS
```

Now the DCOS install package is hosted using the nginx Docker container using the following docker command from the dcos_tmp directory:

```
$ cd /opt/dcos_tmp
$ docker run -d -p 9000:80 -v /opt/dcos_tmp/genconf/serve:/usr/share/nginx/
html:ro nginx
```

The output looks like this:

```
:/usr/share/nginx/html:ro nginx
Unable to find image 'nginx:latest' locally
latest: Pulling from library/nginx
75a822cd7888: Pull complete
0aefb9dc4a57: Pull complete
046e44ee6057: Pull complete
Digest: sha256:fab482910aae9630c93bd24fc6fcecb9f9f792c24a8974f5e46d8ad625ac2357
Status: Downloaded newer image for nginx:latest
77bb9b824edbce6408507a52b8a78263d10444aa0f49130d4e8f67b122e7594c
```

The install server is now ready to be used to install DCOS master and agent servers. In this example, a single master and agent are being installed, but you could need to install thousands of servers. The next step will involve installing the DCOS master server.

Master Server

As the root user on the DCOS master server (192.168.1.120 / hc4r2m3), create a temporary directory /tmp/dcos and move to it.

```
$ mkdir /tmp/dcos
$ cd /tmp/dcos
```

Now use the curl command to download the dcos_install script from the install server:

```
$ curl -O http://192.168.1.119:9000/dcos_install.sh
```

The output following shows the result of the curl command as the file is downloaded:

% Total	%	Received	% Xferd	Average Speed Dload	Upload	Time Total	Time Spent	Time Left	Current Speed
100 13410	100	13410	0 0	4966k	0	--:--:--	--:--:--	--:--:--	6547k

Change the permissions on the install script so that it is executable using the chmod command.

```
$ chmod 755 dcos_install.sh
```

Now run the script with a master parameter so that it will configure the current server as a DCOS master.

```
$ bash ./dcos_install.sh master
```

I would not normally add the output of this script here, as I think generally that this wastes space. However, in this case, I will make an exception, as this output provides a list of all the install tests that DCOS uses. If any one of these fails, then the install will fail.

```
Starting DC/OS Install Process
Running preflight checks
Checking if DC/OS is already installed: PASS (Not installed)
PASS Is SELinux disabled?
Checking if docker is installed and in PATH: PASS
Checking docker version requirement (>= 1.6): PASS (1.12.6)
Checking if curl is installed and in PATH: PASS
Checking if bash is installed and in PATH: PASS
Checking if ping is installed and in PATH: PASS
Checking if tar is installed and in PATH: PASS
Checking if xz is installed and in PATH: PASS
Checking if unzip is installed and in PATH: PASS
Checking if ipset is installed and in PATH: PASS
Checking if systemd-notify is installed and in PATH: PASS
Checking if systemd is installed and in PATH: PASS
Checking systemd version requirement (>= 200): PASS (219)
Checking if group 'nogroup' exists: PASS
Checking if port 80 (required by mesos-ui) is in use: PASS
Checking if port 53 (required by mesos-dns) is in use: PASS
```

```
Checking if port 15055 (required by dcos-history) is in use: PASS
Checking if port 5050 (required by mesos-master) is in use: PASS
Checking if port 2181 (required by zookeeper) is in use: PASS
Checking if port 8080 (required by marathon) is in use: PASS
Checking if port 3888 (required by zookeeper) is in use: PASS
Checking if port 8181 (required by exhibitor) is in use: PASS
Checking if port 8123 (required by mesos-dns) is in use: PASS
Checking Docker is configured with a production storage driver: WARNING:
bridge-nf-call-iptables is disabled
WARNING: bridge-nf-call-ip6tables is disabled
PASS (overlay)
Creating directories under /etc/mesosphere
Creating role file for master
Configuring DC/OS
Setting and starting DC/OS
Created symlink from /etc/systemd/system/multi-user.target.wants/dcos-
setup.service to /etc/systemd/system/dcos-setup.service.
```

As long as the last line ("setup.service") is shown and the preceding output shows that all of the tests have passed, then I can move on and install an agent.

Agent Server

The DCOS agent install is very similar to the master install; the server used will be 192.168.1.121 or hc4r2m4. Initially I will create a working directory on this server called /tmp/dcos and move into that directory.

```
$ mkdir /tmp/dcos && cd /tmp/dcos
```

As with the master install, the config.yaml bootstrap URL is used to download the dcos_install.sh script to the agent server.

```
$ curl -O http://192.168.1.119:9000/dcos_install.sh
```

The downloaded script is then made executable using the Linux chmod command.

```
$ chmod 755 dcos_install.sh
```

The script is then executed in a bash shell as follows. It is possible to give the script the option of slave or slave_public. I have chosen the public option to make a publicly visible slave node.

```
$ bash dcos_install.sh slave_public
```

Again, the install script runs a series of checks, the same set that was carried out for the master install. The output looks very similar, so I have clipped it here:

```
Starting DC/OS Install Process
Running preflight checks
...
Setting and starting DC/OS
Created symlink from /etc/systemd/system/multi-user.target.wants/dcos-
setup.service to /etc/systemd/system/dcos-setup.service.
```

Assuming that the install completes without error and that the last line of the preceding output indicates that it is setting up the service ("setup.service"), then the DCOS interface should be available. This will be examined in the next section.

User Interfaces

The DCOS Mesos Exhibitor ZooKeeper user interface should now be accessible at the following URL. Note that the IP address used for this URL is for the master server:

```
http://192.168.1.120:8181/exhibitor/v1/ui/index.html
```

When accessed, the ZooKeeper Exhibitor DCOS user interface is shown in Figure 4-7. This provides access to the control panel showing the state of the Mesos master servers. Only one server is in operation currently (192.168.1.120), and it has an operation green state as shown following.

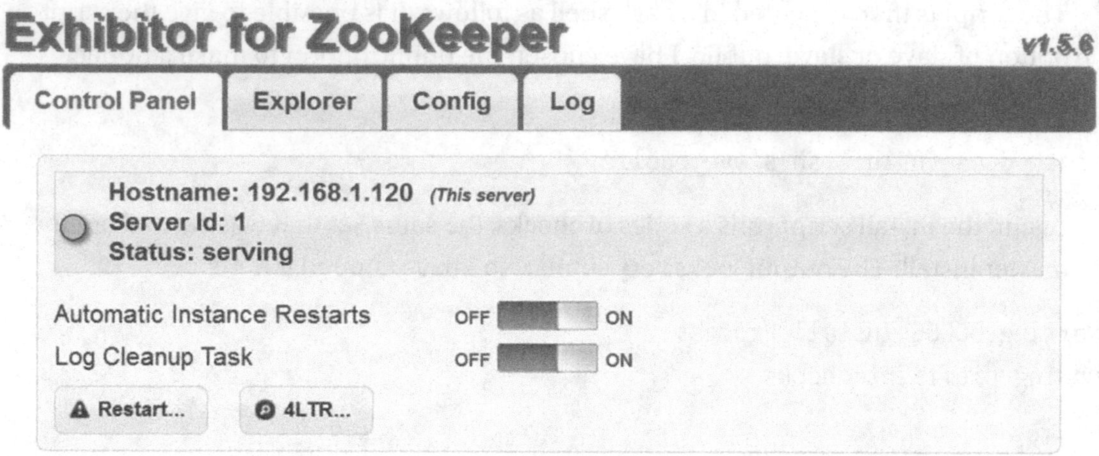

Exhibitor for ZooKeeper

v1.5.6

| Control Panel | Explorer | Config | Log |

Hostname: 192.168.1.120 *(This server)*
Server Id: 1
Status: serving

Automatic Instance Restarts   OFF ▮▮▮ ON

Log Cleanup Task   OFF ▮▮▮ ON

⚠ Restart...   🅾 4LTR...

Figure 4-7. *DCOS Exhibitor for ZooKeeper*

The interface offers a cluster explorer, a configuration detail section, and a logging section. It offers the ability to enable automatic master server restarts and well as log cleanup.

I think that you can try this install for yourself and investigate the configuration and logging options. I will cover access to logging output more fully in the next section. However, I thought that the explorer section warrants further investigation, as it also supplies details about some of the tools available in DCOS.

Figure 4-8 shows the Exhibitor Explorer option. Although I haven't included it here, each option in the preceding list also has associated path, stats, and data details. What is interesting here is the path/tool details available. Marathon is the scheduler for long-running applications. Cronos is the scheduler for tasks of shorter duration. ZooKeeper you are probably already familiarly with; it is used for configuration and master election. The Mesos interface provides an interface to the Mesos cluster and provides details of frameworks and offers.

Exhibitor for ZooKeeper

v1.5.6

Control Panel	Explorer	Config	Log

```
□ ⬛/
    ⊞ ☐ cluster-id
    ⊞ ☐ cosmos
    ⊞ ☐ dcos
    ⊞ ☐ lock
    ⊞ ☐ marathon
    ⊞ ☐ mesos
    ⊞ ☐ zookeeper
```

Figure 4-8. *DCOS Exhibitor Explorer*

The DCOS Marathon user interface is available at the following master URL:

```
http://192.168.1.120:8080/ui/#/apps/
```

The current interface (Figure 4-9) shows an empty Marathon scheduler. It has the ability to show the status of running apps as well as the resources and health of applications. It offers the ability to create applications and groups, search for applications, and organize running applications by their attributes.

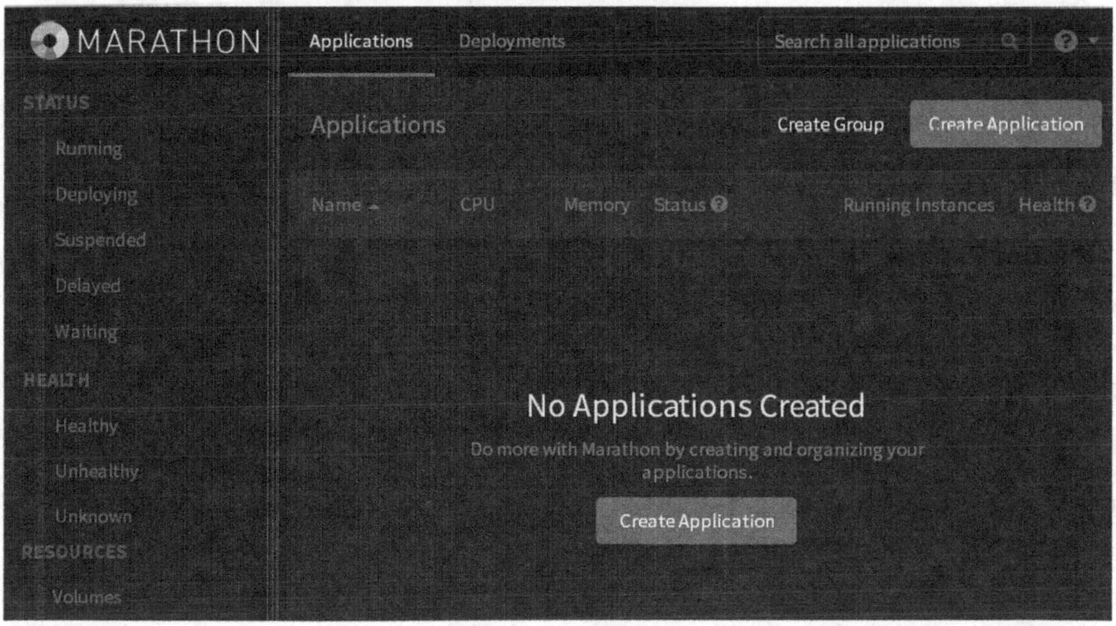

Figure 4-9. *DCOS Marathon*

The DCOS Mesos interface is the same as that shown in the previous section where Mesos was built from source code. It is shown here to make the point that it is the same application that DCOS/Mesosphere uses: DCOS is an integrated environment based on Mesos but with added tools and interfaces. Mesos is available via the URL

`http://192.168.1.120:5050/#/.`

The DCOS Mesos user interface (Figure 4-10) offers options to examine frameworks that are running or have run on the Mesos managed cluster. It offers the ability to examine the Mesos cluster slave (or agents) that reside on cluster nodes, and it allows the offers that Mesos makes to frameworks to be examined.

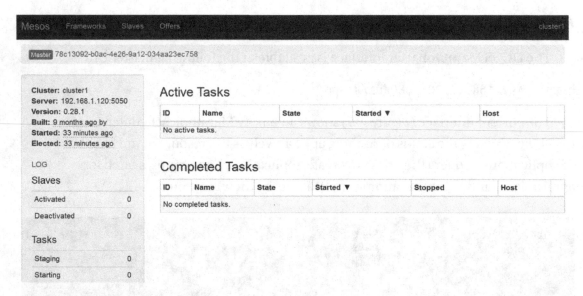

Figure 4-10. *DCOS Mesos*

Remember that the frameworks are the clustered/distributed systems that will share the Mesos cluster with the help of Mesos. The offers are the resource offers from Mesos to those frameworks that, if accepted, allow the frameworks to run on the cluster. The slaves or agents are the nodes in the Mesos cluster that the frameworks will run on.

Examples of potential frameworks might be associated with storage, for instance, Hadoop, Cassandra, or Riak. They might be associated with Apache Spark or Yarn. They might be associated with web-based processing. However, most corporations will probably have a variety of these in operation.

Those of you who are observant might have noticed that I mentioned Apache Yarn on Mesos just now when actually Yarn and Mesos scheduling conflict with one another. This is a topic that I will tackle later in this chapter by examining the Apache Myriad project.

The DCOS install is complicated: it requires multiple nodes and resources as well as time to be completed. I thought that it would be useful to provide sections to cover the issues encountered when installing DCOS and the resources used to solve them. The next two sections will list both the resources and the issues found. I will also expand on why those issues occurred.

Logging and Problem Investigation

Installing DCOS was not a simple process; it took many attempts and much investigation of issues before I finally created a working DCOS system. Given the complexity of the task, I thought that it would be sensible to create a section in this chapter that documented the resources that I used to solve problems apart from Google searches and just asking people. The DCOS troubleshooting page is very useful as it provides journal and logging information associated with each DCOS server. The URL is

https://dcos.io/docs/1.7/administration/installing/custom/troubleshooting/.

DCOS uses the journalctl command to query the systemd CentOS journal. It uses this approach rather than creating log files under /var/log/ like most other Apache systems. The following journal command examples extract journal information for each DCOS server. It was in this way that I tracked and solved many DCOS-related issues. The following command extracts journal entries for the DCOS ZooKeeper Exhibitor; the -b options means extract since boot time.

```
$ journalctl -u dcos-exhibitor -b | more
```

The following command extracts journal information for the Mesos master server. Piping the output to more just allows me to page through the lines of event information that are provided:

```
$ journalctl -u dcos-mesos-master -b | more
```

The following command lists journal entries for the Mesos DNS server:

```
$ journalctl -u dcos-mesos-dns -b | more
```

The following command lists journal entries for the Mesos Marathon server:

```
$ journalctl -u dcos-marathon -b | more
```

The following command lists journal entries for the Mesos admin router server:

```
$ journalctl -u dcos-nginx -b | more
```

The following command lists journal entries for the Mesos gen-resolvconf service, which helps agents locate master servers:

```
$ journalctl -u dcos-gen-resolvconf -b | more
```

The following commands list journal entries for the Mesos slave (or agent) servers whether they are public or not:

```
$ journalctl -u dcos-mesos-slave -b | more
$ journalctl -u dcos-mesos-slave-public -b | more
```

It is also possible to determine the exhibitor cluster status as shown by the URL following. The output shows that the current master is running and is serving the cluster. It shows that the cluster master is leading; but this is not surprising, as there is only one master:

```
http://192.168.1.120:8181/exhibitor/v1/cluster/status
```

```
[{"code":3,"description":"serving","hostname":"192.168.1.120","isLeader":true}]
```

Given the time available to investigate the DCOS system, this is as far as I will take my investigation. I will leave it up to the reader to create applications and launch frameworks onto the DCOS cluster. In the next section, I will investigate some of the errors that occurred during this build.

Build Errors

I think that it is useful to examine the errors that I encountered when attempting to install the DCOS software. It can be helpful to understand why these errors occurred and how they can be resolved. The following error occurred because Docker was not installed when I tried to install DCOS. I assumed that DCOS would install Docker for me:

```
$ bash ./dcos_generate_config.sh
docker should be installed and running. Aborting.
```

The next warning occurred because by default, the initial Docker install that I was using used a loopback device. The solution was to use the DCOS Docker install shown here and layerFS:

```
WARNING: Usage of loopback devices is strongly discouraged for production
use. Use `--storage-opt dm.thinpooldev` to specify a custom block storage
device.
```

The next error occurred because my Docker configuration file, docker.service.d, used a virtual device in its configuration. Following I show the error displayed on investigation by checking Linux journal entries; and following that, I show the original and changed entries for the ExecStart line in the file docker.service.d. The change fixed the problem:

```
$ journalctl -xe

Jan 08 17:09:57 hc4r2m2 dockerd[16236]: time="2017-01-
08T17:09:57.663752772+13:00" level=fatal msg="Error starting daemon: error
initializing graphdriver: devicemapper: Error running device
Jan 08 17:09:57 hc4r2m2 polkitd[10209]: Unregistered Authentication Agent
for unix-process:16230:1246567 (system bus name :1.42, object path /org/
freedesktop/PolicyKit1/AuthenticationAgent,

ExecStart=/usr/bin/docker daemon --storage-driver=overlay -H fd://
ExecStart=/usr/bin/docker daemon --storage-driver=overlay
```

Given more time, I would investigate the Docker configuration further and create dedicated, file-system-based logical volumes that Docker could use for storage. The next error seems complicated due to the volume of errors produced, but was quite simple. The install server must be running when trying to install the master and agent. It is the location from which the master and agent DCOS installs source DCOS:

```
$ bash ./dcos_install.sh master
$ journalctl -xe

Jan 09 16:25:52 hc4r2m2 curl[11516]: * Failed connect to 192.168.56.3:9000;
Connection refused
Jan 09 16:25:52 hc4r2m2 curl[11516]: * Closing connection 0
Jan 09 16:25:52 hc4r2m2 curl[11516]: curl: (7) Failed connect to
192.168.56.3:9000; Connection refused
```

The next error occurred due to the Docker configuration when installing the master and agent. The master and agent DCOS installs run through a series of checks to determine whether components are installed and Docker is configured correctly. The solution was to use layerFS in the Docker install:

```
Docker is configured to use the devicemapper storage driver with a loopback
device behind it. This is highly recommended against by Docker and the
community at large for production use[0][1]. See the docker documentation on
selecting an alternate storage driver, or use alternate storage than
loopback
for the devicemapper driver.
```

The next error occurred again because the install server was not available; ignore the IP address change used here. Some of the DCOS install investigation was carried out using Oracle VirtualBox while travelling, and the IP addresses used reflect that:

```
Jan 12 16:08:00 hc4r2m3 curl[10623]: * Failed connect to 192.168.56.7:9000;
No route to host
Jan 12 16:08:00 hc4r2m3 curl[10623]: * Closing connection 0
Jan 12 16:08:00 hc4r2m3 curl[10623]: curl: (7) Failed connect to
192.168.56.7:9000; No route to host
Jan 12 16:08:00 hc4r2m3 systemd[1]: Failed to start Pkgpanda: Download DC/OS
to this host..
-- Subject: Unit dcos-download.service has failed
```

I will close this section here having given some flavor of the types of problems that occurred while trying to install and configure DCOS. The DCOS install is much more complicated than the basic Mesos code build, but it offers a wealth of extra tools to support a Mesos-based environment. In the next section, I will examine how Apache Yarn and Mesos can be integrated to avoid scheduler contention.

Project Myriad

This chapter has shown how Mesos can be built from source and then how the complex DCOS tool-rich system can be sourced and installed. A Mesos-based cluster control system offers the possibility of running multiple frameworks on a single large cluster and sharing resources between them using Mesos. There might be a Hadoop-based data lake as well as an Apache Spark framework. There might also be a web services framework and possibly a business intelligence layer.

Those of you who have more experience or had noticed comments earlier in this chapter might have noticed a problem. How can you have both Mesos resource-based scheduling and Hadoop-based Yarn scheduling? Won't those two resource schedulers be in conflict? The answer is yes: without some extra layer of integration, there will be conflict between the two systems.

However, a group of people in the big data world have already started investigating the problem and have launched the Apache Myriad project (myriad.apache.org). This is an incubating Apache project that allows the Yarn resource manager and node managers to run inside Mesos containers. Running Yarn on Mesos by using Myriad will enable multiple workloads to share a single cluster. Cluster resources can then be allocated to frameworks on demand as needed. This would also avoid the need to have multiple clusters and move data between them.

I won't install Myriad in this chapter due to a shortage of time, but I want to make you aware of it and allow you to investigate. It is the necessary link between Mesos and Yarn that should allow you to run a full Hadoop stack within a framework on Mesos.

Myriad Architecture

Figure 4-11 is based on the one used on the Apache Myriad web site wiki; just follow the wiki link at myriad.apache.org/docs/.

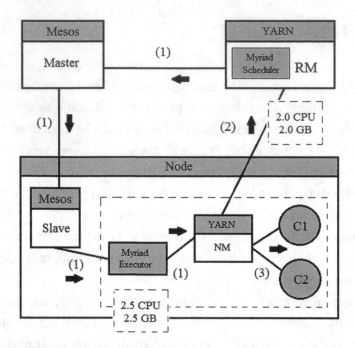

Figure 4-11. *Apache Myriad architecture*

Figure 4-11 shows how Apache Myriad integrates with Apache Mesos so that Mesos manages cluster resources while Yarn is then able to operate via a Myriad executor. The architectural process flow is as follows:

- To launch, a Node Manager Myriad passes the configuration and task launch information to the Mesos Master (1).

- Mesos Master passes this information on to the Mesos Slave (1).

- The Mesos Slave launches a Myriad executor, which manages the life cycle of the Node Manager.

- The Myriad Executor configures the Node Manager resources and launches it (1).

- Upon startup, the Node Manager advertises its configured resources to the Yarn Resource Manager. [Some resources are reserved for Myriad (2).]

- The Yarn Resource Manager can now launch containers (C1 and C2) to process Yarn-based jobs. The containers are mounted under the CentOS kernel cgroups hierarchy (3).

Although I have not had the time to cover Apache Myriad installation and integration with Mesos in this section, I thought that it was important and should be mentioned. I know that I will certainly investigate the install at a later date. I hope that by making you aware of this project, you will be empowered to investigate further.

Conclusion

In this chapter, I have investigated large-scale, cluster-based resource management and sharing by examining the Apache Mesos product. My previous books examined the Apache Hadoop tool eco system and the Apache Spark in memory parallel processing system. Each of these systems could reside within a framework running on Mesos, each carrying out a separate function within an overall corporate computational architecture. I think that Apache Mesos would be a very useful corporate-wide tool to allow these systems to coexist and share resources.

I have concentrated on integration in the big data world because I think it is a bigger problem than some of the other issues, for instance, scaling or security. For example, Apache Spark can use either Yarn or Mesos as its cluster manager. The Myriad project now allows Yarn to integrate with Mesos, but how might that affect a Spark cluster?

I investigated the DCOS project via dcos.io because I think that it provides a much richer tool set than a Mesos source-based build. It is much more complex to use and more difficult to install. I hope that by giving you a basic overview and install guide, I have enabled you to investigate further.

When looking at this chapter in total, I have shown you that Mesos can manage very large clusters and can be the primary resource management system for the cluster. I have shown that multiple types of functional framework can be made to coexist within the Mesos cluster. I have also shown you that a full, Hadoop-based data lake can exist within a Mesos cluster by integrating the Myriad project into your cluster. This means that Yarn-based Hadoop cluster management within a Framework is achievable.

There will be more work to do to create a productionized, cluster-based Mesos system. I'm sure that each corporation will have different requirements and have different framework-based needs. However, I hope that you can use this chapter as a basis to investigate further.

In Chapter 5, I will examine storage-based Mesos frameworks and how they can be created and launched onto a Mesos cluster.

CHAPTER 5

Stack Storage Options

In this chapter, I will examine Mesos-based storage frameworks. I will cover multiple types of framework to show that different types of storage can be used in an Apache Mesos-based big data stack. If you wish to install a traditional Hadoop eco-system-based stack from Hortonworks, Cloudera, or MapR, you just obtain their latest release and install. However, with a Mesos framework, you need to find a suitable framework and install that on Mesos. So whereas a Hortonworks big data stack might install multiple Hadoop eco system tools, a Mesos HDFS framework will only install HDFS. I'm sure that in time the range of frameworks will expand, and companies like Hortonworks will evolve their offerings to include Mesos. However, at this point in time, I will limit my examples to the Mesos-based frameworks available.

So in this chapter, I will show how to obtain and build an HDFS framework on an existing Mesos cluster. You can check the last chapter to determine how to start your cluster. I will examine storage options for HDFS, Riak, and Cassandra. This should provide the reader with a good foundation from which to investigate further.

To remind the reader where this chapter fits in the big data stack architecture, I have again included the big data stack diagram following in Figure 5-1. The components in a gray background have not yet been examined. You will notice that the STORAGE option has now changed the background color to white, as we investigate it in this chapter.

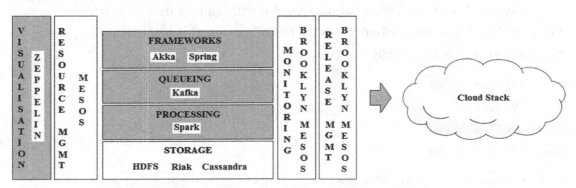

Figure 5-1. *Stack architecture*

© Michael Frampton 2018
M. Frampton, *Complete Guide to Open Source Big Data Stack*, https://doi.org/10.1007/978-1-4842-2149-5_5

Chapter 2 showed how to install Apache CloudStack, create virtual instances, and make them visible to the cluster. To make the point that hybrid clusters can be created to include virtual and physical servers, I have created two CloudStack instances as shown in Figure 5-2. Chapter 2 explains how they can be created, so I will not repeat the instructions here.

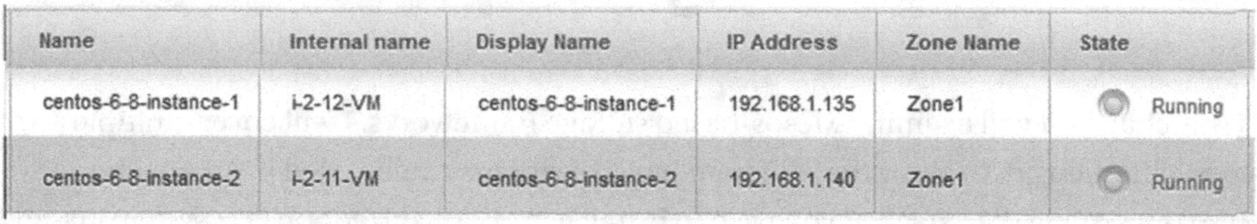

Name	Internal name	Display Name	IP Address	Zone Name	State
centos-6-8-instance-1	i-2-12-VM	centos-6-8-instance-1	192.168.1.135	Zone1	Running
centos-6-8-instance-2	i-2-11-VM	centos-6-8-instance-2	192.168.1.140	Zone1	Running

Figure 5-2. *Virtual CloudStack instances*

This chapter will use the two preceding virtual CentOS instances as well as two physical machines with CentOS 6.8 installed to create a Mesos cluster with one master and four agent nodes. Again, Chapter 4 explains how to create a Mesos cluster, so look there for a reminder. So for the HDFS framework on Mesos, the following servers will be used:

```
192.168.1.135    centos-6-8-instance-1    (cloud)
192.168.1.140    centos-6-8-instance-2    (cloud)
192.168.1.118    hc4r2m1                  (server)  (mesos master)
192.168.1.119    hc4r2m2                  (server)
```

Server hc4r2m1 will be the Mesos master. Riak from basho.com will be installed using a combination of Vagrant and VirtualBox onto the following virtual node:

```
192.168.42.42    vagrant
```

Finally, for Cassandra, Vagrant and VirtualBox will again be used to create the following virtual instances. Where m1 is the DCOS master, a1 is a public agent, p1 is a private agent, and boot is the boot server.

```
m1     192.168.65.90
a1     192.168.65.111
p1     192.168.65.60
boot   192.168.65.50
```

The next section will examine the Mesos HDFS framework installation.

HDFS Mesos Framework

This HDFS Mesos framework example is taken from the Apache 2 licensed Elodina hdfs-mesos example provided on git by Joe Stein at

https://github.com/elodina/hdfs-mesos.

To make this build more coherent, I will break it up into a number of stages, starting with sourcing software and ending with the use of the HDFS framework.

Source Software

I will store all of the system software under /opt, creating symbolic links if necessary to make directory paths easier to read. Before starting the framework install, I have changed the directory to the /opt directory and provided a listing.

```
$ cd /opt
$ ls

mesos  mesos-1.1.0  rh
```

This shows that Mesos is already installed and running on this node (and all of the nodes used for this example). Next, I will use the git clone command to source the Elodina hdfs-mesos GitHub-based code. I then change the directory into the newly created hdfs-mesos directory.

```
$ git clone https://github.com/elodina/hdfs-mesos.git
$ cd hdfs-mesos
```

The wget command will now be used to get the GitHub-based Elodina hdfs-mesos jar file hdfs-mesos-0.0.1.0.jar. The following long listing just shows that this file has been downloaded successfully:

```
$ wget https://github.com/elodina/hdfs-mesos/releases/download/0.0.1.0/
hdfs-mesos-0.0.1.0.jar

$  ls -l
total 4852
-rw-r--r-- 1 root root 4967994 Mar 18  2016 hdfs-mesos-0.0.1.0.jar
```

I will also use wget to source the Hadoop Version 1.2.1 jar file hadoop-1.2.1.tar.gz. The following Linux ls command now shows the contents of the hdfs-mesos directory:

```
$ wget https://archive.apache.org/dist/hadoop/core/hadoop-1.2.1/
hadoop-1.2.1.tar.gz

$ ls

build.gradle  hadoop-1.2.1.tar.gz   lib      src
gradle        hdfs-mesos-0.0.1.0.jar LICENSE  vagrant
gradlew       hdfs-mesos.sh         README.md
```

The eagle-eyed among you may have noticed a couple of points regarding this approach. I have not built the hdfs-mesos module from source, and I am using Hadoop V1 (Version 1.2.1) rather than V2. As ever when writing a book chapter, I always have limited time. I would like to investigate and solve every issue. When building the hdfs-mesos code, I encountered a build error that I did not have time to solve.

```
/opt/hdfs-mesos/src/java/net/elodina/mesos/hdfs/Node.java:205: error:
reference to Base64 is ambiguous
        if (Scheduler.$.config.driverV1()) data = Base64.encode(data);
```

When attempting to use Hadoop Version 2.7.2 in this example, the framework scheduler prompted me to use Version 1.2.1.

```
Exception in thread "main" java.lang.IllegalStateException: Supported
hadoop versions are 1.2.x, current is 2.7.2
```

It is still Hadoop HDFS, so the example is still valid; but given the choice, I would prefer to use Hadoop V2. I also cloned the source from GitHub so that scripts like hdfs-mesos.sh would be available. It will be used throughout this example. The next step will start the framework scheduler.

Start Scheduler

Before starting the framework scheduler, I will create some variables using the Linux export command to define MESOS_HOME, native library locations, and LIBPROCESS_IP to ensure that the scheduler receives resource offers from Mesos.

```
$ export MESOS_HOME=/opt/mesos
$ export MESOS_NATIVE_LIBRARY=/opt/mesos/build/src/.libs/libmesos.so
$ export LIBPROCESS_IP=192.168.1.118
```

I will now start the framework scheduler using the hdfs-mesos.sh script. The first parameter specifies that the scheduler should be started. The second parameter defines the API value to be used for adding HDFS nodes to the framework. The third parameter is the address of the Mesos Master node. The fourth parameter defines the Linux account to be used. Finally, command output is directed to a log file (> hdfs-mesos.log). Standard error output is redirected to standard out (2>&1), and the command is run as a background task (&).

```
$ ./hdfs-mesos.sh scheduler \
    --api=http://192.168.1.118:7000 \
    --master=192.168.1.118:5050 \
    --user=root > hdfs-mesos.log 2>&1 &
```

Now I can check the Mesos user interface, examined in the last chapter by using the following URL and selecting the Frameworks option:

```
http://192.168.1.118:5050
```

The Mesos cluster master node is running on the server 192.168.1.118, and its http port number is 5050. The output following in Figure 5-3 shows that the framework is running on the host hc4r2m1, which has the preceding IP address ending in 118. This figure also provides framework details such as user ID, name, tasks, resources, and so forth.

Active Frameworks

ID ▼	Host	User	Name	Role	Principal	Active Tasks	CPUs	GPUs	Mem	Disk	Max Share
...91c1-0a9de578f40c-0000	hc4r2m1.semtech-solutions.co.nz	root	hdfs	*		4	2	0	2.0 GB	0 B	33.333%

Figure 5-3. Mesos HDFS framework

The next step will involve adding HDFS name nodes and data nodes to the framework.

Create and Start HDFS Nodes

The framework script hdfs-mesos.sh will be used to first add an HDFS name node (nn) to the framework and then three data nodes (dn0, dn1, and dn2). Note the structures of the parameters to the script. The "--api" value is again used to allow the script to connect to the framework scheduler. The first parameter is "node" followed by an action "add nn" then a type of node "--type=namenode."

```
$ ./hdfs-mesos.sh node add nn --type=namenode --api=ht
tp://192.168.1.118:7000

node added:
  id: nn
  type: namenode
  state: idle
  resources: cpus:0.5, mem:512
```

The preceding command output shows that an HDFS framework name node called nn has been added. It also shows the state of that node and the resources that the Mesos cluster will need to offer it so that it can run. The next commands add the three data nodes.

```
$ ./hdfs-mesos.sh node add dn0 --type=datanode --api=ht
tp://192.168.1.118:7000

node added:
  id: dn0
  type: datanode
  state: idle
  resources: cpus:0.5, mem:512

./hdfs-mesos.sh node add dn1 --type=datanode --api=ht
tp://192.168.1.118:7000

./hdfs-mesos.sh node add dn2 --type=datanode --api=ht
tp://192.168.1.118:7000
```

The preceding commands are very similar to the namenode command except for the fact that the node names have changed, and the type is now "--type=datanode." So now the nodes have been added to the framework, but they are in an idle state. The options available for the script hdfs-mesos.sh can be checked using a help parameter as follows:

```
$ ./hdfs-mesos.sh help

Commands:
  help [cmd [cmd]] - print general or command-specific help
  scheduler        - start scheduler
  node             - node management

Run `help <cmd>` to see details of specific command

$ ./hdfs-mesos.sh help node

$ ./hdfs-mesos.sh help node list
```

I won't provide all of the output for the preceding help commands, but you can investigate the various options to determine how to use all of the commands. I can now use the node list command to show that the HDFS framework nodes are idle.

```
$ ./hdfs-mesos.sh node list \* --api=http://192.168.1.118:7000

nodes:
  id: nn
  type: namenode
  state: idle
  resources: cpus:0.5, mem:512
  reservation: cpus:0.5, mem:512, ports:http=31000,ipc=31001

  id: dn0
  type: datanode
  state: idle
  resources: cpus:0.5, mem:512
  reservation: cpus:0.5, mem:512, ports:data=31002,http=31000,ipc=31001
```

```
  id: dn1
  type: datanode
  state: idle
  resources: cpus:0.5, mem:512
  reservation: cpus:0.5, mem:512, ports:data=31004,http=31002,ipc=31003

  id: dn2
  type: datanode
  state: idle
  resources: cpus:0.5, mem:512
  reservation: cpus:0.5, mem:512, ports:data=31005,http=31003,ipc=31004
```

I can use "node start" script options to start the HDFS framework nodes followed by the same preceding list command to show that the HDFS framework-based cluster is starting.

```
$ ./hdfs-mesos.sh node start \*   --api=http://192.168.1.118:7000

$ ./hdfs-mesos.sh node list \* --api=http://192.168.1.118:7000

nodes:
  id: nn
  type: namenode
  state: running
  resources: cpus:0.5, mem:512
  reservation: cpus:0.5, mem:512, ports:http=31000,ipc=31001
  runtime:
    task: 9b232b3f-33e7-45f4-b47b-0bfe75e8f928
    executor: e59da7b2-aa79-4004-ad7d-b37cb8d0cb40
    slave: 4db94e29-59c2-431f-8cc8-92e63abd0110-S3 (hc4r2m1.semtech-
    solutions.co.nz)

  id: dn0
  type: datanode
  state: running
  resources: cpus:0.5, mem:512
  reservation: cpus:0.5, mem:512, ports:data=31002,http=31000,ipc=31001
```

```
runtime:
  task: ba9b2504-0217-42ee-81f9-038d187df8eb
  executor: af91c9f9-ebff-4a59-9971-6d7b5231d481
  slave: 4db94e29-59c2-431f-8cc8-92e63abd0110-S0 (hc4r2m2.semtech-
  solutions.co.nz)

id: dn1
type: datanode
state: running
resources: cpus:0.5, mem:512
reservation: cpus:0.5, mem:512, ports:data=31004,http=31002,ipc=31003
runtime:
  task: f28051f8-9119-47fa-8dc7-99c40831a1eb
  executor: 52358505-0860-4753-8b4f-f4d051ed074e
  slave: 4db94e29-59c2-431f-8cc8-92e63abd0110-S3 (hc4r2m1.semtech-
  solutions.co.nz)

id: dn2
type: datanode
state: starting
resources: cpus:0.5, mem:512
reservation: cpus:0.5, mem:512, ports:data=31002,http=31000,ipc=31001
runtime:
  task: 6db01083-97b7-4bd1-9e13-9c93c414cad5
  executor: f388c8c0-e565-42b6-ab41-e36310937e73
  slave: 4db94e29-59c2-431f-8cc8-92e63abd0110-S2 (centos-6-8-instance-
  2.semtech-solutions.co.nz)
```

I have included all of the output for the preceding node list, even though it takes up space, because it provides useful information. For each node, the name and starting or running status is shown as well as the resources used. Also, details of the task, executor, and slave are given. So given that the HDFS-based cluster is running, I should be able to access it, shouldn't I? The example shows the use of the hadoop command, so I will search the Linux host on which I installed the framework for that command.

Use HDFS Mesos Framework

I will use the Linux `find` command to search the whole file tree starting at the root directory (/) and looking for files (-type f). I will also specify the file name to look for (hadoop).

```
$ find / -type f -name hadoop
```

This provides a very long path name to each instance of the HDFS framework `hadoop` command. The path is defined by the slave, framework, executor, and run IDs for this instance of the framework.

```
/var/lib/mesos/slaves/63894cca-fd52-4082-91c1-0a9de578f40c-S0/
frameworks/63894cca-fd52-4082-91c1-0a9de578f40c-0000/executors/ab80f19a-
02eb-44ea-abd6-5e3c7b8dce82/runs/4e453d13-ef12-4634-82ce-d42592f599e9/
hadoop-1.2.1/bin/hadoop

/var/lib/mesos/slaves/4db94e29-59c2-431f-8cc8-92e63abd0110-S3/
frameworks/63894cca-fd52-4082-91c1-0a9de578f40c-0000/executors/52358505-
0860-4753-8b4f-f4d051ed074e/runs/70ab7b3e-c769-45fc-ae94-e668f9fae332/
hadoop-1.2.1/bin/hadoop

/var/lib/mesos/slaves/4db94e29-59c2-431f-8cc8-92e63abd0110-S3/
frameworks/63894cca-fd52-4082-91c1-0a9de578f40c-0000/executors/e59da7b2-
aa79-4004-ad7d-b37cb8d0cb40/runs/bbd9a0e9-7e47-43fd-a6da-48095133dc6e/
hadoop-1.2.1/bin/hadoop
```

I need to define the value of JAVA_HOME to continue; given that I have Java 1.8 installed, my value is defined using the Linux `export` command.

```
$ export JAVA_HOME=/usr/lib/jvm/java-1.8.0-openjdk.x86_64
```

Also, to simplify the access commands to the HDFS-based cluster that has just been created, I will create a variable called HADOOP_HOME, which will contain most of the path to one of the `hadoop` command instances. I will define the variable using the Linux `export` command.

```
$ export HADOOP_HOME=/var/lib/mesos/slaves/63894cca-fd52-4082-91c1-
0a9de578f40c-S0/frameworks/63894cca-fd52-4082-91c1-0a9de578f40c-
0000/executors/ab80f19a-02eb-44ea-abd6-5e3c7b8dce82/runs/4e453d13-ef12-
4634-82ce-d42592f599e9/hadoop-1.2.1
```

The commands needed to access the HDFS cluster now become more readable using the preceding variable. Also note that when listing the preceding node status, the namenode port values were given as ipc port = 31001 and http port = 31000. The ipc port value will be used in the following commands to access the HDFS cluster. First a directory will be created on HDFS called /misc using the -mkdir option. Then a listing option will be used (-ls) to provide a long listing of the created directory.

```
$ $HADOOP_HOME/bin/hadoop fs -mkdir hdfs://192.168.1.118:31001/misc
$ $HADOOP_HOME/bin/hadoop fs -ls    hdfs://192.168.1.118:31001/

Found 1 items
drwxr-xr-x   - root supergroup          0 2017-01-28 12:58 /misc
```

Next the script hdfs-mesos.sh will be copied from the local file system to the HDFS-based directory /misc. Then an HDFS-based long listing (ls) will be obtained to show that file on HDFS.

```
$ $HADOOP_HOME/bin/hadoop fs \
      -copyFromLocal ./hdfs-mesos.sh   hdfs://192.168.1.118:31001/misc

$ $HADOOP_HOME/bin/hadoop fs -ls    hdfs://192.168.1.118:31001/misc

Found 1 items
-rw-r--r--   3 root supergroup        307 2017-01-28 13:01 /misc/hdfs-
                                                            mesos.sh
```

The preceding output shows that it is possible to use the Mesos framework-based HDFS cluster to create directories and provide HDFS-based listings to add files. It is a fully working, HDFS-based cluster. The HDFS name node, web-based user interface is available on the host on which the framework was installed (192.168.1.118). The http port for the name node was 31000, so the http access URL will be

```
http://192.168.1.118:31000/.
```

Those of you who are familiar with HDFS will recognize this user interface. I added an image of it here (Figure 5-4) not to concentrate on the details but to show that it exists and is accessible on the Mesos HDFS-based framework.

NameNode 'hc4r2m1.semtech-solutions.co.nz:31001'

Started: Sat Jan 28 12:48:12 NZDT 2017
Version: 1.2.1, r1503152
Compiled: Mon Jul 22 15:23:09 PDT 2013 by mattf
Upgrades: There are no upgrades in progress.

<u>Browse the filesystem</u>
<u>Namenode Logs</u>

Cluster Summary

2 files and directories, 0 blocks = 2 total. Heap Size is 150 MB / 889 MB (16%)

Configured Capacity	:	576.75 GB
DFS Used	:	84 KB
Non DFS Used	:	57.32 GB
DFS Remaining	:	519.43 GB
DFS Used%	:	0 %
DFS Remaining%	:	90.06 %
<u>Live Nodes</u>	:	3
<u>Dead Nodes</u>	:	0
<u>Decommissioning Nodes</u>	:	0
Number of Under-Replicated Blocks	:	0

NameNode Storage:

Storage Directory	Type	State
./data/namenode	IMAGE_AND_EDITS	Active

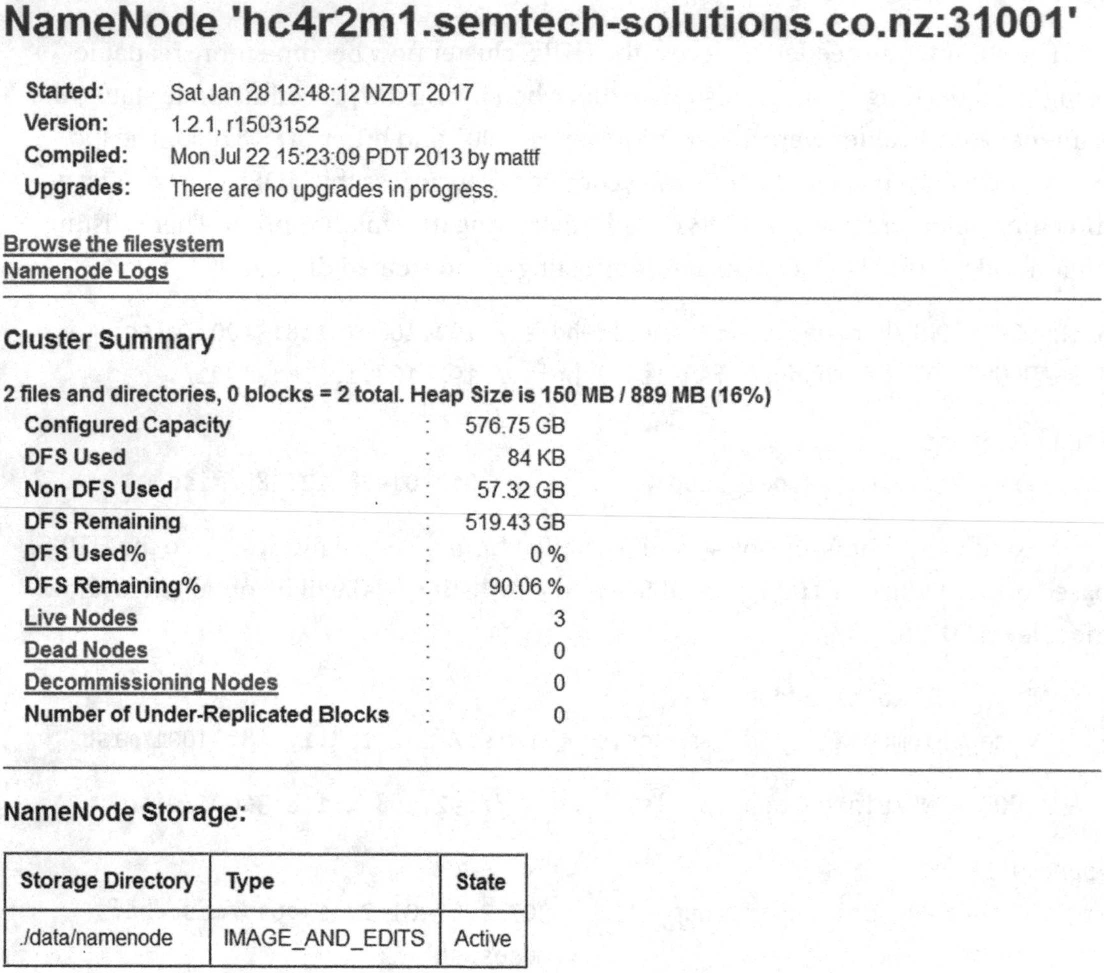

Figure 5-4. *Mesos HDFS Framework NameNode UI*

Given that the Mesos HDFS-based framework is running and has been shown to work, the final task will be to shut it down. The framework-based script hdfs-mesos. sh can again be used for this. The parameters are again the (--api) value for framework scheduler access. The action is now "stop," and the nodes are identified by a wild card value (*) to match all available nodes.

```
$ ./hdfs-mesos.sh node stop \*    --api=http://192.168.1.118:7000

nodes stopped:
  id: nn
  type: namenode
  state: idle
  resources: cpus:0.5, mem:512

  id: dn0
  type: datanode
  state: idle
  resources: cpus:0.5, mem:512

  id: dn1
  type: datanode
  state: idle
  resources: cpus:0.5, mem:512

  id: dn2
  type: datanode
  state: idle
  resources: cpus:0.5, mem:512
```

The output from the preceding command now shows that all of the cluster nodes are idle. In the next section, I will examine the installation of Basho's Riak Mesos framework.

Riak Mesos Framework

The Riak database is an open-source distributed database developed by Basho (basho. com). Whereas the previous example showed an HDFS framework on Mesos, the Riak-based example will be on DCOS. DCOS (dcos.io) is a Mesosphere-based system that is built on top of Mesos but contains many extra tools such as the Marathon scheduler, DNS, and a command line interface (CLI). The main database systems developed by Basho are Riak KV (key value) and TS (time series); TS is the distributed, time-series database variant. This example will deploy Riak KV.

This example will be demonstrated using the Oracle virtualisation tool VirtualBox and the Vagrant environment creation tool. This approach is being taken because the Basho Riak framework is released with a DCOS-based Vagrant environment. This means that this example can use the Vagrant environment supplied and will save time in that DCOS will not have to be installed.

The first step in this process will be the installation of the VirtualBox software on CentOS 7.

VirtualBox Install

To install Oracle's VirtualBox Linux on CentOS 7, I will need to obtain the appropriate yum repository configuration file. To do that, I must first install the wget command. Then I will use the Linux wget command to obtain a copy of the file virtualbox.repo and save it to /etc/yum.repos.d/.

```
$ yum -y install wget
```

```
$ cd /etc/yum.repos.d/
```

```
$ wget http://download.virtualbox.org/virtualbox/rpm/rhel/virtualbox.repo
```

Next I will carry out an update via yum to ensure that all yum-based packages are up-to-date. This can take up to 30 minutes, so be patient.

```
$ yum -y update
```

Having done that, I need to check that the rpm-based kernel version matches the release information for the operating system kernel. Reboot the machine if the values do not match. The rpm command lists the installed kernel versions, while the uname command lists the current one. DCOS requires a minimum kernel version of 3.10, so this check ensures that a 3.10 kernel is installed and current.

```
$ rpm -qa kernel |head -1
kernel-3.10.0-514.6.1.el7.x86_64
```

```
$ uname -r
    3.10.0-514.6.1.el7.x86_64
```

Next I will install the epel repository using the Linux rpm command; the options used are upgrade (U), verbose (v), and hash (h) to print hash marks.

```
$ rpm -Uvh http://dl.fedoraproject.org/pub/epel/7/x86_64/e/epel-
release-7-9.noarch.rpm
```

Now VirtualBox Version 5.1 can be installed using the Linux yum command with a -y switch to avoid the need for confirmations. This install is supported by the repo file that was just downloaded.

```
$ yum -y install VirtualBox-5.1
```

Now rebuild kernel modules using the VirtualBox script vboxdrv.sh under /user/lib/virtualbox/ with a setup parameter.

```
$ /usr/lib/virtualbox/vboxdrv.sh setup
```

If this command fails with an error like this, then execute the following yum-based commands to install gcc, make, and kernel modules.

```
vboxdrv.sh: Building VirtualBox kernel modules.
```

This system is not currently set up to build kernel modules (system extensions).

```
$  yum -y install gcc make

$  yum -y install kernel-devel-3.10.0-514.6.1.el7.x86_64

$ /usr/lib/virtualbox/vboxdrv.sh setup

vboxdrv.sh: Building VirtualBox kernel modules.
vboxdrv.sh: Starting VirtualBox services.
```

Now add the VirtualBox user to the group vboxusers using the Linux usermod command. I am using the root account, but if you are creating a productionized system, you might want to create a user account for VirtualBox.

```
$ usermod -a -G vboxusers root
```

I will now check that that the VirtualBox install can be found by using the Linux type command. This shows that VirtualBox exits under /usr/bin/.

```
$ type VirtualBox
VirtualBox is /usr/bin/VirtualBox
```

153

So now I can start VirtualBox as following and run the command as a background process (&) to free up the console for further commands.

```
$ VirtualBox   &
```

Now that VirtualBox is installed, I can move on to installing the Vagrant package; this will be tackled in the next section.

Vagrant Install

This was a very simple install using the Linux rpm command with a -i switch for install. Version 1.9.1 of Vagrant, a 64-bit variant, was chosen from the Hashicorp site.

```
$ rpm -i  https://releases.hashicorp.com/vagrant/1.9.1/vagrant_1.9.1_
x86_64.rpm
```

It is that simple. Now, by using the Linux type command, I can see that the Vagrant executable is available under /usr/bin/.

```
$ type vagrant
```

```
vagrant is /usr/bin/vagrant
```

So the Riak Mesos framework that will be used in this section is released with a Vagrant configuration, which describes a DCOS environment. The Vagrant application that I have just installed will read that configuration and create the environment to support the framework. The VirtualBox application will be used by Vagrant to create the actual DCOS-based virtual environment.

Now that the necessary supporting software has been installed, the actual Riak Mesos framework can be sourced, installed, and examined. This will be tackled in the next section.

Install Framework

In this section, I will source and install the Riak Mesos framework; the details for this approach are found on the Basho GitHub site at

```
https://github.com/basho-labs/riak-mesos/blob/master/docs/DEVELOPMENT.md
```

To support the install, I first need to install the Linux git command using yum with a -y switch to avoid confirmations.

```
$ yum -y install git
```

Next, I will use the git command to source the Riak-Mesos package from the GitHub site. I will install it to /opt; so I will change the directory to that location first using the Linux cd command.

```
$ cd /opt
```

```
$ git clone https://github.com/basho-labs/riak-mesos
```

Next, I will change the directory using the Linux cd command to the Riak-Mesos code-base directory that was just downloaded. I will then update each of the submodules within the package using the Linux git command with a submodule parameter. The init option will initialize any uninitialized modules and the recursive option will update any nested sub modules.

```
$ cd /opt/riak-mesos
$ git submodule update --init --recursive
```

Now that the Riak-Mesos code base and all of its submodules have been updated, the Vagrant based Linux virtual environment supplied with the framework can be started. The Lunux pwd command following shows that the current location is /opt/riak-mesos/. The following Linux ls command shows the contents of that directory. The point that I wish to make here is that the Riak-Mesos framework contains a Vagrant directory and a Vagrant configuration file called VagrantFile. The contents of the Vagrant directory is shown following. When the Vagrant application is started, it is this configuration information that will be used to create the virtual environment:

```
$ pwd
/opt/riak-mesos

$ ls
docs       LICENSE    packages   tools    Vagrantfile
framework  Makefile   README.md  vagrant
$ ls vagrant
mesos-dns-config.json  mesos-dns-marathon.json  provision.sh  README.md
```

The Vagrant-based virtual environment that contains DCOS can now be started from within the /opt/riak-mesos/ directory using the Linux-based `vagrant` command with a single parameter "up" as follows:

```
$ vagrant up
Bringing machine 'ubuntu' up with 'virtualbox' provider...
==> ubuntu: Box 'ubuntu/trusty64' could not be found. Attempting to find
and install...
    ubuntu: Box Provider: virtualbox
    ubuntu: Box Version: >= 0
.....
==> ubuntu: Successfully uninstalled jsonschema
==> ubuntu: Successfully installed riak-mesos docopt dcos click pager
pygments six toml jsonschema
==> ubuntu: Cleaning up...
```

I have included some of the preceding output to show you what to expect; as long as you see the command output terminate with the preceding Success line, you should be OK. However, be warned: the first time that this environment is brought up, you should expect a lengthy delay, as many required supporting packages are installed. It took my environment around 50 minutes to start the first time.

Now that the virtual Vagrant-based environment has started, it can be accessed via the Linux `vagrant` command with a secure shell (ssh) option. The environment is called Vagrant and is accessed as follows:

```
$ vagrant ssh

Welcome to Ubuntu 14.04.5 LTS (GNU/Linux 3.13.0-107-generic x86_64)

 * Documentation:  https://help.ubuntu.com/

  System information as of Tue Jan 31 17:41:42 UTC 2017

  System load:  0.07              Users logged in:        0
  Usage of /:   13.5% of 39.34GB  IP address for eth0:    10.0.2.15
  Memory usage: 13%               IP address for eth1:    192.168.42.42
  Swap usage:   0%                IP address for docker0: 172.17.0.1
  Processes:    131
```

I have included some useful information from the output of the (preceding) `vagrant` command. The first point is that the virtual environment that has just been started is based on Ubuntu Version 14.04. The second point is the network address for the network interface eth1 (192.168.42.42). It is this address that will be used to access this environment's web-based user interfaces. I will use this address later, but first I will build the Vagrant-based development environment on the virtual environment as follows:

```
$ cd /vagrant/

$ make dev

OK
Building index...
OK
Validating index...
OK
```

The preceding commands build the development environment on the virtual server within the /vagrant/ directory. Next, a directory path $HOME/.config/riak-mesos/ is created using the Linux `mkdir` command. The -p switch just causes the whole directory tree to be created. The ~ character is equivalent to $HOME.

```
$ mkdir -p ~/.config/riak-mesos

$ ln -nsf /vagrant/tools/riak-mesos-tools/config/config.local.json \
        ~/.config/riak-mesos/config.json
```

The preceding Linux `ln` command now creates a symbolic link from the preexisting JSON-based config file config.local.json under /vagrant/tools/riak-mesos-tools/config/. It creates this link named config.json under the directory path that was just created. Now that my virtual environment exists and the development environment has been built, I will test the framework. To do this, I will change the directory to the riak-mesos-tools subdirectory. I will then use the Linux make command to build an environment called env. Finally, I will source an active file under env/bin to set up the working environment.

```
$ cd /vagrant/tools/riak-mesos-tools/

$ make env

virtualenv -q /vagrant/tools/riak-mesos-tools/env --prompt='(riak-mesos)'
echo "Virtualenv created."
Virtualenv created.

$ source env/bin/activate
```

Before installing and running the Riak Mesos framework on this DCOS-based virtual environment, I will make some changes that were kindly advised by Basho's developer Michael Coles. I have modified the file config.local.json under /vagrant/tools/riak-mesos-tools/config/. My scheduler, executor, node, and director sections in this file now look like this. Mesos-based resource requirements for Riak are defined in terms of CPU (cpus), memory (mem), and disk space (disk).

```
"scheduler": {
            "cpus": 0.5,
            "mem": 512.0,
            "constraints": ""
      },
      "executor": {
          "cpus": 0.1,
          "mem": 512.0
      },
      "node": {
          "cpus": 1.0,
          "mem": 512.0,
          "disk": 1000.0
      },
      "director": {
          "use-public": false,
          "cpus": 0.5,
            "mem": 512.0
        }
```

I decreased the resource requirements for the Riak-based cluster in the framework to ensure that the Riak nodes that will shortly be created would start. I also changed the constraints line in the scheduler section. Now I can install the Riak Mesos framework as follows using the `riak-mesos` command. Then I can start the framework and add it to the Marathon scheduler as a long-running process. The second command following does this and uses a time-out to allow for a slow response:

```
$ riak-mesos framework install

Finished adding riak to marathon.

$ riak-mesos framework wait-for-service --timeout 1200

Riak Mesos Framework is ready.
```

The Marathon DCOS environment scheduler can now be accessed via the following URL:

```
http://192.168.42.42:8080/
```

Figure 5-5 shows the Marathon scheduler user interface with the Mesos-DNS and Riak framework processes running.

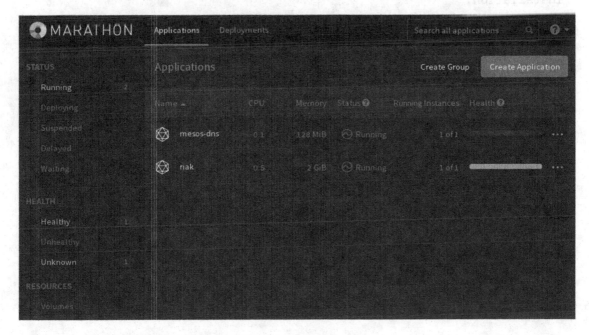

Figure 5-5. *Marathon DCOS scheduler*

Now that the Riak Mesos is installed and running on the virtual Vagrant-based environment, it can be accessed and used. The next section will show how this is achieved.

Use Framework

The Riak Mesos framework is accessed using the `riak-mesos` command, which can be found in the following directory:

```
/vagrant/tools/riak-mesos-tools
```

Riak Mesos framework help can be found by using the --help option with the `riak-mesos` command at multiple levels. For instance, at the topmost level, options and commands are displayed.

```
$ riak-mesos --help

Usage: riak-mesos [OPTIONS] COMMAND [ARGS]...

  Command line utility for the Riak Mesos Framework / DCOS Service. This
  utility provides tools for modifying and accessing your Riak on Mesos
  installation.

Options:
  --home DIRECTORY   Changes the folder to operate on.
  --config PATH      Path to JSON configuration file.
  -v, --verbose      Enables verbose mode.
  --debug            Enables very verbose / debug mode.
  --info             Display information.
  --version          Display version.
  --config-schema    Display config schema.
  --framework TEXT   Changes the framework instance to operate on.
  --json             Enables json output.
  --insecure-ssl     Turns SSL verification off on HTTP requests
  --help             Show this message and exit.
```

```
Commands:
  cluster    Interact with Riak clusters
  config     Interact with configuration.
  director   Interact with an instance of Riak Mesos...
  framework  Interact with an instance of Riak Mesos...
  node       Interact with a Riak node
  riak       Command line utility for the Riak Mesos...
```

Now the same help option can be used to determine how to use the Riak Mesos framework cluster option.

```
$ riak-mesos cluster --help
```

There are also options to determine the version of the framework (1.4) and information about the command riak-mesos.

```
$ riak-mesos --info
```

```
Start and manage Riak nodes in Mesos.
```

```
$ riak-mesos --version
```

```
Riak Mesos Framework Version 1.4.0
```

I can now create a Riak-based cluster on the framework by using the options cluster and create with the riak-mesos command. The cluster will be called riak-kv1, and the version of Riak used will be riak-kv-2-2 (Version 2.2 of Riak KV).

```
$ riak-mesos cluster create riak-kv1  riak-kv-2-2
{"success":true}
```

I can add nodes to the Riak cluster using the cluster and add-node options with the riak-mesos command. The final parameter in the following commands will be the Riak node name:

```
$ riak-mesos cluster add-node riak-kv1-1
```

```
{"success":true}
```

```
$ riak-mesos cluster add-node riak-kv1-2
```

```
{"success":true}
```

If I now call the `riak-mesos` command with the cluster and info options followed by the cluster name riak-kv1, I can determine the structure of the cluster that was just created.

```
$ riak-mesos cluster info riak-kv1
```

```
{"riak-kv1":{"nodes":[
{"name":"riak-riak-kv1-2",
"status":"requested","container_path":"","persistence_id":""},
{"name":"riak-riak-kv1-1",
"status":"requested","container_path":"","persistence_id":""}
],"name":"riak-kv1","riak_version":"riak-kv-2-2",
"riak_config":null,"advanced_config":null,"generation":3}
}
```

Note that the preceding nodes are in the requested state and that the node names have been created as "riak-riak-kv1-1" and "riak-riak-kv1-2." If I wait awhile, the Riak nodes will start. I have used the cluster and list options following to show that the first node now has a status of starting:

```
$ riak-mesos cluster list
```

```
{"clusters":[{"nodes":[
{"name":"riak-riak-kv1-2",
"status":"starting","container_path":"data","persistence_id":
"43f20f78-e5b3-4074-a9a9-3c046761fe3e"},
{"name":"riak-riak-kv1-1",
"status":"reserved","container_path":"data","persistence_id":
"8d90574b-933e-4c7c-aa02-d7343090e5ba"}
],"name":"riak-kv1","riak_version":"riak-kv-2-2",
"riak_config":null,"advanced_config":null,"generation":3}]}
```

If I now check the Riak cluster endpoints using the cluster, endpoints, and cluster name riak-kv1 option, I can see that both Riak nodes have started.

```
$ riak-mesos cluster endpoints riak-kv1
```

```
{"riak-riak-kv1-1": {"status": "started", "pb_direct": "ubuntu.
local:31491", "alive": true, "http_direct":
```

```
"ubuntu.local:31490"}, "riak-riak-kv1-2": {"status": "started",
"pb_direct": "ubuntu.local:31718", "alive": true,

"http_direct": "ubuntu.local:31717"}}
```

From previous sections in this chapter, and previously, I know that the Mesos user interface in this DCOS-based environment should be available on port 5050. In fact, the URL to access the interface is

```
http://192.168.42.42:5050/
```

Figure 5-6 shows the active tasks section of the Mesos DCOS-based environment user interface. It shows that there are two tasks running on the Mesos framework: riak and mesos-dns. These tasks match those that were shown in the Marathon scheduler earlier.

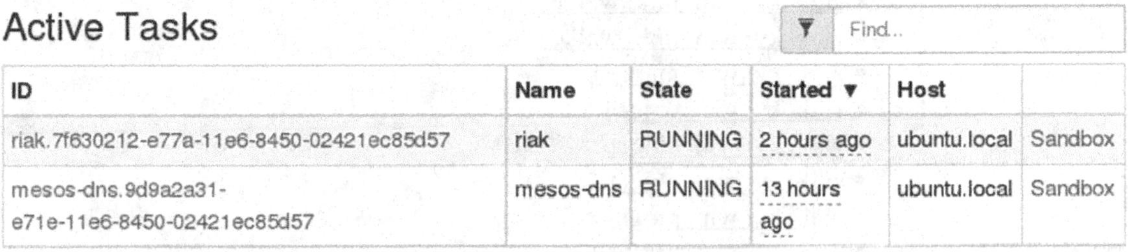

Active Tasks

ID	Name	State	Started ▼	Host	
riak.7f630212-e77a-11e6-8450-02421ec85d57	riak	RUNNING	2 hours ago	ubuntu.local	Sandbox
mesos-dns.9d9a2a31-e71e-11e6-8450-02421ec85d57	mesos-dns	RUNNING	13 hours ago	ubuntu.local	Sandbox

Figure 5-6. *Mesos DCOS user interface*

The last item that I will mention here is the http_direct information that was displayed in the preceding cluster endpoint commands. They show that there are two http-based interfaces available for the Riak nodes at ports 31490 and 31717. Figure 5-7 shows the options available on that user interface for each Riak node. As Figure 5-7 shows, there is a rich list of options for determining information on this Riak node.

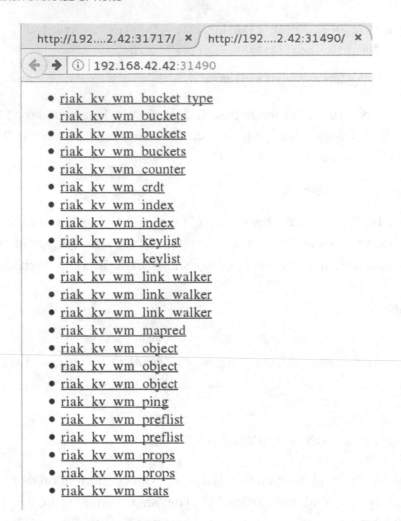

Figure 5-7. *Framework Riak node http direct interface*

I will conclude the examination of Basho's Mesos Riak framework here to examine the Mesos Cassandra framework. This will be covered in the next section.

Cassandra Mesos Framework

This section examines the creation and install of a Vagrant-based DCOS environment created by mesosphere.io. It will show how to install Cassandra onto the DCOS environment using the DCOS CLI. I am using a Linux-based CentOS 7.2 environment for this install. Many of the Mesos-based framework providers seem to be moving to Vagrant-based DCOS environments since DCOS was open sourced. Given that the DCOS environment is complex, this section will by necessity concentrate on environment preparation. The install of Cassandra at the end of the section is minimal compared to the amount of preparation needed to reach that point.

This section is based on the Apache 2 licensed mesosphere.io, github-based, dcos-vagrant module maintained by Karl Isenberg at

```
https://github.com/dcos/dcos-vagrant/tree/master/examples/oinker
```

The following sections walk through the environment preparation.

Install Prerequisites

This section covers the prerequisite packages that need to be installed before moving on to prepare the environment. I've included a couple of graphics tools in this section such as GIMP (GNU Image Manipulation Program) and KSnapshot (K desktop environment [K] snapshot). When things go wrong, I find that screenshots can be very useful. There isn't much to this section: just install gcc, wget, git, and make using the Linux yum command. I always use the -y switch to avoid the need for confirmations.

```
$ yum -y install git wget gcc make
```

Next, install firefox, ksnapshot, and gimp in the same way. The Firefox browser will be needed to both authenticate and examine the DCOS GUI environment.

```
$ yum -y install firefox  ksnapshot  gimp
```

The next section will examine the preparation of a minimal X Windows system to support the X-based tools used in this section.

Install X Windows

Given that the DCOS environment is resource hungry when installing CentOS, I generally choose a minimal CentOS release. This means that there is no X Windows system included. Given that many of the tools used in this section—that is, VirtualBox— have an X interface, then an X Windows system needs to be installed to support them. However, this will not be a full desktop install. Only those components needed will be installed, leaving more resources for DCOS.

All Linux yum-based installs in this section will use the -y switch to avoid confirmation prompts. First, I will do a group install of the "X Windows System," followed by an install of Gnome classic and Gnome terminal. (Gnome is the name of the CentOS-based X Windows system.)

```
$ yum -y groupinstall "X Window System"
```

```
$ yum -y install gnome-classic-session gnome-terminal
```

Next, I will install the nautilus open terminal, the control center, and some fonts.

```
$ yum -y install nautilus-open-terminal control-center liberation-mono-fonts
```

The next command unlinks the systemd default target and then creates a new symbolic link (ln -sf) to the file graphical.target. This sets up the environment to boot with an X Windows-based GUI. It groups together components like the Gnome display manager and the accounts service. Finally, the host is rebooted.

```
$ unlink /etc/systemd/system/default.target
```

```
$  ln -sf /lib/systemd/system/graphical.target
        /etc/systemd/system/default.target
```

```
$ reboot
```

The last action in this section is to execute a yum update command to ensure that all yum packages are up-to-date. This can take up to 30 minutes but provides an up-to-date environment from which to continue.

```
$ yum -y update
```

The next section will cover the installation of Vagrant and Oracle VirtualBox virtualisation tool.

Install VirtualBox and Vagrant

To recap, many Mesos-based framework providers offer their frameworks as Vagrant- or Docker-based environments. This does not mean that they advise that Vagrant-based environments be used in a production environment, but it does provide a shortened path to bring up a DCOS-based environment.

Vagrant provides a way to configure a virtual environment and release that configuration as part of the framework release. Vagrant-configured environments can be used in association with other virtualisation tools like VirtualBox (as in this case, or AWS). The Riak Mesos framework showed how to install VirtualBox and Vagrant, so I will not repeat the steps here. I will, however, mention that I installed Version 5.0 of VirtualBox instead of Version 5.1, having seen some warnings in the install output. So I installed VirtualBox as follows:

```
$ yum -y install VirtualBox-5.0
```

I also installed the Vagrant hostmanager plug-in for managing host files in a multi-machine environment.

```
$ vagrant plugin install vagrant-hostmanager
```

```
Installing the 'vagrant-hostmanager' plugin. This can take a few minutes...
Fetching: vagrant-hostmanager-1.8.5.gem (100%)
Installed the plugin 'vagrant-hostmanager (1.8.5)'!
```

The next section will show how Vagrant DCOS can be installed.

Install Vagrant-Based DCOS

The Vagrant-based DCOS install will be sourced from the Apache 2 licensed GitHub-based path dcos/dcos-vagrant. It has been developed by mesosphere.io and will be cloned from GitHub using the Linux git command.

```
$ cd /opt
```

```
$ git clone https://github.com/dcos/dcos-vagrant
```

```
Cloning into 'dcos-vagrant'...
remote: Counting objects: 2147, done.
remote: Total 2147 (delta 0), reused 0 (delta 0), pack-reused 2146
Receiving objects: 100% (2147/2147), 14.97 MiB | 1.47 MiB/s, done.
Resolving deltas: 100% (1283/1283), done.
```

Moving into the dcos-vagrant directory followed by a Linux ls shows the directory contents. Of initial interest are the Vagrant yaml-based config files that will specify how the DCOS-based environment is created.

```
$ cd dcos-vagrant

# ls
ci                      LICENSE                 VagrantConfig-1m-3a-1p.yaml
dcos-versions.yaml      NOTICE                  VagrantConfig-3m-1a-1p.yaml
docs                    patch                   VagrantConfig-3m-6a-3p.yaml
etc                     provision               Vagrantfile
examples                README.md
lib                     VagrantConfig-1m-1a-1p.yaml
```

The file that Vagrant will use needs to be copied to VagrantConfig.yaml. In this case, one master, one private agent, and one public agent node (1m-1a-1p) will be created.

```
$ cp VagrantConfig-1m-1a-1p.yaml VagrantConfig.yaml
```

Finally, the Vagrant-based environment is started with the vagrant up command; this can take a long time, as many extra packages are installed.

```
$ vagrant up
```

At this point, Oracle VirtualBox can be checked to see whether the DCOS-based environments exist.

Figure 5-8 taken from the VirtualBox tool shows that the environments a1.dcos, p1.dcos, m1.dcos, and boot.dcos have been created. This image was captured before the environment was fully started, so these virtual instances are still powered off. Examining the yaml-based configuration file provides some insight into the node resources.

Figure 5-8. *DCOS-based VirtualBox environments*

```
$ more VagrantConfig.yaml

m1:
  ip: 192.168.65.90
  cpus: 2
  memory: 1024
  type: master
a1:
  ip: 192.168.65.111
  cpus: 4
  memory: 6144
  memory-reserved: 512
  type: agent-private
p1:
  ip: 192.168.65.60
  cpus: 2
  memory: 1536
  memory-reserved: 512
  type: agent-public
  aliases:
  - spring.acme.org
  - oinker.acme.org
boot:
  ip: 192.168.65.50
  cpus: 2
  memory: 1024
  type: boot
```

It can be seen in the preceding that each node has been described in terms of an IP address, aliases, CPUs, memory, and a type. From this point, the DCOS-based GUI can be accessed at the URL

```
http://m1.dcos/.
```

However, before that is done, the DCOS CLI tool should also be sourced because both the GUI and the CLI will be used in tandem. Change directory using the Linux cd command to /usr/bin/. Then use curl to download Version 1.8 of the DCOS CLI tool from the site dcos.io.

```
$ cd /usr/bin/

$ curl -O https://downloads.dcos.io/binaries/cli/linux/x86-64/dcos-1.8/dcos
  % Total    % Received % Xferd Average Speed  Time    Time    Time    Current
                                Dload  Upload Total   Spent   Left    Speed
100 8674k 100 8674k     0        0 1336k  0        0:00:06 0:00:06 --:--:-- 1794k
```

Next make the DCOS CLI executable using the Linux chmod command (+x means add execute).

```
$ chmod +x dcos
```

Next, configure the DCOS CLI tool to use the DCOS master node URL. This sets the dcos core.dcos_url configuration value.

```
$ ./dcos config set core.dcos_url http://m1.dcos

[core.dcos_url]: set to 'http://m1.dcos'
```

It should be noted at this point that the DCOS install alters the /etc/hosts file to define the Vagrant node names and IP addresses.

```
$ tail /etc/hosts

## vagrant-hostmanager-start id: 72624615-2568-40c8-929a-e4f0639e18ce
192.168.65.90    m1.dcos

192.168.65.111  a1.dcos

192.168.65.60    p1.dcos
192.168.65.60    spring.acme.org oinker.acme.org
192.168.65.50    boot.dcos

## vagrant-hostmanager-end
```

When accessing the URL http://m1.dcos, the user is now presented with DCOS login options for Google, GitHub, and Microsoft (Figure 5-9).

Figure 5-9. *DCOS login options*

As I have a GitHub account, I used those credentials to log in. Once logged in, I was able to obtain an authentication token, which is then used to authenticate a dcos cli command line session as follows. The authentication token obtained from the DCOS GUI on first login is a very long alphabetic string. Use the auth and login parameters to the dcos cli command and follow the prompts. Enter the authentication string obtained from the DCOS GUI. I have truncated my auth string to save space. Look for the success line following:

```
$ ./dcos auth login
```

Please go to the following link in your browser:

```
http://m1.dcos/login?redirect_uri=urn:ietf:wg:oauth:2.0:oob
```

```
Enter OpenID Connect ID Token:eyJOTRPRVpGTO6OlpoS8P8KtJ4v9KZ9f2iDFpmA
Login successful!
```

This DCOS CLI session is now authenticated with the DCOS master node, and so further commands can be executed to modify the DCOS-based Vagrant environment. The next section will show how Cassandra can be installed.

Install Cassandra

Compared to the setup of the Vagrant-based DCOS environment, the installation of the DCOS Cassandra framework is trivial. A JSON-based Cassandra DCOS configuration file is created as cassandra.json under the /tmp directory (see following). The statement following uses the Linux cat command to concatenate all of the text between the EOF (end-of-file) markers into the file:

```
$ cat >/tmp/cassandra.json <<EOF
{
        "service": {
            "cpus": 0.1,
            "mem": 512,
            "heap": 256
        },
        "executor": {
            "cpus": 0.1,
            "mem": 512,
            "heap": 256
        },
        "nodes": {
            "cpus": 0.5,
            "mem": 2048,
            "disk": 4096,
            "heap": {
                "size": 1024,
                "new": 100
            },
            "count": 1,
            "seeds": 1
        },
        "task": {
            "cpus": 0.1,
            "mem": 128
        }
}
EOF
```

This cassandra json configuration file defines the Cassandra nodes in terms of CPU, memory, disk, and heap space. I have executed a Linux long listing following to show that the file exists:

```
$ ls -l /tmp/cassandra.json
-rw-r--r-- 1 root root 538 Feb  6 16:26 /tmp/cassandra.json
```

Now in the already authenticated DCOS CLI session, the Cassandra package can be installed using the cassandra.json file created previously. The package option allows DCOS packages to be managed. The install option will install Cassandra, while the --options attribute allows the configuration file to be used. Cassandra is the DCOS package to be installed, while the --yes option switches off interactive mode.

```
$ dcos package install --options=/tmp/cassandra.json cassandra --yes

DC/OS Cassandra Service default configuration requires 3 nodes each with
1.5 CPU shares, 5376MB of memory and 11264MB of disk for running Cassandra
Nodes. And, 1 node with 0.5 CPU shares, 2048MB of memory for running the
service scheduler.
Installing Marathon app for package [cassandra] version [1.0.24-3.0.10]
Installing CLI subcommand for package [cassandra] version [1.0.24-3.0.10]
New command available: dcos cassandra
DC/OS Apache Cassandra has been successfully installed!
```

There are a couple of points to make here: to be installed, the Cassandra package must be available in the DCOS user interface. Figure 5-10 taken from the DCOS user interfaces packages page shows the available DCOS GUI menu options and their meaning.

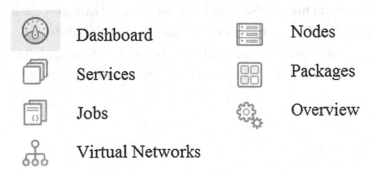

Figure 5-10. *DCOS menu icons (left)*

Having selected the packages option in the GUI, it can be seen without filtering that the Cassandra package is available for install. So what the preceding dcos cli install command did was install this package via the CLI with extra configuration specified.

Check the DCOS services page at the following URL to monitor the Cassandra DCOS service status. The Cassandra package with the configuration shown in Figure 5-11 should deploy one scheduler task and one Cassandra node on private DCOS nodes. Check the service details to see more information about these tasks.

```
http://m1.dcos/#/services/
```

Figure 5-11. *DCOS available packages*

I am fully aware that that this section has concentrated more on the installation and preparation of the DCOS environment rather than Cassandra. However, with DCOS being as complex as it is, that was unavoidable. As I progress through the later chapters in this book, I will begin to link some of the frameworks into a cohesive whole and use them in concert.

Conclusion

My intention in this chapter was to introduce some of the possible big data frameworks available in Mesos and DCOS. I have concentrated on HDFS, Basho's Riak-distributed database, and Cassandra. I have also examined the Vagrant-based release options offered by organisations such as Basho and mesosphere.io. Although I would like to delve more deeply into the actual use of these frameworks, the complexity of setting up the environments to support them limits this. I have a time and size limit when writing this chapter, and I also need to provide a repeatable set of instructions for the reader to use. In later chapters, I will show how frameworks can be accessed to use the functionality that they contain.

You may have noticed already that the Mesos frameworks that are being used in the chapters to this point are being developed by organisations that maintain or support a product. For instance, Basho has created the Mesos-based Riak database frameworks. In this way, the people that know and understand the product create the Mesos framework that will deploy it to a Mesos-based cluster.

The Vagrant-based environments used in this chapter have been possible because the framework suppliers release Vagrant modules within their frameworks. Such modules might be offered for Vagrant or say Docker. They might use Oracle VirtualBox or perhaps AWS for the underlying virtualisation. These approaches provide a quick means to enable a development or test environment to be created to access the framework. They are not intended for production release but for preproduction use, development, and testing of the framework that they support.

The next chapter will examine a Mesos-based processing framework to add the next layer to the big data processing stack.

CHAPTER 6

Processing

In this chapter, I will examine the processing function within a big data stack. I will concentrate on Apache Spark because it integrates well with both Apache Mesos and DCOS (dcos.io). I will expand on the work carried out in Chapter 4 to show how both Mesos and DCOS can be installed so that Apache-Spark-based frameworks can be installed into those environments and used.

This chapter will not teach you how to use Apache Spark; the aim here is to show how it can be integrated into a Mesos/DCOS environment and made ready to use. There are many books available that explain the Spark-based modules, including mine, *Mastering Apache Spark* (Packt, 2015).

To recap on the topics covered thus far in terms of a big data stack, the same stack architecture diagram is shown in Figure 6-1. The processing component, which specifies Apache Spark, has now been highlighted in white to indicate that it will be covered in this topic.

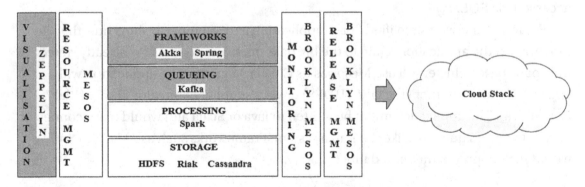

Figure 6-1. *Stack architecture*

© Michael Frampton 2018

M. Frampton, *Complete Guide to Open Source Big Data Stack*, https://doi.org/10.1007/978-1-4842-2149-5_6

Figure 6-1 describes the big data stack at a very high level. I think it is worth briefly examining the relationships between the stack components and how they can be used together. I have said previously that I will not explain how to use Spark here, but I will provide a little detail about its modules and cluster management options. The next section will cover these areas.

Stack Architecture

Apache Spark is shown as the main processing module for this big data stack; but why is that? Spark is an open-source, distributed cluster processing system that offers in-memory processing. It allows a wide range of cluster management options, that is, Standalone, Yarn (client and server), and Mesos. In this case, Mesos will be used as the Spark-based cluster manager, as it is already being used as a stack component. Spark has been widely adopted, is widely supported, and is the successor to Map/Reduce, being many times faster and far more flexible as a processing paradigm.

Spark provides a wide range of functionality within its modules. The mllib (machine learning library) library provides a range of machine-learning functions, while the streaming module can be used to process streamed data. The SQL module allows in-memory tables to be created and SQL to be used against them. Finally the GraphX module allows graph processing to be executed against the data. The modules can be used in sequence within an application, for instance, streamed data can be accessed via SQL.

Figure 6-2 shows a simplified Spark application and attempts to show how the functions of the application relate to the big data stack components. As already stated, the Spark-based cluster will use Mesos as its Cluster Manager. The application will connect to storage either via a URL (HDFS) or via a supplier connector library (Riak/ Cassandra). The application might be written in Java or Scala and would use a connector library to access queueing like the Kafka system. Frameworks such as Akka and Spring would then supply extra canned functionality.

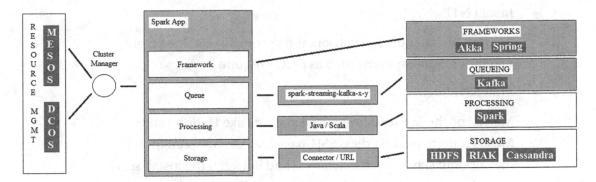

Figure 6-2. *Spark application architecture*

Using the same format as Chapter 4, Apache Mesos, I want to show and compare two methods for using Mesos and Spark together in this chapter. The first method will build and install Mesos onto a cluster; the second will install DCOS, the Data Center Operating System, the aim being to show how DCOS improves on a basic Mesos install.

The next section will examine the creation of a Mesos-based environment for the use of Apache Spark after having briefly examined server preparation. The examples shown here will expand on the work carried out in Chapter 4 and provide extra detail.

Server Preparation

Before moving on to the Mesos-based cluster management system installs, it is worth considering the preparation of the servers used for these installs. The previous chapters have already covered many of these topics in detail, but I think a recap is a good idea.

- Operating System

  Many people have a favorite operating system; I prefer CentOS Linux—it is free, widely supported, and robust. I use Centos 6.x and 7.x in this book and chapter.

- FQDN Server Names

  Fully qualified domain names need to be used for the servers; each machine must have a name and a domain name, e.g., hc4nn.semtech-solutions.co.nz. You can test this by using the "hostname -f" command.

- Install NTP

  I always install the NTP (network time protocol) service on my machines. Some systems such as DCOS require it.

- Auto SSH Login

  Many Apache Master/Slave-based systems like Hadoop and Mesos require passwordless SSH-based access between the master- and slave-based machines (and between the install server and all master and slave servers for DCOS). If necessary, I set this up using commands like "`ssh-keygen`" and "`ssh-copy-id`".

- Disable SE Linux

  Many Apache-based systems operate better with SE Linux disabled; I edit the file /etc/selinux/config and set SELINUX=disabled.

- Java Install

  I always install the Open JDK (Java Development Kit) version of Java on my servers, being careful to install the version required by the system that it will support.

- Set Up Hosts File

  Finally I set up the /etc/hosts file on each server to ensure that every machine hosts file has an entry describing every machine in the cluster. I am reiterating these points because Mesos, and especially DCOS-based environments, are complex. By spending time now to properly prepare the cluster servers, time can be saved later by avoiding problems that are hard to track and solve.

The next section will examine the install and build of a Mesos-based environment followed by the install and use of Apache Spark. This work builds on and extends that presented in Chapter 4.

Mesos and Spark

This section will use three servers to support the Mesos build: hc4nn (192.168.1.109), hc4r1m1 (192.168.1.113), and hc4r1m2 (192.168.1.114). The first server will be used for the master process, whereas all servers will be used to run Mesos agents. This section will provide a simplified list of commands based on those used in Chapter 4. For further detail of their meaning, please consult that chapter. I have divided the Mesos environment build into a number of logical sections to reduce complexity. The following Build Steps will be carried out on all servers used. The build will be carried out by the root user.

Build Mesos Part 1

This section of the build starts with a newly installed CentOS 6.8 server along with the extra steps described in the "Server Preparation" section. It then modifies the kernel to support the use of Mesos and ends with a server reboot. The first step involves using the Linux rpm command to import some updated kernel files.

```
$ rpm --import https://www.elrepo.org/RPM-GPG-KEY-elrepo.org
```

```
$ rpm -Uvh http://www.elrepo.org/elrepo-release-6-6.el6.elrepo.noarch.rpm
```

The Linux yum command is then used to install and enable the kernel updates.

```
$ yum --enablerepo=elrepo-kernel install -y kernel-lt
```

The Linux sed command is used to modify the /boot/grub/grub.conf file; this is the grub boot loader config file. The "-i" sed option allows files to be edited in place. This will cause the new Linux kernel to be used after a reboot, which is initiated by the last command following:

```
$ sed -i 's/default=1/default=0/g' /boot/grub/grub.conf
```

```
$ reboot
```

Build Mesos Part 2

After each server has been rebooted, log back into the server as root and continue. Use the Linux yum command to install the tar, wget, git, which, and nss commands. The -y options avoids the need for confirmation prompts.

```
$ yum -y install tar wget git which nss
```

Next obtain a yum-based repository file for the devtoolset component that will support the install of a wide range of functionality like GCC. The Linux wget command is used to obtain repo file and supporting GPG key from the Linuxsoft site.

```
$ wget -O /etc/yum.repos.d/slc6-devtoolset.repo  http://linuxsoft.cern.ch/
cern/devtoolset/slc6-devtoolset.repo
```

```
$ rpm --import http://linuxsoft.cern.ch/cern/centos/7/os/x86_64/RPM-GPG-
KEY-cern
```

Next wget is used to get a yum-based repo file for Apache Maven, sourced from the repos.fedorapeople.org site.

```
$ wget http://repos.fedorapeople.org/repos/dchen/apache-maven/epel-apache-
maven.repo   -O  /etc/yum.repos.d/epel-apache-maven.repo
```

A WANdisco SVN repo file is then created as wandisco-svn.repo under the directory /etc/yum.repos.d. This is to support the use and install of SVN source control with Mesos.

```
$ bash -c 'cat > /etc/yum.repos.d/wandisco-svn.repo <<EOF
[WANdiscoSVN]
name=WANdisco SVN Repo 1.8
enabled=1
baseurl=http://opensource.wandisco.com/centos/6/svn-1.8/RPMS/$basearch/
gpgcheck=1
gpgkey=http://opensource.wandisco.com/RPM-GPG-KEY-WANdisco
EOF'
```

The next step uses the Linux yum command to carry out a group install of the "Development Tools" module. This will install a set of tools such as gcc, flex, make, and so forth.

```
$ yum groupinstall -y "Development Tools"
```

The devtoolset-2-toolchain module is then installed using yum to install development and debugging tools.

```
$ yum install -y devtoolset-2-toolchain
```

The next three yum commands install a range of modules to support the Mesos build, starting with Apache Maven:

```
$ yum install -y apache-maven python-devel java-1.7.0-openjdk-devel

$ yum install -y zlib-devel libcurl-devel openssl-devel cyrus-sasl-devel

$ yum install -y cyrus-sasl-md5 apr-devel subversion-devel apr-util-devel
```

Finally, in this section, a devtoolset-2 bash session is started using the Linux scl command. This command allows the execution of applications not located in the root file system.

```
$ scl enable devtoolset-2 bash
```

Build Mesos Part 3

This section sets up the cgconfig.conf file under the /etc/ directory. A perf_event line is added to the file to support the use of config groups.

```
$ vi /etc/cgconfig.conf

mount {
        cpuset  = /cgroup/cpuset;
        cpu     = /cgroup/cpu;
        cpuacct = /cgroup/cpuacct;
        memory  = /cgroup/memory;
        devices = /cgroup/devices;
        freezer = /cgroup/freezer;
        net_cls = /cgroup/net_cls;
        blkio   = /cgroup/blkio;
        perf_event = /cgroup/perf_event;
}
```

The libcgroup (control group library) module is then installed using the Linux yum command; this library abstracts CentOS group management.

```
$ yum install -y libcgroup
```

Finally, in this section, the cgconfig service is started and configured to start after reboot using the chkconfig (check configuration) command. The same process is carried out for the CentOS 6.x firewall service iptables. This is only done for environment development simplification and because this is not a productionized server.

```
$ service cgconfig start ; chkconfig cgconfig on
```

```
$ service iptables stop ; chkconfig iptables off
```

Building the Mesos Source

Having prepared the CentOS 6-based server and installed all of the prerequisite components, the Mesos system itself can now be sourced and built. At the time of this writing (March 2017), Mesos Version 1.1 is the latest available. I will build the source under /tmp and so create a temporary directory and move to that location. Then I use wget to source Version 1.1 of the Mesos code from apache.org in a gzipped and tarred format.

```
$ mkdir /tmp/mesos ; cd /tmp/mesos
```

```
$ wget http://www.apache.org/dist/mesos/1.1.0/mesos-1.1.0.tar.gz
```

The code package is unpacked in a single step using the Linux tar command with the options f (file), x (extract), and z (gzip). This creates an unpacked directory called mesos-1.1.0, which contains the unbuilt code.

```
$ tar -zxf mesos-1.1.0.tar.gz
```

I move this directory to /opt so that it has a more appropriate permanent home and cd to that location.

```
$ mv mesos-1.1.0 /opt ; cd /opt
```

I also create a symbolic link using the Linux `ln` command called `mesos` under `/opt` to point to the new Mesos-based source directory. Then I use that link to move into the Mesos source directory.

```
$ ln -s mesos-1.1.0 mesos
```

```
$ cd mesos
```

Now I execute the bootstrap command, which is required when building from a git-based repository. I also set the JAVA_HOME variable to ensure that it exists and is assigned to the version of Java that is installed (1.7).

```
$ ./bootstrap
```

```
$ export JAVA_HOME=/usr/lib/jvm/java-1.7.0-openjdk-1.7.0.131.x86_64
```

The next step involves creating a build directory to support the Mesos code build and changing the directory to that location.

```
$ mkdir build
```

```
$ cd build
```

The configure script (run from the level above the build directory) is executed to prepare the build environment, creating make files and allowing the build to be started.

```
$ ../configure
```

Now the source can be built using the make command following; the -j switch allows the number of cores present to be specified. The V option specifies the verbose level. This stage of the build will take at least 30 minutes.

```
$ make -j 2 V=0  #  time aprox 30 mins
```

The `make check` command executed next will run unit tests against the Mesos build and then create the necessary binaries for Mesos to be run. This will also create the src/test-framework tree under the build directory.

```
$ make check
```

Finally, the make install option run next will install Mesos components, binaries, and libraries into the expected CentOS-based system locations so that when running Mesos, all of its components are easily found.

```
$ make install
```

Mesos is now ready to use as the next section will show.

Starting Mesos

Now that Mesos has been built, checked, and installed, a Mesos-based cluster can be started. I have used the Linux cd command to ensure that I am in the /opt/mesos/build/ directory. I have then used the ./bin/mesos-master.sh script to start a Mesos master server.

```
$ cd /opt/mesos/build

$ ./bin/mesos-master.sh \
   --ip=192.168.1.109 \
   --advertise_ip=192.168.1.109 \
   --advertise_port=5055 \
   --work_dir=/var/lib/mesos >    ./master.log 2>&1  &
```

This master server has been started on the server hc4nn, IP address 192.168.1.109. The --ip switch allows the master IP address to be specified. The next two options allow the IP address and port to be advertised to the Mesos agents that will connect to this master. The work_dir options specifies that all data should reside under /var/lib/mesos. While the redirection option redirects output to the log file master.log., STDERR (standard error) is redirected to the log as well (2>&1), and the server is run as a background task (&).

It is possible to ensure that the Mesos master server is running correctly on the node hc4nn by using the Linux ps command to create a process listing and piping this to grep with a search for mesos-master as shown following:

```
$ ps -ef | grep mesos-master

root      8027  2514  0 15:05 pts/0    00:00:00 /opt/mesos/build/src/.libs/
lt-mesos-master --ip=192.168.1.109 --work_dir=/var/lib/mesos
```

This provides the Mesos master process listing (process 8027) as shown previously. On each server that will host a Mesos agent process, an agent is started, as shown following. The execution location is again under /opt/mesos/build/, and again the agent script is executed in the same way.

```
$ cd /opt/mesos/build
```

```
$ ./bin/mesos-agent.sh \
  --master=192.168.1.109:5050 \
  --launcher=posix   \
  --work_dir=/var/lib/mesos > ./agent.log 2>&1  &
```

A working directory is specified as well as a log file (agent.log). A posix launcher option is used to specify a posix-based location of Linux cgroups. Also a master switch is used to tell the Mesos agent process which IP address and port number to use to access the Mesos master. As with the master process, the Mesos agent process can be checked to ensure it is running.

```
$ ps -ef | grep mesos-master
```

```
root      8027  2514  0 15:05 pts/0    00:00:00 /opt/mesos/build/src/.libs/
lt-mesos master --ip-192.168.1.109 --work_dir=/var/lib/mesos
```

The Mesos user interface can now be accessed from the following URL using the master IP address and port specified when starting the master process. I won't provide any Mesos user interfaces images here because they have already been shown in previous chapters.

```
http://192.168.1.109:5050
```

The next steps will involve installing a Hadoop HDFS framework on Mesos and then installing Apache Spark and showing how the two frameworks can be used together on Mesos.

Installing the HDFS Framework

I will install the HDFS Mesos framework under the /opt directory on the master node hc4nn, so initially I cd to that location.

```
$ cd /opt
```

I then use the git command to clone a copy of the Elodina hdfs-mesos code to a directory under /opt. This creates a source directory called hdfs-mesos.

```
$ git clone https://github.com/elodina/hdfs-mesos.git
```

I cd to the new HDFS Mesos directory hdfs-mesos using the Linux cd command and then examine the README.md file in that directory.

```
$ cd hdfs-mesos
```

```
$ vi README.md
```

This readme file explains how the HDFS-Mesos framework can be used. It provides the details of its dependencies.

```
Project requires:
- Mesos 0.23.0+
- JDK 1.7.x
- Hadoop 1.2.x or 2.7.x
```

This readme file provides a few methods for using the framework, that is, a Vagrant-based environment, downloading the framework binary or the method that I will use building the framework using the gradlew (gradle wrapper) script. I chose to build the framework rather than download a hdfs-mesos binary from GitHub because when I tried that, I encountered an error when starting the scheduler, which stated the following:

```
Exception in thread "main" java.lang.IllegalStateException: Supported
hadoop versions are 1.2.x, current is 2.7.2
```

I was attempting to use a Hadoop V2 binary, and I found that the only way to do so without error was to follow the gradlew approach to the build. Remember that similar errors were encountered in the last chapter when using HDFS-Mesos. The framework is built using gradlew as follows:

```
$ ./gradlew jar
```

Version 2.7.2 of the hadoop binary is then downloaded to the HDFS-Mesos directory using the wget command from the archive.apache.org site.

```
$ wget https://archive.apache.org/dist/hadoop/core/hadoop-2.7.2/hadoop--
2.7.2.tar.gz
```

Some variables are now set up to support the running of the HDFS-Mesos scheduler process. The MESOS_HOME variable indicates where the Mesos system has been installed. The MESOS_NATIVE_LIBRARY variable provides the path to the lib mesos library, while the LIBPROCESS_IP variable provides the IP address of the Mesos master host. All of these variables are defined in the current session using the Linux export command.

```
$ export MESOS_HOME=/opt/mesos
$ export MESOS_NATIVE_LIBRARY=/opt/mesos/build/src/.libs/libmesos.so
$ export LIBPROCESS_IP=192.168.1.109
```

The HDFS-Mesos scheduler process is started using the hdfs-mesos.sh script with the first parameter as scheduler. The second parameter defines the host and port on which the scheduler will be accessible. The master parameter defines the host and port for Mesos access, while the user parameter states that the scheduler will be run as root. Output is redirected to the log hdfs-mesos.log.

```
$ ./hdfs-mesos.sh scheduler \
     --api=http://192.168.1.109:7000 \
     --master=192.168.1.109:5050 \
     --user=root > hdfs-mesos.log 2>&1 &
```

Now that the hdfs-mesos framework is running as well as Mesos, a Hadoop cluster can be created. First a name node is created using the following command:

```
$ ./hdfs-mesos.sh node add nn --type=namenode
--api=http://192.168.1.109:7000
```

Again the hdfs-mesos.sh script is called but with the add command this time. The next parameter is nn, which provides the name of the Hadoop Name Node. The type parameter specifies that it is a Name Node, while the api parameter provides access to the HDFS-Mesos framework scheduler.

Once the Hadoop Name Node is created, Hadoop Data Nodes can be created in the same way. This time the type is datanode, and the Data Node names are dn0 to dn2.

```
$ ./hdfs-mesos.sh node add dn0 --type=datanode --api=http://192.168.1.109:7000
$ ./hdfs-mesos.sh node add dn1 --type=datanode --api=http://192.168.1.109:7000
$ ./hdfs-mesos.sh node add dn2 --type=datanode --api=http://192.168.1.109:7000
```

Once the Hadoop cluster has been created on the HDFS-Mesos framework that is running on Mesos, the cluster must be started. This is carried out as follows:

```
$ ./hdfs-mesos.sh node start \*    --api=http://192.168.1.109:7000
```

The command is again node, but this time the next option is start, followed by an escaped wild card character (*). This means start all, whereas we could have replaced this wild option with actual cluster member names (nn dn0 dn1 dn2). Once started, we can check the status of the cluster using the list option.

```
$ ./hdfs-mesos.sh node list nn --api=http://192.168.1.109:7000
```

The preceding command lists the status of the Name Node and provides the output following. This is useful because it shows the state is running, the resources used, as well as the node the Name Node is running on and the ports used. These details will be used shortly.

```
node:
  id: nn
  type: namenode
  state: running
  resources: cpus:0.5, mem:512
  stickiness: period:30m, hostname:hc4nn.semtech-solutions.co.nz
  failover: delay:3m, max-delay:30m
  reservation: cpus:0.5, mem:512, ports:http=31000,ipc=31001
  runtime:
    task: 909829e1-f6ba-430a-a03c-2fcf37d877f2
    executor: 479dde06-c9e8-462e-b412-2d04447512b6
    slave: 23dfd5f6-f354-4008-9054-4d50907898c5-S2 (hc4nn.semtech-solutions.
    co.nz)
```

The IPC port for the Name Node is 31001, and the host name is hc4nn, so I know the IP address is 192.168.1.109. Now if I use the same list command with a wild card and grep for state, I can see that all Hadoop cluster nodes that were just created are running.

```
$ ./hdfs-mesos.sh node list \* --api=http://192.168.1.109:7000 | grep state

  state: running
  state: running
  state: running
  state: running
```

Those of you that are familiar with Hadoop may have realized that by starting the Hadoop cluster in this way, I have no control over where the cluster nodes will be started on a Mesos cluster. So how can I access Hadoop if I don't know where it's cluster nodes exist ? Well luckily, the preceding list command showed the host and port by which the Hadoop Name Node could be accessed, hc4nn. So we can search on that host using the Linux find command following to find the hadoop command:

```
$ find / -type f -name hadoop
```

This provides the following output, which represents a Hadoop task running on the HDFS-Mesos framework, which is itself running on the Mesos cluster.

```
/var/lib/mesos/slaves/23dfd5f6-f354-4008-9054-4d50907898c5-S2/
frameworks/23dfd5f6-f354-4008-9054-4d50907898c5-0000/executors/479dde06-
c9e8-462e-b412-2d04447512b6/runs/696e38fb-1ff8-4ddc-8963-cb30e1b13376/
hadoop-2.7.2/bin/hadoop
```

This path can be used to specify a HADOOP_HOME variable as follows, which will simplify Hadoop access. The variable is defined using the Linux export command as shown following:

```
$ export HADOOP_HOME=/var/lib/mesos/slaves/23dfd5f6-f354-4008-9054-
4d50907898c5-S2/frameworks/23dfd5f6-f354-4008-9054-4d50907898c5-0000/
executors/479dde06-c9e8-462e-b412-2d04447512b6/runs/696e38fb-1ff8-4ddc-
8963-cb30e1b13376/hadoop-2.7.2
```

Before attempting to access Hadoop, I ensure that JAVA_HOME is set and if not, assign it to a Java 1.7-based path.

```
$ echo $JAVA_HOME
$ export JAVA_HOME=/usr/lib/jvm/java-1.7.0-openjdk-1.7.0.131.x86_64
```

Now I can access the hadoop command using the HADOOP_HOME variable as shown following. The fs option means "file system," whereas the -ls option is for a long listing of HDFS. The command following will not provide any output because the HDFS/ file system is empty:

```
$ $HADOOP_HOME/bin/hadoop fs -ls    hdfs://192.168.1.109:31001/
```

The HDFS-based command following creates a directory on HDFS called /misc, while the following ls-based `hdfs` command shows that it exists:

```
$  $HADOOP_HOME/bin/hadoop fs -mkdir  hdfs://192.168.1.109:31001/misc
$  $HADOOP_HOME/bin/hadoop fs -ls    hdfs://192.168.1.109:31001/

drwxr-xr-x   - root supergroup          0 2017-03-14 13:33
hdfs://192.168.1.109:31001/misc
```

Note that Hadoop HDFS is being access via port 31001, the IPC port on hc4nn provided in the `list` command for the preceding Name Node. Like any Hadoop installation, the Hadoop Name Node user interface can be access via the Name Node host name and port, in this case

```
http://192.168.1.109:31000.
```

The next step will be to obtain a version of Apache Spark that will be compatible with the version of Hadoop that was just installed and run. First, I will create a directory /spark on HDFS in the same way that I created the /misc directory previously. I will then list the directories to show that they both exist.

```
$  $HADOOP_HOME/bin/hadoop fs -mkdir    hdfs://192.168.1.109:31001/spark

$  $HADOOP_HOME/bin/hadoop fs -ls    hdfs://192.168.1.109:31001/

Found 2 items
drwxr-xr-x   - root supergroup          0 2017-03-14 13:33
hdfs://192.168.1.109:31001/misc
drwxr-xr-x   - root supergroup          0 2017-03-14 13:35
hdfs://192.168.1.109:31001/spark
```

Running Spark

I now create a directory /opt/spark/ on the Linux file system as a working directory and home for Apache Spark. I will download Version 2.1.0 of Spark for Hadoop 2.7 using the `wget` command as shown following:

```
$ cd /opt ; mkdir spark ; cd spark
$ wget  http://d3kbcqa49mib13.cloudfront.net/spark-2.1.0-bin-hadoop2.7.tgz
```

Then I check the downloaded Spark package using the Linux ls command, which shows that it is in .tgz format or gzipped tar.

```
$ ls -l spark*.tgz
```

```
-rw-r--r-- 1 root root 195636829 Dec 29 13:49 spark-2.1.0-bin-hadoop2.7.tgz
```

I now copy the Spark package to HDFS into the /spark directory using the Hadoop put command.

```
$ $HADOOP_HOME/bin/hadoop fs -put ./spark*.tgz hdfs://192.168.1.109:31001/spark/
```

I then check it is on HDFS using the Hadoop ls command; as shown following, the package resides in the /spark directory:

```
$ $HADOOP_HOME/bin/hadoop fs -ls  hdfs://192.168.1.109:31001/spark/
```

```
-rw-r--r--   3 root supergroup  195636829 2017-03-14 13:45
hdfs://192.168.1.109:31001/spark/spark-2.1.0-bin-hadoop2.7.tgz
```

Now to use Spark, I need to set up some variables: MESOS_NATIVE_JAVA_LIBRARY specifies the path to the libmesos library. The SPARK_EXECUTOR URI variable specifies the path to the Spark package on HDFS.

```
$ export MESOS_NATIVE_JAVA_LIBRARY=/usr/local/lib/libmesos.so
$ export SPARK_EXECUTOR_URI=hdfs://192.168.1.109:31001/spark/spark-2.1.0-
bin-hadoop2.7.tgz
```

I will now unpack the Spark package using the gunzip command initially to create the Spark tar file following shown by the Linux ls command:

```
$ gunzip spark-*.tgz
$ ls -l
```

```
total 219512
-rw-r--r-- 1 root root 224778240 Dec 29 13:49 spark-2.1.0-bin-hadoop2.7.tar
```

I then use the Linux tar command to unpack the tar file that was just created. I'm doing this because I want access to the Spark-based spark-shell command so that I can run a Spark shell that will access Spark on HDFS/Mesos. The tar command following

unpacks the tar package to the directory spark-2.1.0-bin-hadoop2.7, and I use the Linux
ln command to create a symbolic link called spark. This points to the Spark package
directory and simplifies Spark access.

```
$ tar xf spark-*.tar

$ ln -s spark-2.1.0-bin-hadoop2.7 spark
```

The Linux ls long listing following shows the original tar file, the Spark package
directory, and the link that was just created:

```
$ ls -l

total 219516
lrwxrwxrwx  1 root root            25 Mar 14 13:48 spark -> spark-2.1.0-bin-
                                       hadoop2.7
drwxr-xr-x 12  500  500          4096 Dec 16 15:18 spark-2.1.0-bin-hadoop2.7
-rw-r--r--  1 root root 224778240 Dec 29 13:49 spark-2.1.0-bin-hadoop2.7.tar
```

To run Apache Spark against Mesos, I need to set up some Spark configuration files.
The first file to be set up will be spark-env.sh. I use the Linux cd command to move to the
Spark conf directory. I then create the spark-env.sh file from its template via Linux cp.

```
$ cd /opt/spark/spark/conf
$ cp spark-env.sh.template spark-env.sh
```

I vi this new file and add the following lines to the bottom of the file:

```
$ vi spark-env.sh

export MESOS_NATIVE_JAVA_LIBRARY=/usr/local/lib/libmesos.so
export SPARK_EXECUTOR_URI=hdfs://192.168.1.109:31001/spark/spark-2.1.0-bin-
hadoop2.7.tgz
```

This specifies the location of the libmesos library (as before) and the location
on HDFS of the Spark package. Next, I set up the file spark-defaults.conf in the same
directory, again creating it from its preexisting template file using the Linux cp (copy)
command. The following lines are added to the bottom of the new file using a vi session:

```
$ cp spark-defaults.conf.template spark-defaults.conf
$ vi spark-defaults.conf
```

```
spark.master mesos://192.168.1.109:5050
spark.executor.uri hdfs://192.168.1.109:31001/spark/spark-2.1.0-bin-
hadoop2.7.tgz
```

This specifies the URL for the Spark master; note that this a Mesos-based URL. The Spark cluster manager is now Mesos! The spark.executor.ui variable specifies the full path to the Spark package on HDFS. The next step is to create the file spark-env.cmd in the conf directory. I use the touch command for this. I then make the file executable using the Linux chmod command.

```
$ touch spark-env.cmd ; chmod 755 spark-env.cmd
```

Using a vi session, I edit the file

```
$ vi spark-env.cmd
```

and add the following lines, which define the HADOOP_HOME variable, define the PATH variable, and set the SPARK_DIST_CLASSPATH to be the Hadoop classpath:

```
export HADOOP_HOME=$HADOOP_HOME
export PATH=$HADOOP_HOME/bin:$PATH

# assign output of this command
#   $HADOOP_HOME/bin/hadoop classpath
# to the variable SPARK_DIST_CLASSPATH

export SPARK_DIST_CLASSPATH=`$HADOOP_HOME/bin/hadoop classpath`
```

I am now ready to run a Spark shell as follows: I move to the /opt/spark/spark/ directory and execute the ./bin/spark-shell command. The master option indicates that the Spark cluster manager will be Mesos followed by the Mesos master IP address and port.

```
$ cd  /opt/spark/spark/
```

```
$ ./bin/spark-shell --master mesos://192.168.1.109:5050
```

I have limited the output from the spark shell start up following to save space, but you will recognize the Spark shell credentials with the Mesos master URL:

```
I0314 13:55:30.260362  8327 sched.cpp:330] New master detected at
master@192.168.1.109:5050
Spark context Web UI available at http://192.168.1.109:4040
```

```
Spark context available as 'sc' (master = mesos://192.168.1.109:5050, app
id = 23dfd5f6-f354-4008-9054-4d50907898c5-0001).
Spark session available as 'spark'.
Welcome to


      ___              __
     / __/__  ___ _____/ /__
    _\ \/ _ \/ _ `/ __/  '_/
   /__ / .__/\_,_/_/ /_/\_\   version 2.1.0
      /_/

Using Scala version 2.11.8 (OpenJDK 64-Bit Server VM, Java 1.7.0_131)
Type in expressions to have them evaluated.
Type :help for more information.

scala>  :quit
```

Now that I have Spark running against Mesos, I can run a Scala shell script against it. The file test1.scala shown by the Linux cat command following just lists the first one hundred positions in the Fibonacci series:

```
$ cat test1.scala

import org.apache.spark.SparkContext
import org.apache.spark.SparkContext._
import org.apache.spark.SparkConf

  val appName = "Fibonacci 1"
  val conf = new SparkConf()

  conf.setAppName(appName)

  val sparkCxt = new SparkContext(conf)

  var seed1:BigInt = 1
  var seed2:BigInt = 1
  val limit = 100
  var resultStr = seed1 + " " + seed2 + " "
```

```
for( i <- 1 to limit ){

  val fib:BigInt = seed1 + seed2
  resultStr += fib.toString + " "

  seed1 = seed2
  seed2 = fib
}

println()
println( "Result : " + resultStr )
println()
```

I execute this script against Spark and Mesos using the Spark shell command following with a Mesos master URL as described previously. The "-i" option allows the test1.scala file to be included at the command line:

```
$ ./bin/spark-shell -i    test1.scala    --master mesos://192.168.1.109:5050
```

The output from the script is the list of Fibonacci values.

```
Result : 1 1 2 3 5 8 13 21 34 55 89 144 233 377 610 987 1597 2584 4181
6765 10946 17711 28657 46368 75025 121393 196418 317811 514229 832040
1346269 2178309 3524578 5702887 9227465 14930352 24157817 39088169
63245986 102334155 165580141 267914296 433494437 701408733 1134903170
1836311903 2971215073 4807526976 7778742049 12586269025 20365011074
32951280099 53316291173 86267571272 139583862445 225851433717 365435296162
591286729879 956722026041 1548008755920 2504730781961 4052739537881
6557470319842 10610209857723 17167680177565 27777890035288 44945570212853
72723460248141 117669030460994 190392490709135 308061521170129
498454011879264 806515533049393 1304969544928657 2111485077978050
3416454622906707 5527939700884757 8944394323791464 14472334024676221
23416728348467685 37889062373143906 61305790721611591 99194853094755497
160500643816367088 259695496911122585 420196140727489673 679891637638612258
1100087778366101931 1779979416004714189 2880067194370816120
4660046610375530309 7540113804746346429 12200160415121876738
19740274219868223167 31940434634990099905 51680708854858323072
83621143489848422977 135301852344706746049 218922995834555169026
354224848179261915075 573147844013817084101 927372692193078999176
```

So Spark has been successfully run against Mesos using a Mesos cluster built from source and manually installed on each node. In the next section, DCOS (Data Center Operating System) will be built and can be compared against this section and the approach used.

DCOS and Spark

DCOS is the open-sourced data center operating system that has been created and released via the dcos.io site. It was introduced in Chapter 4; the work presented in this chapter will build on the earlier work and go further. As per the previous section, the DCOS installation here will be a trimmed-down version of that presented in Chapter 4. However, this section will go further, showing how to use the DCOS CLI and install and use DCOS modules like HDFS and Spark. The servers used in this section have been prepared as described in the "Server Preparation" section. Each server has been installed with CentOS 7.2 and Java 1.8.

I have divided the DCOS server build into three parts to simplify the process, each of which is described by a section following. This install will use an install server hc4nn (192.168.1.109), a master server hc4r1m1 (192.168.1.113), and a number of agents hc4r1m2 (192.168.1.114) to hc4r1m5 (192.168.1.117). The next sections will describe the parts of the DCOS install.

DCOS Build Part 1

This section of the build installs some prerequisite components via yum, runs an upgrade, and sets up an overlay file to support the later Docker install. It ends with a server reboot and is executed on all servers. The first command installs tar, xz, unzip, ipset, and curl using the Linux yum command.

```
$ yum -y install tar xz unzip  ipset curl wget
```

This is followed by a Linux yum upgrade command to ensure that all yum-based components are up-to-date.

```
$ yum -y upgrade --assumeyes --tolerant
```

A file called overlay.conf is then created under /etc/modules-load.d/ to contain a single word "overlay." This is needed to support Docker.

```
$ tee /etc/modules-load.d/overlay.conf <<-'EOF'
overlay
EOF
```

Finally, the server is rebooted to enable the changes.

```
$ reboot
```

DCOS Build Part 2

The commands in this section are executed on all servers. It creates the configuration for Docker and then installs and executes Docker. Docker will provide container support for DCOS. The first command creates a repository configuration file called docker.repo under /etc/yum.repos.d/. This will support the later yum-based Docker install.

```
$ bash -c 'cat > /etc/yum.repos.d/docker.repo <<EOF
[dockerrepo]
name=Docker Repository
baseurl=https://yum.dockerproject.org/repo/main/centos/7/
enabled=1
gpgcheck=1
gpgkey=https://yum.dockerproject.org/gpg
EOF'
```

The next command creates a directory docker.service.d under /etc/systemd/system/ using the Linux mkdir command. The -p option means that any subdirectory in the path is also created.

```
$ mkdir -p /etc/systemd/system/docker.service.d
```

A file called override.conf is then created within this directory, which specifies how the Docker service will start and that it will use the overlay file system created earlier for storage.

```
$ bash -c 'cat > /etc/systemd/system/docker.service.d/override.conf <<EOF
[Service]
ExecStart=/usr/bin/docker daemon --storage-driver=overlay
EOF'
```

Next, a directory /var/lib/docker/ is created using mkdir to contain Docker libraries, and setenforce is used to ensure that SELinux is disabled.

```
$ mkdir /var/lib/docker/
```

```
$ setenforce 0
```

Docker engine is then installed using the Linux yum command; it is enabled with systemctl and executed via a systemctl start command.

```
$ yum -y install --assumeyes --tolerant docker-engine
```

```
$ systemctl enable docker
```

```
$ systemctl start docker
```

Finally, a group called "nogroup" is added to the Linux groups file /etc/group to support DCOS install checks.

```
$ echo "nogroup:x:5000:" >>    /etc/group
```

DCOS Build Part 3—Install Server

This section forms the third part of the DCOS install and is only carried out on the install server, in this case, hc4nn (192.168.1.109). The install server is only used during the DCOS install and acts to provide services and configuration scripts to the other DCOS machines during installation, as you will see. The first set of commands creates a working directory /opt/dcos_tmp/ using mkdir. The current directory is then changed to that location, and a subdirectory called genconf is created.

```
$ mkdir /opt/dcos_tmp/
```

```
$ cd /opt/dcos_tmp/
```

```
$ mkdir genconf
```

Now a script called ip-detect is created under the genconf directory. The important line in this file is the last line, starting with the echo command. This line uses the CentOS 7-based "ip addr show" command to list the IP address information for the network port enp0s25. The grep command then searches the output for an IP address, while the head command limits the output to one line, the IP address.

```
$ cat <<EOF > /opt/dcos_tmp/genconf/ip-detect

#!/usr/bin/env bash
set -o nounset -o errexit
export PATH=/usr/sbin:/usr/bin:$PATH
echo $(ip addr show enp0s25| grep -Eo '[0-9]{1,3}\.[0-9]{1,3}\.[0-9]{1,3}\.
[0-9]{1,3}' | head -1)
EOF
```

Take care with the preceding script, as your network entry may not be called enp0s25 on CentOS 7. Check under the directory /etc/sysconfig/network-scripts for files called ifcfg-*. The contents of these files will start with the line

```
TYPE=Ethernet,
```

And the full file name will indicate the value to be used in the "ip addr show" command shown previously. For instance, my file is called ifcfg-enp0s25. The next command makes the ip-detect script executable.

```
$ chmod 755 ./genconf/ip-detect
```

When run, this script returns the IP address of the server on which it is executed; for instance, the output following run on hc4nn returns 192.168.1.109:

```
$ ./genconf/ip-detect
192.168.1.109
```

The next cat command creates the file /opt/dcos_tmp/genconf/config.yaml, which is the DCOS cluster yaml-based configuration file. It specifies a bootstrap address and port to be used by all other servers in the cluster during installation. It specifies the cluster name and static storage type. It specifies the location of the ip-detect script as well as the location of the Mesos master and DNS server values.

```
$ cat <<EOF > /opt/dcos_tmp/genconf/config.yaml
---
bootstrap_url: http://192.168.1.109:9000
cluster_name: 'cluster1'
exhibitor_storage_backend: static
ip_detect_filename: /opt/dcos_tmp/genconf/ip-detect
```

```
master_discovery: static
master_list:
- 192.168.1.113
resolvers:
- 8.8.4.4
- 8.8.8.8
EOF
```

Now the dcos_generate_config.sh command shell script is downloaded to the directory /opt/dcos_tmp/ using curl. This is a large script that will take some time to completely download, as it contains binary data.

```
$ cd  /opt/dcos_tmp/
```

```
$ curl -O https://downloads.dcos.io/dcos/EarlyAccess/commit/14509fe1e7899f4
39527fb39867194c7a425c771/dcos_generate_config.sh
```

The script is made executable via a Linux chmod (change mode) command and then executed via a bash shell.

```
$ chmod 755 dcos_generate_config.sh
```

```
$ bash ./dcos_generate_config.sh
```

Finally, nginx, the high-performance http server, is executed in a Docker container to support DCOS.

```
$ cd /opt/dcos_tmp
```

```
$ docker run -d -p 9000:80 -v /opt/dcos_tmp/genconf/serve:/usr/share/nginx/
html:ro nginx
```

Now that the DCOS install server is running, the remaining DCOS servers can have their installs completed. That means that the DCOS master server needs to be prepped first, and then the agent servers will be prepared. The next sections will describe how this is done.

DCOS Master Server Install

There may be multiple DCOS master servers, but in this cluster, I will only create one, as I have limited machines. This install will be carried out on the server hc4r1m1 (192.168.1.113). The DCOS Build part 1 and part 2 sections will already have been carried out on this server. The final step involves downloading a DCOS install script from the install server and running it. The first command involves creating a directory /opt/dcos using mkdir and moving to that location.

```
$ mkdir /opt/dcos && cd /opt/dcos
```

The curl command is then used to obtain the script dcos_install.sh from the install server using the bootstrap URL defined in the yaml file earlier.

```
$ curl -O http://192.168.1.109:9000/dcos_install.sh
```

Finally, the script is made executable using the chmod command and executed in a bash shell. The master parameter indicates that this node is the DCOS master server.

```
$ chmod 755 dcos_install.sh
```

```
$ bash ./dcos_install.sh master
```

The DCOS master server is now running and is ready to receive agents into the DCOS cluster. The next section will complete that process.

DCOS Agent Server Install

This section will be executed for all agent servers to be added to the DCOS cluster. The DCOS Build part 1 and part 2 sections will already have been carried out on these servers. The final steps for the agents are similar to those of the master. The first command involves creating a directory /opt/dcos using mkdir and moving to that location.

```
$ mkdir /opt/dcos && cd /opt/dcos
```

The curl command is then used to obtain the script dcos_install.sh from the install server using the bootstrap URL defined in the yaml file earlier.

```
$ curl -O http://192.168.1.109:9000/dcos_install.sh
```

Finally, the script is made executable using the chmod command and executed in a bash shell. The dcos_install.sh script can be executed with the parameter slave_public or slave. The first option creates a public slave or agent node, whereas the second creates a private node. I found that the nodes had to be private to execute DCOS-framework-based tasks.

```
$ chmod 755 dcos_install.sh   ; ls -l
$ bash ./dcos_install.sh  slave
```

DCOS can now be accessed via a series of web- based user interfaces as shown in Chapter 4.

User Interfaces

The ZooKeeper Exhibitor interface is available at the following URL, based on the IP address of the master host hc4r1m1 (192.168.1.113) at port 8181.

```
http://192.168.1.113:8181/exhibitor/v1/ui/index.html
```

The DCOS Marathon scheduler application is available at the following URL, again based on the IP address of the master host hc4r1m1 (192.168.1.113) at port 8080.

```
http://192.168.1.113:8080/ui/#/apps/
```

The DCOS user interface can be accessed from the master server via the URL following.

```
http://192.168.1.113/
```

Finally the Mesos web based user interface is available on port 5050 on the master server IP address.

http://192.168.1.113:5050/#/

To gain more information about and access to the DCOS cluster, the DCOS CLI tool needs to be installed. The next section will show how this is carried out.

DCOS CLI Command Install

The DCOS CLI tool can be installed as a binary from the mesosphere.com site and allows command line access to the DCOS system. It is useful because it allows greater control of functionality like installs. It also appears to provide a greater level of debug information when installs fail. The detail for this CLI install can be found at the following URL:

```
https://docs.mesosphere.com/1.8/usage/cli/install/
```

I will install the DCOS CLI binary on the DCOS master node hc4r1m1. The first step is to create a directory called bin under /opt/dcos/ using the `mkdir` command. The `curl` command is then used to obtain the dcos binary from the dcos.io site.

```
$ cd /opt/dcos ; mkdir bin ; cd bin
```

```
$ curl -O https://downloads.dcos.io/binaries/cli/linux/x86-64/dcos-1.8/dcos
```

The Linux `chmod` command is then used to make the `dcos` command executable.

```
$ chmod +x dcos
```

To connect to the installed DCOS system, the CLI needs to know where the master node is located. This is determined by setting the CLI variable core.dcos_url to the web-based URL for DCOS as follows:

```
$ ./dcos config set core.dcos_url http://192.168.1.113
```

Next, a DCOS authorized login session needs to be set up so that later CLI commands are authorized to access DCOS. This is possible by executing the DCOS CLI binary (dcos) and passing two parameters, auth and login.

```
$ ./dcos auth login
```

The output to this command is shown following; it provides the web-based login URL that you should use to access DCOS. This in turn will provide you with a DCOS Connect ID Token that you can enter at the prompt. You will see that I have pasted my alphanumeric connect string following. The ID is truncated to save space:

```
Please go to the following link in your browser:

   http://192.168.1.113/login?redirect_uri=urn:ietf:wg:oauth:2.0:oob

Enter OpenID Connect ID Token:eyJ0eXAiOiJKV1QiLCJh.......ko9-spjldck8q_cuwA
```

If the login is successful, you will see a success message like that shown following:

```
Login successful!
```

Now you can use the DCOS CLI to install DCOS packages like Spark as shown following. The DCOS CLI binary has been executed with the package option followed by the install command and the name of the package to install "spark."

```
$  ./dcos package install spark
```

The output for the Spark install is shown following; note that I encountered an error, shown here, which stated that the virtualenv component was missing:

```
Unable to install CLI subcommand. Missing required program 'virtualenv'.
Please see installation instructions: https://virtualenv.pypa.io/en/latest/
installation.html
```

This was corrected by installing virtualenv using the Python (Pip installs Python) pip-based command following:

```
$ pip install virtualenv
```

This provided the following output after a successful install:

```
Installing collected packages: virtualenv
Successfully installed virtualenv-15.1.0
After a successful install of the DCOS Spark package using the CLI you
should see the following output.
Installing Marathon app for package [spark] version [1.0.9-2.1.0-1]
Installing CLI subcommand for package [spark] version [1.0.9-2.1.0-1]
New command available: dcos spark
DC/OS Spark is being installed!

        Documentation: https://docs.mesosphere.com/current/usage/service-
        guides/spark/
        Issues: https://docs.mesosphere.com/support/
```

Chapter 4 provided quite a few images of the DCOS user interface, so I don't want to waste space here by repeating detail that was already provided. However, when DCOS private agent nodes are deployed and working correctly, you will see resource-based activity on the UI. Figure 6-3, taken from the Nodes menu option, shows resource usage in terms of the CPU allocation rate.

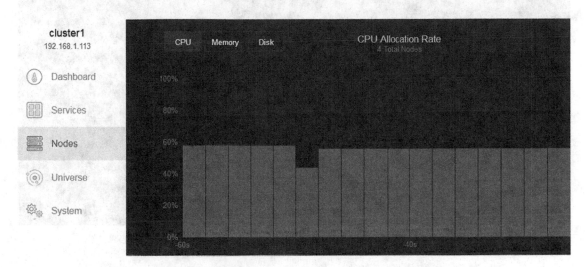

Figure 6-3. *DCOS UI CPU allocation*

The same UI Nodes-based page shows the status of the DCOS agent nodes in terms of the resources used by each agent server on the cluster. Figure 6-4 shows the health of each agent along with the number of tasks and the resources used. One agent is shown as unhealthy because it was still starting.

4 Nodes						
All 4 ● Healthy 3 ● Unhealthy 0 Filter by Service ▾					List	Grid
HOSTNAME ▴	HEALTH	TASKS	CPU	MEM		DISK
192.168.1.114	N/A	0	50%	37%		23%
192.168.1.115	Healthy	1	50%	35%		23%
192.168.1.116	Healthy	1	50%	35%		23%
192.168.1.117	Healthy	2	75%	21%		0%

Figure 6-4. *DCOS UI agent status*

The DCOS UI Services menu option shows the status of the services that are currently installed. As Figure 6-5 shows, I currently have three services installed: Marathon, HDFS, and Spark. The health of each service is shown as well as the number of tasks involved. Finally, the resources used by each service are displayed.

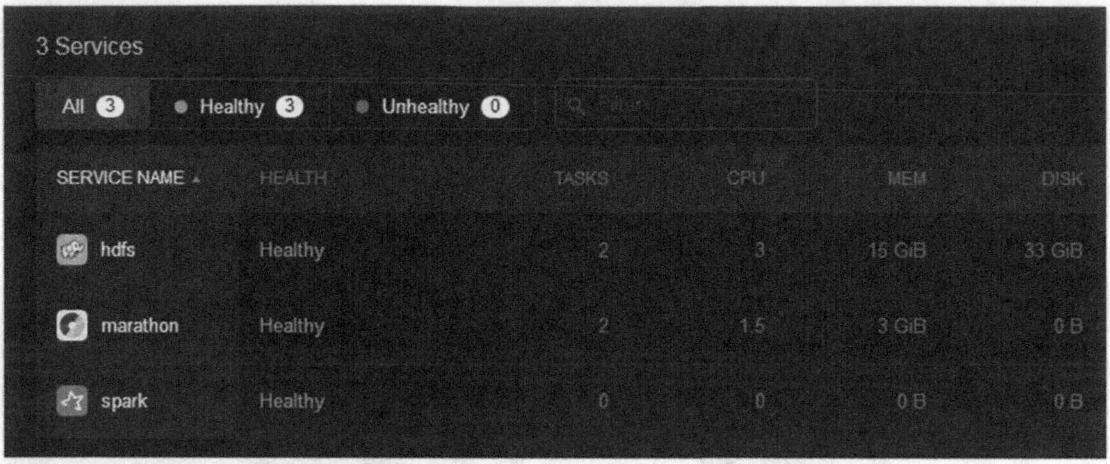

Figure 6-5. *DCOS UI services status*

The last image that I will include in this section is from the Marathon UI showing the Marathon application status. Figure 6-6 shows that spark has been deployed and is running. It also shows that the HDFS package is deploying.

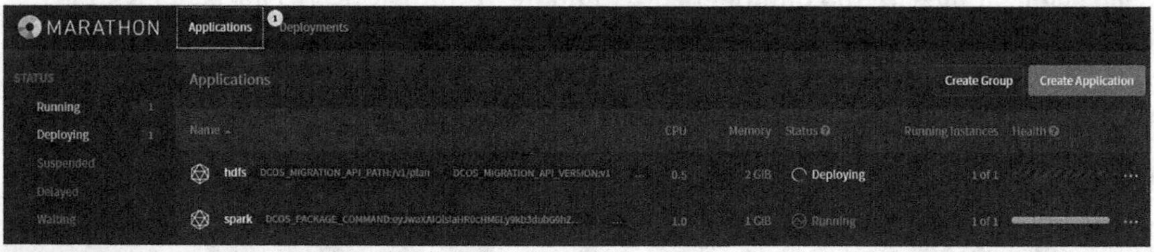

Figure 6-6. *DCOS Marathon Applications*

Now that the Apache Spark framework is running on DCOS, it can be used to run a Spark application. The next chapter will show how this can be done as well as how the supporting tools can be installed.

Running a Spark Application

In this section, I will show how to run a Scala-based application against the Apache Spark framework that has been installed on DCOS. I will use the SBT (Simple Build Tool) to install the application, so I will show how these tools are installed and how to build the code. To create a yum-based repository file on CentOS 7.2 to support the sbt command install, do the following:

```
$ curl https://bintray.com/sbt/rpm/rpm |  tee /etc/yum.repos.d/bintray-sbt-rpm.repo
```

The preceding curl command downloads the bintray-sbt-rpm.repo file from the bintray.com site and saves it to the /etc/yum.repos.d/ directory. This means that when the Linux yum command following is run, yum knows where to find the executable. The tee command used previously allows the output of the curl command to be piped to the .repo file as well as the console.

```
$ yum -y install sbt
```

A quick check using sbt to get its installed version shows that Version 0.13.13 of SBT is installed.

```
$ sbt -version
Getting org.scala-sbt sbt 0.13.13 ...
```

The SBT tool provides the method to compile and package the Scala code into a library, but now the Scala application is needed to support compilation. I change the directory to /tmp/ and use wget to source the scala-2.11.6.rpm Scala install package.

```
$ cd /tmp/
```

```
$ wget http://downloads.typesafe.com/scala/2.11.6/scala-2.11.6.rpm
```

I then use rpm to install the scala-2.11.6.rpm package and clean up afterward by removing the unneeded package file once Scala is installed. A check of the Scala version shows that Scala version 2.11.6 is installed.

```
$ rpm -ivh ./scala-2.11.6.rpm
```

```
$ rm -f scala-2.11.6.rpm
```

```
$ scala -version

Scala code runner version 2.11.6 -- Copyright 2002-2013, LAMP/EPFL
```

To provide continuity, I will run the same Scala-based example code on the DCOS-based Spark framework as I did for the Mesos cluster example. The Scala example code will list the first 100 entries of the Fibonacci series. I have created an sbt source code structure called ex1 on the DCOS master server hc4r1m1 as shown following:

```
$ pwd
/opt/src

$ ls
ex1
```

The sbt-based example code directory ex1 exists under the /opt/src/ directory. As the listing of the ex1 directory shows following, the ex1 directory contains an sbt configuration file called example1.sbt whose contents have been listed via a Linux cat command:

```
$ ls ex1
example1.sbt  project  src  target

$ cat ex1/example1.sbt

name := "Example1"

version := "1.0"

scalaVersion := "2.11.6"

libraryDependencies += "org.apache.hadoop" % "hadoop-mapreduce-client-core"
% "2.1.0" from "file:///root/.dcos/spark/dist/spark-2.1.0-1-bin-2.6/jars/
hadoop-mapreduce-client-core-2.6.4.jar"

libraryDependencies += "org.apache.hadoop" % "hadoop-client" % "2.1.0" from
"file:///root/.dcos/spark/dist/spark-2.1.0-1-bin-2.6/jars/hadoop-client--
2.6.4.jar"

libraryDependencies += "org.apache.spark" %% "spark-core"  % "2.1.0" from
file:///root/.dcos/spark/dist/spark-2.1.0-1-bin-2.6/jars/spark-core_2.11--
2.1.0.jar
```

```
$ ls ex1/src/main/scala
```

```
example1.scala
```

The example1.sbt sbt configuration file provides the name, version, and Scala version of the application. It also provides paths to Hadoop and Spark jar files needed for the compilation. The application source itself exists under the ex1/src/main/scala/ directory and is called example1.scala.

I won't dwell on the Scala application code itself, as you have seen it before. But I have listed it following via the Linux cat command. My intention here is to show that Spark is working and can be used. Any Spark application would provide that proof:

```
$ cat ex1/src/main/scala/example1.scala
```

```scala
import org.apache.spark.SparkContext
import org.apache.spark.SparkContext._
import org.apache.spark.SparkConf

object example1  extends App
{
  val appName = "example 1"
  val conf - new SparkConf()

  conf.setAppName(appName)

  val sparkCxt = new SparkContext(conf)

  var seed1:BigInt = 1
  var seed2:BigInt = 1
  val limit = 100
  var resultStr = seed1 + " " + seed2 + " "

  for( i <- 1 to limit ){

    val fib:BigInt = seed1 + seed2
    resultStr += fib.toString + " "

    seed1 = seed2
    seed2 = fib
  }
```

```
    println()
    println( "Result : " + resultStr )
    println()

    sparkCxt.stop()

} // end application
```

The Scala-based application can be compiled via the `sbt` command using the package option. This will compile the source, download any required modules, and package the result into a jar file.

```
$ cd ex1 ; pwd
/opt/src/ex1

$ sbt package
```

Upon successful compilation, the jar file for the application can be found under the ./target/scala-2.11/ directory within the ex1 sbt directory.

```
$ ls target/scala-2.11
classes  example1_2.11-1.0.jar
```

This jar file and the application it contains can now be used to test the Spark cluster framework running on DCOS. I will use the DCOS CLI to execute the application.

```
$ /opt/dcos/bin/dcos spark run --submit-args='-Dspark.mesos.coarse=true
--driver-cores 1 --driver-memory 1024M --class example1 /opt/src/ex1/
target/scala-2.11/example1_2.11-1.0.jar'
```

The preceding command shows how the DCOS CLI binary under the /opt/dcos/bin/ directory is used to execute the Spark submit. The DCOS CLI binary receives two parameters, spark and run, followed by a final parameter submit-args, which contains the bulk of the call detail.

The spark.mesos.coarse option means that each Spark executor runs as a Mesos task. The driver-cores options sets the number of cores to be used for the driver process. The driver memory options sets a memory limit for the driver process. Finally, the application class example1 is specified as well as the full path to the jar file example1_2.11-1.0.jar, which contains that application. Upon successful execution, you will see output like that following:

```
Run job succeeded. Submission id: driver-20170331221309-0001
```

I won't provide any further detail here, as the Mesos section showed the output of this task. The important issue is that the method of installing Apache Spark on a DCOS cluster has been provided. A method of compiling a Scala-based application and launching onto the Spark cluster has also been provided and shown to work.

I will discuss the comparison between the Mesos and DCOS clusters at the end of this chapter, but I hope that this brief introduction to DCOS has shown you that it has more to offer that a basic Mesos cluster. It provides an integrated cluster management environment, schedulers, and a range of pre-provided applications.

The next section examines the approach to problem investigation if an error is encountered with your DCOS system.

Problem Tracking

This section will examine the steps needed to track problems with DCOS-based systems. The steps in this section will be executed at the command line level, involving searching process logs and ensuring DCOS components are operating correctly.

Check IP Detect

It is important that the detect_ip script is running correctly. On each node in the cluster, execute the command detect_ip, which resides under /opt/mesosphere/bin/ as shown following. Ensure that it returns the IP address of the host:

```
$ /opt/mesosphere/bin/detect_ip
192.168.1.114
```

Check FQDN

On each node in the cluster, check that the FQDN is defined correctly. Execute the hostname command with a -f switch as shown following. Make sure that it returns a full hostname with domain name as shown here:

```
$ hostname -f
hc4r1m5.semtech-solutions.co.nz
```

Check Exhibitor Log

Attempt to access the ZooKeeper-based Exhibitor user interface at the master server as shown following:

```
http://192.168.1.113:8181/exhibitor/v1/ui/index.html
```

If the interface is not accessible or the DCOS server is not shown with a green state, then check the exhibitor status using the `journalctl` command as shown following:

```
$ journalctl -flu dcos-exhibitor
```

Check /tmp

Verify that /tmp is mounted without noexec (not execute). If it is mounted with noexec, Exhibitor will fail to bring up ZooKeeper. To repair /tmp, use the following command:

```
$ mount -o remount,exec /tmp
```

Check Leader

Check that the correct number of Mesos master processes exist and that a leader has been elected. The /exhibitor/v1/cluster/status path can be used to obtain this information as shown following from the Mesos master server. The output in JSON format shows that a single Mesos master as a leader exists as expected:

```
$ curl -fsSL http://localhost:8181/exhibitor/v1/cluster/status
```

```
[{"code":3,"description":"serving","hostname":"192.168.1.113","isLeader":true}]
```

Check ready.spartan Process

Make sure that the ready.spartan entity is pingable on the Mesos cluster by executing the following command:

```
$ ping ready.spartan
```

If an error occurs, then check the spartan log via the following `journalctl` command.

```
$ journalctl -flu dcos-spartan
```

Check leader.mesos and master.mesos

Make sure that the leader.mesos and master.mesos entities are pingable on the Mesos cluster. Execute the following commands:

```
$ ping leader.mesos
```

```
$ ping master.mesos
```

If an error occurs, then check the mesos dns log via the following `journalctl` command:

```
$ journalctl -flu dcos-mesos-dns
```

Check Mesos master

Next check the Mesos master log via the following `journalctl` command:

```
$ journalctl -flu dcos-mesos-master
```

Check Mesos DNS

Next check the Mesos dns log via the following `journalctl` command:

```
$ journalctl -u dcos-mesos-dns -b
```

Check DC/OS Marathon

The marathon scheduler process is started on the Mesos master nodes; use the following `journalctl` command to check the marathon log:

```
$ journalctl -u dcos-marathon -b
```

Check Admin Router

The Admin router is started on the master nodes and provides authentication to services within the cluster. Use the following `journalctl` command to check the Admin log.

```
$ journalctl -u dcos-adminrouter -b
```

Check gen_resolvconf

This is a process that helps agent nodes locate the master node; use the following journalctl command to check the gen_resolvconf log:

```
$ journalctl -u dcos-gen-resolvconf -b
```

Check Slaves

You can check the slave logs depending on their type, public or private. The following two journalctl-based commands show how the logs can be checked:

```
$ journalctl -u dcos-mesos-slave -b
```

```
$ journalctl -u dcos-mesos-slave-public -b
```

Check /var/log/messages

You can also check the contents of the following message logs:

```
/var/log/messages*
```

On each node, look for potential errors.

Check NTP

Use the following NTP-based command to ensure that the NTP service is running on CentOS 7:

```
$ ntptime
```

Check User Interfaces

Finally, check the user interfaces to make sure that they are accessible and contain no obvious errors. DCOS can be accessed via the master nodes, that is,

```
http:/ 192.168.1.113/.
```

Mesos can be accessed via the master node via its DNS path.

```
http://192.168.1.113/mesos/
```

Marathon can be accessed at the master node using its DNS-based name.

```
http://192.168.1.113/marathon/
```

If an error is encountered, then solve the problem and start at the top of the list again to ensure that no further problems exist.

Conclusion

This chapter has shown two methods of adding a processing component to a big data stack based on Apache Spark. Much of the work shown in this chapter has involved preparing the cluster on which Spark and the Spark application would run. I think that this is necessary because if a small mistake is made or a detail missed, then it can be very difficult to track and solve problems.

I have shown two methods of building a Mesos-based cluster. The first involved building Mesos from source. The second involved installing the DCOS Mesos-based open-source system from dcos.io. I hope that it is apparent to you that DCOS is the more functionally complete and resilient system. I worked through the two approaches to provide a contrast. DCOS provides a series of management tools such as Marathon, DNS, and Cosmos. It provides a series of user interfaces through which you can monitor your system. Also, more importantly it has a large user community that can be approached when hard-to-resolve problems are encountered.

Chapter 7 will examine queuing in a Mesos-based big data stack and build on the work carried out so far.

CHAPTER 7

Streaming

In this chapter, I concentrate on the queueing/streaming component of the big data stack provided by Apache Kafka—certainly one of the most successful Apache projects in this area. After a brief overview of the Kafka project, this chapter presents installation procedures using either the DCOS UI or directly from the command line. Both are informative, and the chapter includes detailed discussion on some of the issues that may arise in integrating this component into the big data stack. Management of the Kafka cluster is discussed as well as looking at various ways of producing and consuming records in Kafka topics. The chapter ends with a discussion of how one can use Scala to interact with Kafka topics. This chapter highlights the value created through the use of DCOS in cluster management, which facilitates both Kafka installation and management.

For big-data-based queue processing, the queueing component must have a "big data" heritage. A big data queueing component must

- Be able to process large data volumes

- Be able to scale

- Offer distributed processing

- Integrate with other big data components

I have reproduced the big data stack diagram (Figure 7-1) seen in other chapters as a reminder. Note that the queueing component has changed color from gray to white; this stack module will be the subject of this chapter.

© Michael Frampton 2018
M. Frampton, *Complete Guide to Open Source Big Data Stack*, https://doi.org/10.1007/978-1-4842-2149-5_7

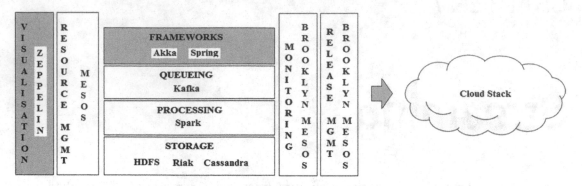

Figure 7-1. *Stack architecture*

The big data queueing component Kafka (`https://kafka.apache.org/`) will provide the queueing functionality for the queueing module described in this stack. It has been chosen because it meets the criteria discussed previously and has been designed by Apache. It has the following attributes:

- Processing large data volumes

  As of 2015, the Kafka-based system at linkedin.com processed 800 billion messages a day or 175 terabytes of data.

- Scaling

  Kafka scales by using a system of broker processors to process queued data in a distributed fashion. By 2015, there were 1,100 Kafka brokers in use at linkedin.com. Linear scaling for Kafka is achieved by scaling the number of active brokers and reassigning Kafka topic partitions across the Kafka broker cluster.

- Distributed processing

  As mentioned previously, Kafka offers distributed topic, queue data processing by using brokers. Queue-based data and the actions on it are dispersed across a network of broker processors.

- Integration

  Apache Kafka integrates with Apache Spark, which will be demonstrated later in this chapter. Library functionality has been built into Apache Spark to enable Kafka-based stream processing.

The preceding section describes the attributes of the queueing module needed for the big data stack. It also explains why Apache Kafka has been chosen. More detail will be provided for Kafka in subsequent sections. I just wanted to explain the direction that this chapter will take before we get started. In the big data, open-source world, when people think about distributed configuration, ZooKeeper is an obvious choice. Where big-data-based, open-source queueing is needed, then in the same way Kafka is an obvious choice.

Before delving into the detail of Kafka, I wanted to remind you that this big data stack is based on Spark for processing and Mesos for cluster management. Spark can be run in a number of cluster management modes, for example, standalone, yarn (client/cluster), and Mesos/ZooKeeper. Given that Mesos is being used as the cluster manager for this stack, then it makes sense that Mesos will act as the Spark cluster manager.

This chapter will be based on DCOS (dcos.io), the open-source, Mesos-based, big data processing environment. Although there is overhead to learning and installing DCOS, it is worth it. DCOS provides a more robust and self-healing, scaling, Mesos-based environment. I have already explained how to install a DCOS cluster; but before I move on to examining the Kafka project, I wanted to point out some potential issues with a DCOS-based install and system. The next section will examine DCOS and some potential issues with its install and use.

DCOS Issues

The process of writing this book has taken more than a year, largely due to the complexity of Mesos-based clusters, particularly DCOS. As I develop each chapter, I have installed the latest version of DCOS available. I wanted to point out some issues that have become apparent with DCOS across versions. This issues list assumes that you are using CentOS 7.2 and DCOS 1.7–1.9.

Port Conflict Issues

From DCOS 1.8 onward, there is a port conflict in that port 53, which is needed by the CentOS dnsmasq process, is also used by the dcos-spartan.service process. Without any remedial action, the result of this conflict for a DCOS cluster are dns-related issues and routing issues. It means that DCOS-based processes cannot communicate, and the

DCOS user interface cannot be reached remotely. The solution to this problem is to do as follows. Use the Linux yum command to install the psmisc module. This makes the fuser command available.

```
$ yum -y install psmisc
```

Use the fuser command to check the port number 53; this will probably show that the dnsmasq is using that port.

```
$ fuser -v 53/tcp
```

If the preceding command does return some process-based output, do as follows. Use the systemctl command to disable and stop the dnsmasq process.

```
$ systemctl disable dnsmasq &&  systemctl stop dnsmasq
```

If necessary, use the killall command to kill all dnsmasq-related processes.

```
$ killall dnsmasq
```

Now remove the dnsmasq process using the yum command as follows:

```
$ yum -y remove dnsmasq
```

Restart the ntpd (NTP daemon) process for NTP processing. The network-based time across the Mesos-based cluster needs to be in sync for DCOS to function properly.

```
$ service ntpd restart
```

Check that the NTP process is working correctly by using the ntptime command. The output should show no errors.

```
$ ntptime
```

Firewall Issues

There can also be firewall-related issues between CentOS 7.x servers and DCOS 1.8+-based clusters. At least on my nonproduction DCOS clusters, I prefer to disable the CentOS firewall. I would prefer to have a firewall outside of the cluster between the

Internet and the cluster. I would prefer this arrangement to reduce complexity. So on my nonproduction systems, I do as follows on each server. I use the systemctl command to disable and stop the iptables process.

```
$ systemctl disable iptables &&  systemctl stop iptables
```

Because I restart my DCOS-based cluster multiple times when writing a book like this, after each restart, I need to flush the firewall configuration on each server after startup. If I don't do this as follows, then server routing will not work, and DCOS dns will fail.

```
$ iptables -F
```

Network Time Synchronisation

I wanted to mention DCOS network time-based synchronisation, as it can cause issues. Part of the DCOS installation requires that the NTP server ntpd be installed on each CentOS 7.2 server. Although DCOS is generally a self-healing system, meaning that over time it can solve issues itself, timing issues can occur.

An indication of this is that the DCOS navstar process can fail. This can be seen on the DCOS user interface when the navstar process is no longer healthy. The log output that identifies the error can be found either from the DCOS user interface or from the Linux DCOS cluster server command line using the journalctl command as shown following:

```
$ journalctl -u dcos-navstar

May 07 13:01:21 hc4r1m4.semtech-solutions.co.nz systemd[1]: Starting
Navstar: A distributed systems & network overlay orchestration engine...
May 07 13:01:22 hc4r1m4.semtech-solutions.co.nz check-time[670]: Checking
whether time is synchronized using the kernel adjtimex API.
May 07 13:01:22 hc4r1m4.semtech-solutions.co.nz check-time[670]: Time
can be synchronized via most popular mechanisms (ntpd, chrony, systemd-
timesyncd, etc.)
May 07 13:01:22 hc4r1m4.semtech-solutions.co.nz check-time[670]: Time is
not synchronized / marked as bad by the kernel.
May 07 13:01:22 hc4r1m4.semtech-solutions.co.nz systemd[1]: dcos-navstar.
service: control process exited, code=exited status=1
```

```
May 07 13:01:22 hc4r1m4.semtech-solutions.co.nz systemd[1]: Failed to start
Navstar: A distributed systems & network overlay orchestration engine.
May 07 13:01:22 hc4r1m4.semtech-solutions.co.nz systemd[1]: Unit dcos-
navstar.service entered failed state.
May 07 13:01:22 hc4r1m4.semtech-solutions.co.nz systemd[1]: dcos-navstar.
service failed.
```

The preceding log error shows that although we are using the ntpd service on each DCOS-based server, time is not synchronized across servers. If this issue does not resolve itself over time, then the solution is to install the chrony service on the offending server(s) as follows:

```
$ yum -y install chrony
```

ZooKeeper Issues

In nonproduction DCOS-based clusters that may be frequently restarted, there can be associated ZooKeeper issues. I know that when writing, I constantly stop and start my cluster to make changes. I mention this to assist the reader in the full knowledge that production-based systems would be configured to run without interruption.

Frequently when restarting a DCOS cluster, I have found that the exhibitor process or Mesos-based master would not start; the master would indicate red and not green. The exhibitor can be found at the following address:

```
http://<master>:8181/exhibitor/v1/ui/index.html
```

Here "<master>" is either the IP address or name of one of your master servers. I found that this might be because ZooKeeper did not restart properly and left an old "pid" file or process identification file from the last session. The solution would be to do as follows on each master that is in a red state:

```
$ cd /var/lib/dcos/exhibitor; rm -f zk.pid
```

That would remove the old "pid" file and allow the exhibitors and so the Mesos master and finally the DCOS UI to start.

Having examined some potential issues that would impact a DCOS cluster's operation, I will now examine the Kafka system. It is important for this chapter to progress that DCOS be functioning without error.

The Kafka System

Kafka has been designed as a best of breed, open-source, distributed big data queueing/streaming system. It has been developed under the Apache umbrella and is distributed via an Apache V2 license (kafka.apache.org). It is a ubiquitous big data system, so much so that when people think of big data queueing/streaming, they think of Kafka. It is not my intention of rewrite the contents of the Kafka web site (see preceding link). But before I move on to use Kafka with DCOS and Spark, I should provide an overview. See the Kafka web site for further reading and access to the Kafka community.

Figure 7-2 shows an overview of a Kafka cluster.

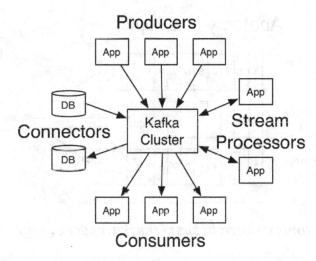

Figure 7-2. *Kafka Architecture (Source: https://kafka.apache.org/documentation/)*

Kafka is formed from a cluster of broker processors that manage streams of record-based data called topics. Each record in a topic is comprised of a key, a value, and a timestamp.

As shown in the preceding diagram, Kafka has four main APIs: producer, consumer, streams, and Connector. The API details are as follows:

- The producer API allows providers of data to publish a stream of records to Kafka-based topic queues.

- The consumer API allows stream-based record consumers to register to read topic-based queues.

- The stream's API allows an application to read input topic queues, process the data, and send the resulting stream data to output queues. It could be performing some ETL against the queue to process the data.

- The connector API allows the creation of reusable producers or consumers to connect to storage systems. In this way, a storage system could populate or be populated by a Kafka based topic queue.

Kafka topic queues are divided into partitions of ordered sequenced records. Figure 7-3 shows the structure of a Kafka topic.

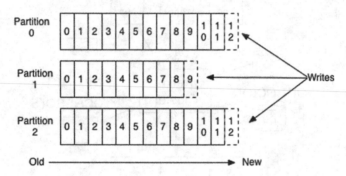

Figure 7-3. *Kafka topic (Source: https://kafka.apache.org/documentation/)*

Records are written to partitions in a sequential manner, with each record being given a unique offset number. Depending on the retention policy for the topic, the record will be available for consumption in a topic partition before finally being removed. This is a publish/subscribe-based system, so there can be multiple producers and consumers.

The number of partitions for a topic is defined when the topic is created or scaled. It is the responsibility of the message producer to assign messages to topic partitions. Partitions are assigned to topic consumers, and the assignment is rebalanced as consumers come and go.

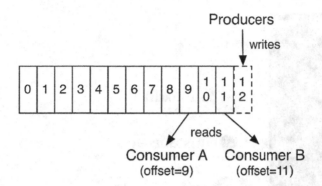

Figure 7-4. *Kafka topic offsets (Source:* `https://kafka.apache.org/` `documentation/`)

Figure 7-4 shows how multiple consumers of a topic partition use the stream-based record offset to maintain their read position in the queue. Producers will always write to the end of a partition, while multiple consumers will have a unique read position in the topic partition.

I will not go into any further detail for Kafka queueing. If you would like to gain further insight, then please read the Kafka site. Also, connect with the Kafka community and ask questions. I think it is much more important to provide practical examples. The next section will explain how to install Kafka on DCOS.

Installing Kafka

There are two main ways to install Kafka on DCOS: the first is via the DCOS user interface and the second is by using the DCOS CLI. I will show both, as both can be useful. It is worthwhile learning to use the DCOS CLI, especially when building and launching Spark-based tasks.

In this section, I will first install Kafka via the web-based user interface; then I will remove the application and install using the CLI.

DCOS UI Kafka Install

Due to the nature of this user interface install, it will mostly involve images of the DCOS user interface. From the DCOS UI Universe ➤ Packages option, find the Kafka package and click install (Figure 7-5).

Figure 7-5. Kafka package install: Step 1

A DCOS package install is defined via a JSON-based configuration file. The next step allows the installer to install a default configuration or change the JSON configuration via an advanced install (Figure 7-6).

Figure 7-6. Kafka package install: Step 2

Step 3 of the install, having chosen the advanced option, will allow the installer to alter the install configuration (Figure 7-7). This actually presents the contents of the JSON configuration file divided into four sections: service, brokers, executors, kafka.

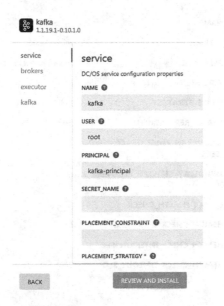

Figure 7-7. Kafka package install: Step 3

Upon selecting the "REVIEW AND INSTALL" button, the installer is able to check the full JSON configuration for the install and start the actual install (Figure 7-8). There is also a useful option here to download the JSON-based configuration file, which I have already done. This can then be used for a later DCOS CLI-based Kafka install.

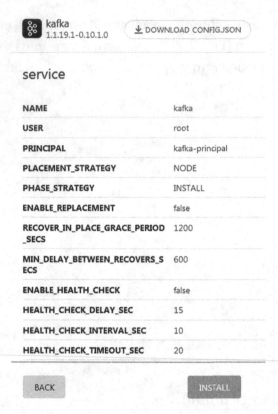

Figure 7-8. *Kafka package install: Step 4*

If the install goes well, the installer will be prompted with a success message (Figure 7-9).

Success!

DC/OS Kafka Service is being installed.

Documentation: https://docs.mesosphere.com /current/usage/service-guides/kafka/ Issues: https://dcosjira.atlassian.net/projects/KAFKA/is- sues

OK

Figure 7-9. *Kafka package install: Step 5*

Now by selecting the Universe ➤ Installed DCOS UI menu option, it can be seen that the Kafka package 1.1.19.1 has been installed (Figure 7-10).

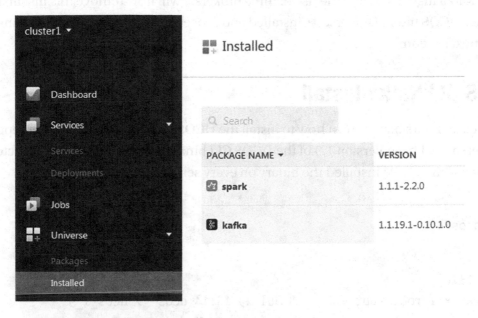

Figure 7-10. *Kafka package install: Step 6*

Finally, by selecting the DCOS UI menu option Services ➤ Services and selecting the installed Kafka service (Figure 7-11), it is possible to see the components within the service.

Services > kafka Running (4 of 1)

Instances Configuration Debug

Showing 4 of 4 tasks (Clear)

ID	NAME	HOST	STATUS	HEALTH	CPU	MEM	UPDATED ▼	VERSION
broker-2__4de17f3d-8aec-4ba4-8663-dc1f8895164e	broker-2	192.168.1.120	Running		1	2.3 GiB	22 minutes ago	
broker-1__40f06c4b-0fb3-4151-bd1f-33df74770c1b	broker-1	192.168.1.109	Running		1	2.3 GiB	23 minutes ago	
broker-0__dd7bac31-b37a-4806-bb7d-5c8cafb7f16e	broker-0	192.168.1.122	Running		1	2.3 GiB	24 minutes ago	
kafka.a64ad5bc-8541-11e7-bdea-de64d2257cda	kafka	192.168.1.114	Running	●	1	1.2 GiB	26 minutes ago	20/08/2017, 12:51:06 PM

Figure 7-11. *Kafka package install: Step 7*

Figure 7-11 shows three Kafka brokers and a Kafka process running along with their resource usage in terms of CPUs and memory used. The default configuration for the DCOS Kafka install involves the use of three brokers. I will now remove this installation from the DCOS menu Universe ➤ Installed and proceed with a DCOS CLI Kafka install in the next section.

DCOS CLI Kafka Install

Previous chapters have shown how to install the DCOS CLI binary, so I will not repeat that step here. I have Version 1.9 of the DCOS CLI binary installed under the directory /opt/dcos/bin. I have installed the binary on every server in my DCOS cluster.

```
$ pwd
/opt/dcos/bin

$ ls -l
total 13168
lrwxrwxrwx 1 root root        8 Jul 29 18:14 dcos -> dcos_1_9
-rwxr-xr-x 1 root root 13483440 Jul 29 18:14 dcos_1_9
```

I also use a symbolic link called dcos to link the name dcos to a binary named dcos_1_9. This serves to remind me that I am using a version of the binary that matches my DCOS cluster version. The next step involves altering the Linux server environment variable PATH to add the value /opt/dcos/bin/. This means that the DCOS CLI executable is now accessible no matter where I execute commands in the file system.

```
$ export PATH=$PATH:/opt/dcos/bin/
```

To use the CLI, it is necessary to log in to DCOS; this is done with the following command using the auth login dcos options:

```
$ dcos auth login

Please go to the following link in your browser:

  http://192.168.1.112/login?redirect_uri=urn:ietf:wg:oauth:2.0:oob
```

Use the link provided in the preceding output to obtain a login token for the DCOS CLI. There are three DCOS login options: Google, GitHub, and Microsoft. I generally use the GitHub option, as I have an account. This will provide a long token that can be entered at the command line as shown.

```
Enter OpenID Connect ID Token:eyJOeXAiOiJKV1QiLC
```

```
Login successful!
```

The DCOS CLI session is now authenticated and able to access the DCOS cluster. During the previous DCOS UI Kafka install, I downloaded a copy of the Kafka JSON configuration file, which I have stored as /opt/dcos/json/kafka-config1.json. I will now use this file as follows to install Kafka via the CLI:

```
$ dcos package install --options=/opt/dcos/json/kafka-config1.json kafka
```

```
Installing Marathon app for package [kafka] version [1.1.19.1-0.10.1.0]
Installing CLI subcommand for package [kafka] version [1.1.19.1-0.10.1.0]
New command available: dcos kafka
DC/OS Kafka Service is being installed.
```

> Documentation: https://docs.mesosphere.com/current/usage/service-
> guides/kafka/
> Issues: https://dcosjira.atlassian.net/projects/KAFKA/issues

Note that the preceding install states that it has also installed the CLI kafka command. This make commands like "dcos kafka" possible via the CLI. If this had to be done manually, then the command would be as follows:

```
$ dcos package install --cli kafka
```

```
Installing CLI subcommand for package [kafka] version [1.1.19.1-0.10.1.0]
New command available: dcos kafka
```

It may be necessary to wait a short time while the Kafka application actually installs. This can be checked via the Kafka UI as in the previous section. The functionality of the DCOS CLI kafka command can be checked using the --help option as shown following:

```
# dcos kafka --help
```

```
usage: kafka [<flags>] <command> [<args> ...]
```

```
Deploy and manage Kafka clusters
```

Flags:
```
  -h, --help              Show context-sensitive help (also try --help-long and
                          --help-man).
      --version           Show application version.
  -v, --verbose           Enable extra logging of requests/responses
      --info              Show short description.
      --force-insecure    Allow unverified TLS certificates when querying service
      --custom-auth-token=DCOS_AUTH_TOKEN
                          Custom auth token to use when querying service
      --custom-dcos-url=DCOS_URI/DCOS_URL
                          Custom cluster URL to use when querying service
      --custom-cert-path=DCOS_CA_PATH/DCOS_CERT_PATH
                          Custom TLS CA certificate file to use when querying
                          service
      --name="kafka"      Name of the service instance to query
```

Commands:
```
  help [<command>...]
    Show help.
  config list
    List IDs of all available configurations
  config show <config_id>
    Display a specified configuration
  config target
    Display the target configuration
  config target_id
    List ID of the target configuration
  connection [<type>]
    View connection information (custom types: address, dns)
  plan
    Display full plan
  continue
    Continue a currently Waiting operation
  interrupt
    Interrupt a currently Pending operation
  force <phase> <step>
```

    Force the current operation to complete
restart <phase> <step>
    Restart the current operation
state framework_id
    Display the mesos framework ID
state status <name>
    Display the TaskStatus for a task name
state task <name>
    Display the TaskInfo for a task name
state tasks
    List names of all persisted tasks
broker list
    Lists all running brokers in the service
broker replace [<broker_id>]
    Replaces a single broker job, moving it to a different agent
broker restart [<broker_id>]
    Restarts a single broker job, keeping it on the same agent
topic create [<flags>] [<topic>]
    Creates a new topic
topic delete [<topic>]
    Deletes an existing topic
topic describe [<topic>]
    Describes a single existing topic
topic list
    Lists all available topics
topic offsets [<flags>] [<topic>]
    Returns the current offset counts for a topic
topic partitions [<topic>] [<count>]
    Alters partition count for an existing topic
topic producer_test [<topic>] [<messages>]
    Produces some test messages against a topic
topic unavailable_partitions
    Gets info for any unavailable partitions
topic under_replicated_partitions
    Gets info for any under-replicated partitions

The preceding list provides all of the commands available to manage the Mesos-based Kafka framework using the DCOS CLI. In the next section, I will use some of these commands to show by example how these commands work.

Kafka Management Using the CLI

Before using the DCOS CLI to manage the Kafka framework, it is important to ensure that the Kafka Framework is running correctly. This can be checked by using the DCOS Marathon scheduler URL

```
http://<master>:8080/ui/#/apps,
```

where <master> is the full name or IP address of your DCOS master server. Select the top most "Applications" menu option, and you should see the Kafka framework in the state shown in Figure 7-12.

Figure 7-12. *Marathon Kafka framework state*

Figure 7-12 shows the Kafka framework in a green and running state. That means that if CLI commands are run, they should connect to the framework without error. This may not provide a full indication of the Kafka framework state. To check that the Kafka framework is running correctly, the Mesos user interface should be checked at the following URL:

```
http://<master>/mesos/#/
```

Note that Figure 7-13 shows a Kafka framework task running as well as three brokers.

Active Tasks

Framework ID	Task ID	Task Name	State	Started ▼	Host	
7c0fee71-1704-4713-9a9b-867a74dea20f-0000	broker-2__2adf2cb6-5765-4516-9f14-e2a3561918ef	broker-2	RUNNING	9 minutes ago	192.168.1.117	Sandbox
7c0fee71-1704-4713-9a9b-867a74dea20f-0000	broker-1__605cc369-cb62-4303-9474-9512710f9c10	broker-1	RUNNING	11 minutes ago	192.168.1.109	Sandbox
7c0fee71-1704-4713-9a9b-867a74dea20f-0000	broker-0__3a7c6890-67bc-45b4-86ce-590885624ed8	broker-0	RUNNING	14 minutes ago	192.168.1.122	Sandbox
1fc9d2fc-e5c5-4d9a-8e17-6cff7c49cc23-0001	kafka.bb0399a8-8615-11e7-b84f-26ba07702c3f	kafka	RUNNING	16 minutes ago	192.168.1.113	Sandbox
1fc9d2fc-e5c5-4d9a-8e17-6cff7c49cc23-0001	spark.906edb4e-8602-11e7-b84f-26ba07702c3f	spark	RUNNING	2 hours ago	192.168.1.114	Sandbox

Figure 7-13. *Mesos Kafka Active Tasks*

I encountered a situation with the Kafka framework where the brokers were not created when Kafka was installed. I solved this by executing the following steps:

- From the DCOS UI, go to Universe ➤ Installed menu option and destroy Kafka.

- Examine the ZooKeeper Exhibitor at the following URL: `http://<master-ip>:8181/exhibitor/v1/ui/index.html`

- Expand the Explorer section

- Remove the dcos-service-kafka entry

- Reinstall Kafka via the DCOS UI

Figure 7-14 shows the Exhibitor interface and gives you an idea of the entry that you will need to delete if you encounter the same issue.

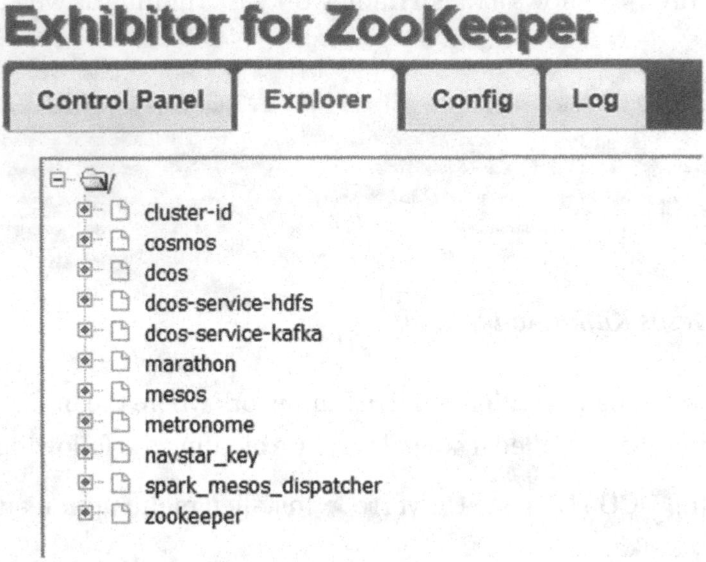

Exhibitor for ZooKeeper

Control Panel	Explorer	Config	Log

```
⊟ 📁/
   ⊞ 🗋 cluster-id
   ⊞ 🗋 cosmos
   ⊞ 🗋 dcos
   ⊞ 🗋 dcos-service-hdfs
   ⊞ 🗋 dcos-service-kafka
   ⊞ 🗋 marathon
   ⊞ 🗋 mesos
   ⊞ 🗋 metronome
   ⊞ 🗋 navstar_key
   ⊞ 🗋 spark_mesos_dispatcher
   ⊞ 🗋 zookeeper
```

Figure 7-14. *Exhibitor Kafka Explorer entry*

So now the Kafka framework is running correctly, the DCOS CLI can be used to access it. By default, three Kafka brokers are created when Kafka is installed; the plan command used with the CLI gives details of the Kafka architecture and status in a JSON format.

```
$ dcos kafka plan

{
  "phases": [
    {
      "id": "2d43c64f-e143-4f9a-acd1-1b642e5e0714",
      "name": "Reconciliation",
      "steps": [
        {
          "id": "1996303a-64e7-46ef-9772-42d7dd49e534",
          "status": "COMPLETE",
          "name": "Reconciliation",
          "message": "Reconciliation complete"
        }
```

```
      ],
      "status": "COMPLETE"
    },
    {
      "id": "fe40d43b-9bbf-44ec-a978-5f48017700f9",
      "name": "Deployment",
      "steps": [
        {
          "id": "68ea1529-5ae7-42c1-8775-dad3e76ce37d",
          "status": "COMPLETE",
          "name": "broker-0",
          "message": "Broker-0 is COMPLETE"
        },
        {
          "id": "9d3d39fe-ca76-498e-b29e-83e59629ef25",
          "status": "COMPLETE",
          "name": "broker-1",
          "message": "Broker-1 is COMPLETE"
        },
        {
          "id": "89677ede-6caa-4e27-ac38-50f07372f1c0",
          "status": "COMPLETE",
          "name": "broker-2",
          "message": "Broker-2 is COMPLETE"
        }
      ],
      "status": "COMPLETE"
    }
  ],
  "errors": [],
  "status": "COMPLETE"
}
```

The preceding output shows the broker names, statuses, and identification numbers. It also shows that the brokers are numbered 0, 1, and 2. The CLI broker list command following displays the current Kafka brokers:

```
$ dcos kafka broker list
[
  "0",
  "1",
  "2"
]
```

The CLI allows the brokers in the Kafka cluster to be controlled; they can be either restarted or replaced. Restarting a broker causes the broker on a given DCOS agent to be restarted. If a broker is replaced, then a broker is stopped on one DCOS agent and started on another. Here are some examples of broker restarts and replacements.

```
$ dcos kafka broker restart 0
[
  "broker-0__dd7bac31-b37a-4806-bb7d-5c8cafb7f16e"
]
$ dcos kafka broker replace 0
```

Remember that Kafka streamed data is stored in queues, which are called topics, and each topic is automatically partitioned. Currently no topics have been created in the Kafka cluster created on this DCOS system, as the DCOS CLI topic list command shows following:

```
$ dcos kafka topic list
[]
```

If you attempt to use the CLI to create topics, then the brokers must be installed and running. I mentioned an error earlier in this section where they were not installed. The result of this installation error caused the following error when trying to create a topic called "topic1" as follows:

```
$ dcos kafka topic create topic1
{
  "message": "Output: Error while executing topic command :
  replication factor: 3 larger than available brokers: 0\n
```

```
Error: [2017-08-21 12:57:45,919] ERROR
org.apache.kafka.common.errors.InvalidReplicationFactorException:
replication factor: 3 larger than available brokers: 0\n
(kafka.admin.TopicCommand$)\n"
}
```

Once the Kafka cluster framework was running along with its three brokers, topics could be created. The cluster state can be checked using the kafka `plan` command shown previously or by checking the Mesos, Marathon, or DCOS UI Service interfaces. The command following shows the topic "topic1" successfully being created, followed by "topic2."

```
$ dcos kafka topic create topic1
{
  "message": "Output: Created topic \"topic1\".\n"
}

dcos kafka topic create topic2
{
  "message": "Output: Created topic \"topic2\".\n"
}
```

The topic list CLI command is then used to list the current Kafka topics that exist and the result is the two that have just been created.

```
$ dcos kafka topic list
[
  "topic1",
  "topic2"
]
```

It is also possible to specify attributes when creating a topic. The following example creates a topic, "topic3," with two partitions and a replication factor of two. So data in the queue is duplicated across brokers.

```
$ dcos kafka topic create topic3 --partitions 2 --replication 2
{
  "message": "Output: Created topic \"topic3\".\n"
}
```

The official DCOS Kafka documentation shows how the Kafka CLI command can be used. The details can be found by using this URL for DCOS 1.9:

```
https://github.com/dcos/examples/tree/master/kafka/1.9
```

To follow the example that DCOS provides, an ssh-agent must be running. When started, the agent dumps some variable values to standard output.

```
$ ssh-agent
```

Copy and execute the definitions for the variables SSH_AUTH_SOCK and SSH_AGENT_PID. The actual values in your instance will vary.

```
$ SSH_AUTH_SOCK=/tmp/ssh-SiHwHNP2AIzP/agent.6251; export SSH_AUTH_SOCK;
$ SSH_AGENT_PID=6252; export SSH_AGENT_PID;
```

Run the CLI kafka connection command to determine broker names, IP addresses, and the vip value. Remember these values for later in this section.

```
$ dcos kafka connection
{
  "address": [
    "192.168.1.122:9529",
    "192.168.1.109:9609",
    "192.168.1.117:9680"
  ],
  "zookeeper": "master.mesos:2181/dcos-service-kafka",
  "dns": [
    "broker-0.kafka.mesos:9529",
    "broker-1.kafka.mesos:9609",
    "broker-2.kafka.mesos:9680"
  ],
  "vip": "broker.kafka.l4lb.thisdcos.directory:9092"
}
```

Now use the DCOS CLI node command to ssh to the master leader server. I have specified the root account for the ssh access. Remember that a Mesos cluster will always have an odd number of master processes. By a system of voting, the masters will elect a single leader server.

```
$ dcos node ssh --master-proxy --leader --user=root
```

```
Running `ssh -A -t root@192.168.1.112 - `
root@192.168.1.112's password:
Last login: Mon Aug 21 14:42:07 2017 from hc4r2m1.semtech-solutions.co.nz
[root@hc4r1m0 ~]#
```

The ssh CLI command has now moved the session to the master node in my cluster called hc4r1m0. As per the DCOS documentation, I now run the Docker kafka-client to gain access to Kafka client scripts and commands.

```
$ docker run -it mesosphere/kafka-client
```

```
Unable to find image 'mesosphere/kafka-client:latest' locally
latest: Pulling from mesosphere/kafka-client
efd26ecc9548: Pull complete
a3ed95caeb02: Pull complete
d1784d73276e: Pull complete
52a884c93bb2: Pull complete
070ee56a6f7e: Pull complete
f8b8b1302b4f: Pull complete
e71221cc9598: Pull complete
349c9e35d503: Pull complete
0686c3f0e36a: Pull complete
Digest: sha256:92eacfe5cf19bb194d3b08e92a3bde985777da765a3aa5398f275cfc8d7e27c7
Status: Downloaded newer image for mesosphere/kafka-client:latest
```

Using the kafla client script kafka-topic.sh like this, I am able to list details of the three topics that have been created: topic 1, 2, and 3.

```
$ ./bin/kafka-topics.sh --describe --zookeeper master.mesos:2181/dcos-
service-kafka --topic  topic1
```

```
Topic:topic1    PartitionCount:1        ReplicationFactor:3     Configs:
        Topic: topic1    Partition: 0    Leader: 0       Replicas: 0,1,2
                                                         Isr: 0,1,2
```

```
$ ./bin/kafka-topics.sh --describe --zookeeper master.mesos:2181/dcos-
service-kafka --topic  topic2
```

```
Topic:topic2     PartitionCount:1        ReplicationFactor:3    Configs:
        Topic: topic2    Partition: 0    Leader: 1        Replicas: 1,2,0
                                                          Isr: 1,2,0
```

```
$ ./bin/kafka-topics.sh --describe --zookeeper master.mesos:2181/dcos-
service-kafka --topic  topic3
```

```
Topic:topic3     PartitionCount:2        ReplicationFactor:2    Configs:
        Topic: topic3    Partition: 0    Leader: 2        Replicas: 2,0
                                                          Isr: 2,0
        Topic: topic3    Partition: 1    Leader: 0        Replicas: 0,1
                                                          Isr: 0,1
```

Note that "topic3" has two partitions, as were defined when it was created. The documentation states that I can use the kafka-console-producer.sh and kafka-console-consumer.sh scripts within this Docker-based client to send data to Kafka queues and read data from queues. An example of this would be the command following that echos some text to the kafka-console-producer.sh script. This script uses the Kafka cluster vip value and port number to send this data to the topic1 queue.

```
$ echo "message1" | ./bin/kafka-console-producer.sh --broker-list broker.
kafka.l4lb.thisdcos.directory:9092 --topic "topic1"
```

I could never get this to work; remember that the Kafka client is running within a Docker session on the DCOS master server. In my environment, the client session could never see the Kafka brokers, and I received errors such as this:

```
[2017-08-21 03:16:34,417] ERROR Error when sending message to topic
topic1 with key: null, value: 8 bytes with error: Failed to update
metadata after 60000 ms. (org.apache.kafka.clients.producer.internals.
ErrorLoggingCallback)
```

To populate the Kafka-based queues that I had created, I decided to exit out of the Docker-based Kafka client as follows and try a different approach.

```
$ exit
```

I downloaded a version of Kafka as follows that matches the version that was installed on DCOS. I decided to install it under the directory /opt/kafka on my DCOS master server. I used the `mkdir` command to set up the directory structure and the `wget` command to obtain the tarred package.

```
$ mkdir -p /opt/kafka ; cd /opt/kafka
$ wget http://download.nextag.com/apache/kafka/0.10.1.0/kafka_2.11--
0.10.1.0.tgz
```

I then used the `tar` command with the options x (extract) and f (file) to unpack the binaries. I then changed the directory into the unpacked package.

```
$ tar xf kafka_2.11-0.10.1.0.tgz
$ cd kafka_2.11-0.10.1.0/bin
```

Using two separate sessions on my master server, I was now able to both populate the queue "topic1" using the kafka-console-producer.sh script. I specified the Kafka vip value and port number as well as the topic name. I then entered a series of message data lines that were sent to the queue "topic1."

```
$ ./kafka-console-producer.sh --broker-list broker.kafka.l4lb.thisdcos.
directory:9092 --topic topic1

message1
message2
message3
message4
message5
message6
message7
```

Having populated the Kafka queue-based topic, I needed to try to read from the queue. The kafka-console-consumer.sh script following was used this time with the master Mesos value and port number of 2181. The ZooKeeper/Exhibitor Kafka service name of dcos-service-kafka was also specified. A topic queue name was added to the command ("topic1"); and finally, a flag was used (--from-beginning) to receive all data in the queue.

```
$ ./kafka-console-consumer.sh --zookeeper master.mesos:2181/dcos-service-
kafka --topic topic1 --from-beginning
```

```
Using the ConsoleConsumer with old consumer is deprecated and will be
removed in a future major release. Consider using the new consumer by
passing [bootstrap-server] instead of [zookeeper].
message1
message2
message3
message4
message5
message6
message7
```

```
Processed a total of 7 messages
```

As you can see, the command was successful, as all data that was added to the queue was also read from it. That completes this section and explains how the DCOS kafka CLI command can be used to manage queues. The next step will involve writing Spark Scala-based code to access Kafka-based queues.

Kafka Management Using Spark

So now that a DCOS Kafka cluster has been created and Apache Spark is already running on DCOS, it is time to create some Spark Scala code to show how Kafka can be used from Spark. In this section, a development environment will be set up using SBT, Spark, and Scala. (SBT, the Simple Build Tool is an open-source build tool for Scala and Java projects, similar to Java's Maven and Ant.) On my DCOS install server, I have created an SBT project directory as follows:

```
$ pwd
/opt/dev/kafcom1
```

```
$ ls
build.sbt  project  src
```

A project directory called "kafcom1" has been created along with project and src subdirectories. The build process to create the Kafka-based class needs to create a "fat" jar file. What I mean by that is that everything that this class needs must reside in this jar file. To achieve this build, the following extra SBT configuration file is needed:

```
$ more project/assembly.sbt
addSbtPlugin("com.eed3si9n" % "sbt-assembly" % "0.12.0")
```

The assembly.sbt file within the project subdirectory contains a reference to sbt-assembly, which will be used during the build to include all linked classes. The main build.sbt build configuration file looks like this:

```
$      cat  build.sbt

lazy val root = (project in file(".")).
  settings(
    name := "kafcom1",
    version := "1.0",
    scalaVersion := "2.11.8",
    mainClass in Compile := Some("myPackage.MyMainObject")
  )

libraryDependencies ++= Seq(

  "org.apache.kafka" % "kafka-clients"  % "0.10.1.0" from
"file:///opt/dev/kafka_2.11-0.10.1.0/libs/kafka-clients-0.10.1.0.jar",

  "org.apache.spark" % "spark-core"  % "2.1.1" from
"file:///opt/dev/spark-2.1.1-bin-hadoop2.6/jars/spark-core_2.11-2.1.1.jar"

)


// META-INF discarding
mergeStrategy in assembly <<= (mergeStrategy in assembly) { (old) =>
    {
    case PathList("META-INF", xs @ _*) => MergeStrategy.discard
    case x => MergeStrategy.first
    }
}
```

This is similar to previous .sbt files used in my other books in that the project name, version, and Scala version have been defined. Also, library dependencies have been defined for kafka-clients and spark-core. A merge strategy has been defined for the assembly process. Now let's look at the Scala code that will access the Kafka queue data. A Scala source file called kafcom1.scala has been created under the project directory within a subdirectory called src/main/scala. I will dump the file using the cat command and then explain it line by line.

```
$  cat src/main/scala/kafcom1.scala
```

```scala
import scala.collection.JavaConverters._
import java.util.{Properties,Collections}
import org.apache.kafka.clients.consumer.KafkaConsumer
```

The preceding section imports the classes to be used, that is, the Kafka queue consumer, collection, and properties classes. The object class KafCom1 is then defined.

```scala
object KafCom1 extends App {

  // set up some Kafka configuration values

  val broker4    = "broker.kafka.l4lb.thisdcos.directory:9092"

  val brokerList = broker4

  val groupId       = "test-consumer-group"
  val consTimeOut   = "5000"
  val zooConTimeOut = "6000"
  val topicName     = "topic1"
  val pollPeriod    = 500
  var printStr      = ""
```

Properties and variables have been defined for the Kafka queue access task. A properties object is then created, and the preceding properties are assigned to it. Key and value deserializer classes are also specified to be able to read the Kafa queue data. Remember that a queue record contains a key, value, offset, and timestamp.

```
// define the kafka properties

val properties = new Properties()

properties.put("bootstrap.servers", brokerList)
properties.put("group.id", groupId)
properties.put("consumer.timeout.ms", consTimeOut)
properties.put("zookeeper.connection.timeout.ms", zooConTimeOut)

properties.put("key.deserializer",
          "org.apache.kafka.common.serialization.StringDeserializer")
properties.put("value.deserializer",
          "org.apache.kafka.common.serialization.StringDeserializer")
```

A consumer is then created from the KafkaConsumer class, and that is used to subscribe to the Kafka topic, "topic1." Note that a group ID has also been specified.

```
val consumer = new KafkaConsumer[String, String](properties)

consumer.subscribe(Collections.singletonList(topicName))
```

Now the consumer is polled using a poll period value specified earlier to obtain queue-based data for the given topic name and group ID. While records are found, the record key, value, and offset are printed.

```
while(true) {

  val records=consumer.poll( pollPeriod )

  for (record<-records.asScala){

    printStr = "Read record - "
    printStr = printStr + " key='"    + record.key() + "'   "
    printStr = printStr + " value='"  + record.value() + "'   "
    printStr = printStr + " offset='" + record.offset() + "'   "

    println( printStr )

  } // for

} // while

} // end KafkaConsumer
```

Note also that if no group ID is specified, then the following error will occur when the DCOS Spark task is executed.

```
ERROR AbstractCoordinator: Attempt to join group  failed due to fatal
error: The configured groupId is invalid Exception in thread "main" org.
apache.kafka.common.errors.InvalidGroupIdException: The configured groupId
is invalid
```

This task can now be built using the sbt command with an assembly option; this will build a "fat" jar file as follows:

```
$ sbt assembly
[info] Assembly up to date: /opt/dev/kafcom1/target/scala-2.11/kafcom1-
assembly-1.0.jar
[success] Total time: 1 s, completed Aug 24, 2017 12:31:17 PM
```

You may be familiar with running Spark tasks on non-DCOS Spark clusters. In that case, Spark will distribute your class jar file for you. However, when running on DCOS, you need to place your jar file in a location from which it will be accessible. I placed mine in a subdirectory of my web site as follows:

```
http://www.semtechsolutions.co.nz/spark/kafcom1-assembly-1.0.jar
```

To submit this task to the DCOS-based Spark cluster, I will use the DCOS Spark CLI command. Note that I have added the export and "dcos auth login" commands here to remind you of the steps that are needed to set a DCOS CLI session for use:

```
$ export PATH=$PATH:/opt/dcos/bin/
```

```
$ dcos auth login
```

```
$ dcos spark run --verbose \
--submit-args=' --driver-cores 1 --driver-memory 1024M --class KafCom1
http://www.semtechsolutions.co.nz/spark/kafcom1-assembly-1.0.jar'
```

The Spark task execution uses the DCOS spark run command, and most of the submission detail is specified with the "submit-args" option. The number of cores and memory to be used for the task are specified. Also, the class to be called and the location of the "fat" jar file is given. When submitted, and because a verbose option has been used, the following output is dumped to the terminal (I have clipped the output to save space):

```
127.0.0.1 - - [24/Aug/2017 14:29:42] "POST /v1/submissions/create HTTP/1.1" 200
Stderr:
Using Spark's default log4j profile: org/apache/spark/log4j-defaults.
properties
17/08/24 14:29:42 INFO RestSubmissionClient: Submitting a request to launch
an application in mesos://localhost:44760.
17/08/24 14:29:42 INFO RestSubmissionClient: Submission successfully
created as driver-20170824022942-0002. Polling submission state...
17/08/24 14:29:42 INFO RestSubmissionClient: Submitting a request for the
status of submission driver-20170824022942-0002 in mesos://localhost:44760.
17/08/24 14:29:42 INFO RestSubmissionClient: State of driver
driver-20170824022942-0002 is now QUEUED.
17/08/24 14:29:42 INFO RestSubmissionClient: Server responded with
CreateSubmissionResponse:
{
  "action" : "CreateSubmissionResponse",
  "serverSparkVersion" : "2.2.0",
  "submissionId" : "driver-20170824022942-0002",
  "success" : true
}

Run job succeeded. Submission id: driver-20170824022942-0002
```

The preceding output states that the task has been queued and gives the Mesos cluster address "mesos://localhost:44760." It also gives the resulting submission ID of the task that was created "driver-20170824022942-0002." This submission ID can be used to obtain further details on this task's run. Access the Marathon UI at the following:

```
http://<master>:8080/ui/#/apps
```

Select the applications menu option, and then select the "spark" application. Finally, select the instance ID of the spark application within Marathon; for example, mine was called "spark.c6e7ba9d-8861-11e7-b0a0-8ee2450f1bf1." Within this Marathon spark page, you will see Spark endpoints specified. Clicking on one of these provides the Spark cluster Drivers UI as shown in Figure 7-15.

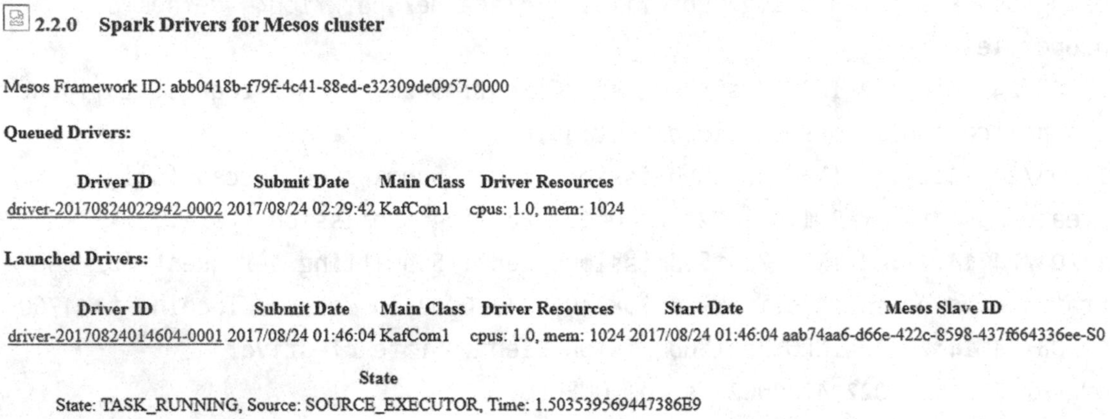

2.2.0   Spark Drivers for Mesos cluster

Mesos Framework ID: abb0418b-f79f-4c41-88ed-e32309de0957-0000

Queued Drivers:

Driver ID	Submit Date	Main Class	Driver Resources
driver-20170824022942-0002	2017/08/24 02:29:42	KafCom1	cpus: 1.0, mem: 1024

Launched Drivers:

Driver ID	Submit Date	Main Class	Driver Resources	Start Date	Mesos Slave ID
driver-20170824014604-0001	2017/08/24 01:46:04	KafCom1	cpus: 1.0, mem: 1024	2017/08/24 01:46:04	aab74aa6-d66e-422c-8598-437f664336ee-S0

State

State: TASK_RUNNING, Source: SOURCE_EXECUTOR, Time: 1.503539569447386E9

Figure 7-15. *DCOS Spark cluster driver UI*

Figure 7-15 shows two instances of this task running 0001 and 0002. The 0001 task instance has started because it has a start date and time. The second instance 0002 is queued and waiting for cluster resources. I used the DCOS Spark CLI to kill off the first instance of this job because it was poorly configured and hanging. This is how I did it using the submission ID:

```
$ dcos spark kill driver-20170824014604-0001

127.0.0.1 - - [24/Aug/2017 15:14:46] "POST /v1/submissions/kill/
driver-20170824014604-0001 HTTP/1.1" 200 -
Kill job succeeded.
Message: Killing running driver
```

Once the first instance was killed, the second instance started, and the driver details page from Figure 7-15 gave the Mesos agent node on which it was being executed as follows:

```
Node  192.168.1.113 (aab74aa6-d66e-422c-8598-437f664336ee-S0)
```

I wanted to access the Mesos agent cluster node to access the task log files as they are created. I did this because generally these are short-running tasks. For long-running tasks, it is possible to access spark task logs using the following command for a given submission ID:

```
$ dcos spark log <submissionId>
```

By using the dcos node command and piping (|) the output to the grep command, I am able to determine the Mesos agent IP address for the node S0. I can then get the hostname (hc4r1m1) for this IP address from the host configuration file on my servers (/etc/hosts).

```
$ dcos node | grep S0
192.168.1.113   192.168.1.113   aab74aa6-d66e-422c-8598-437f664336ee-S0

$ grep 113 /etc/hosts
192.168.1.113   hc4r1m1.semtech-solutions.co.nz   hc4r1m1
```

This allows me to navigate to that host using the ssh command and the host name as follows:

```
$ ssh hc4r1m1
```

I know that when a DCOS Spark job runs, it downloads the class jar file to be used to the Mesos agent node. So to find the Spark task logs, I needed to search for the jar file kafcom1-assembly-1.0.jar that was created earlier. I will use the following find command to do this:

```
$ find / -name kafcom1-assembly-1.0.jar
```

This provides the following path-based output from which I can see the second value relates to the driver ID "driver-20170824022942-0002" that I am interested in:

```
/var/lib/mesos/slave/slaves/aab74aa6-d66e-422c-8598-437f664336ee-S0/
frameworks/abb0418b-f79f-4c41-88ed-e32309de0957-0000/executors/
driver-20170824014604-0001/runs/70f75bb1-8a5a-4155-afd7-45c6223ca7c8/
kafcom1-assembly-1.0.jar
/var/lib/mesos/slave/slaves/aab74aa6-d66e-422c-8598-437f664336ee-S0/
frameworks/abb0418b-f79f-4c41-88ed-e32309de0957-0000/executors/
driver-20170824022942-0002/runs/74d9f6ab-1316-473b-b820-4968a4cac503/
kafcom1-assembly-1.0.jar
```

I navigate to that directory using the cd (change directory) command:

```
cd /var/lib/mesos/slave/slaves/aab74aa6-d66e-422c-8598-437f664336ee-S0/
frameworks/abb0418b-f79f-4c41-88ed-e32309de0957-0000/executors/
driver-20170824022942-0002/runs/74d9f6ab-1316-473b-b820-4968a4cac503/
```

This gives me access to the task logs as shown by the log listing of the task directory following. I am only interested in two log files: stderr to obtain task error messages and stdout to obtain the task's non-error output:

```
$ ls -lh
total 19M
-rw-r--r-- 1 root root  19M Aug 24 15:15 kafcom1-assembly-1.0.jar
-rw-r--r-- 1 root root 6.5K Aug 24 15:15 stderr
-rw-r--r-- 1 root root  234 Aug 24 15:15 stderr.logrotate.conf
-rw-r--r-- 1 root root  255 Aug 24 15:15 stderr.logrotate.state
-rw-r--r-- 1 root root   85 Aug 24 15:15 stdout
-rw-r--r-- 1 root root  234 Aug 24 15:15 stdout.logrotate.conf
-rw-r--r-- 1 root root  255 Aug 24 15:15 stdout.logrotate.state
```

If you remember in the last section I installed the Kafka client package on the master server under the directory /opt/kafka/kafka_2.11-0.10.1.0/. I have used the kafka-console-producer.sh script from the bin directory following to populate the Kafka-based queue "topic1" for the Kafka broker "roker.kafka.l4lb.thisdcos.directory:9092." The queue is populated with message values message1 . . . message5:

```
$ ./kafka-console-producer.sh   --broker-list broker.kafka.l4lb.thisdcos.
directory:9092   --topic topic1
message1
message2
message3
message4
message5
```

I then use the Linux tail command with a -f switch (continuous updates) to monitor the task output in the file stdout. As you can see, the messages populated to the topic queue "topic1" have been read by this task and output. The queue records have been output as key, value, and offset parameters as the Scala code specified.

```
$ tail -f stdout

Registered docker executor on 192.168.1.113
Starting task driver-20170824022942-0002
Read record - key='null'    value='message1'    offset='7'
Read record - key='null'    value='message2'    offset='8'
Read record - key='null'    value='message3'    offset='9'
Read record - key='null'    value='message4'    offset='10'
Read record - key='null'    value='message5'    offset='11'
```

The stderr log file contains any errors that occur as well as details of the task execution in terms of activities associated with the task jar file:

```
I0824 15:15:07.883760 13100 fetcher.cpp:442] Fetching URI 'http://www.
semtechsolutions.co.nz/spark/kafcom1-assembly-1.0.jar'
I0824 15:15:07.883774 13100 fetcher.cpp:283] Fetching directly into the
sandbox directory
I0824 15:15:07.883791 13100 fetcher.cpp:220] Fetching URI 'http://www.
semtechsolutions.co.nz/spark/kafcom1-assembly-1.0.jar'
I0824 15:15:07.883807 13100 fetcher.cpp:163] Downloading resource from
'http://www.semtechsolutions.co.nz/spark/kafcom1-assembly-1.0.jar' to

'/var/lib/mesos/slave/slaves/aab74aa6-d66e-422c-8598-437f664336ee-S0/
frameworks/abb0418b-f79f-4c41-88ed-e32309de0957-0000/executors/
driver-20170824022942-0002/runs/74d9f6ab-1316-473b-b820-4968a4cac503/
kafcom1-assembly-1.0.jar'
```

It also specifies the full Kafka consumer configuration for this task; I have trimmed the output following to save space:

```
I0824 15:15:23.672859 13118 exec.cpp:162] Version: 1.2.1
I0824 15:15:23.679325 13125 exec.cpp:237] Executor registered on agent
aab74aa6-d66e-422c-8598-437f664336ee-S0
17/08/24 03:15:25 INFO ConsumerConfig: ConsumerConfig values:
        auto.commit.interval.ms = 5000
        auto.offset.reset = latest
        bootstrap.servers = [broker.kafka.l4lb.thisdcos.directory:9092]
        check.crcs = true
```

```
client.id =
connections.max.idle.ms = 540000
enable.auto.commit = true
exclude.internal.topics = true
fetch.max.bytes = 52428800
fetch.max.wait.ms = 500
fetch.min.bytes = 1
group.id = test-consumer-group
heartbeat.interval.ms = 3000
```

Finally, there are some queue-based actions for the topic and consumer group that may be of interest. The stderr file should be examined first to check for task issues before the stdout file is checked. Also, the task status should be checked in the DCOS services and Marathon user interfaces.

```
17/08/24 03:15:25 INFO AppInfoParser: Kafka version : 0.10.1.0
17/08/24 03:15:25 INFO AppInfoParser: Kafka commitId : 3402a74efb23d1d4
17/08/24 03:15:26 INFO AbstractCoordinator: Discovered coordinator
192.168.1.117:9486 (id: 2147483647 rack: null) for group test-consumer-group.
17/08/24 03:15:26 INFO ConsumerCoordinator: Revoking previously assigned
partitions [] for group test-consumer-group
17/08/24 03:15:26 INFO AbstractCoordinator: (Re-)joining group test-
consumer-group
17/08/24 03:15:26 INFO AbstractCoordinator: Successfully joined group test-
consumer-group with generation 1
17/08/24 03:15:26 INFO ConsumerCoordinator: Setting newly assigned
partitions [topic1-0] for group test-consumer-group
```

The preceding Scala code consumed Kafka-based topic data. Before closing this section, I wanted to provide a link to a blog that shows how queues can be populated. With Marcin Kuthan's permission I am providing a link (following) to his blog, which describes how to create Kafka producer Scala code to write to a Kafka queue:

http://mkuthan.github.io/blog/2016/01/29/spark-kafka-integration2/

This concludes the Scala-based Kafka queue access. This section has shown that Scala code can be written to consume Kafka queue-based messages. Check the Kafka web site (kafka.apache.org) for further information.

Conclusion

This chapter has examined potential issues with a DCOS-based build using DCOS Version 1.9. It has examined how the DCOS CLI and the Kafka client package can be used to create, manage, and populate Kafka topic-based queues. Finally, a Scala-based section has shown how Kafka client code can be written and submitted to Apache Spark on DCOS to read from these queues. These are simple examples, and you will need to investigate further to use DCOS, Spark, and Kafka in depth. Remember that the Google DCOS group is available at the following URL:

`https://groups.google.com/a/dcos.io/forum/#!forum/users`

Even though my original big data stack diagram specified the use of Mesos, my use of DCOS was inevitable. I say that because dcos.io open sourced their cluster-based operating system, and it provides a rich and robust Mesos-based experience. Although, as I have shown, there are issues associated with its use, it is worth investigating. It is self-healing, provides powerful user interfaces, and is more robust and rich than Mesos alone. I think that inevitably it will become the go to Mesos-based environment.

Having said that, I must express that I have found it difficult, very time consuming, and expensive to complete this chapter due to the complexity of a DCOS-based environment in comparison to say a standalone Spark cluster or a Hadoop stack. It has taken months to build a cluster and successfully install frameworks and tasks to run on it. I am glad to have completed the task, but individuals and corporations need to be aware of the potential costs involved.

The next steps or chapters in this book will involve examining library-based packages that will provide extra task functionality such as Akka and Spring. After that, visualisation of data needs to be considered, and this will be accomplished by examining the Zeppelin package. Finally, the last chapter will look at the big data stack as a whole.

CHAPTER 8

Frameworks

In this chapter, I will concentrate on frameworks that can be used to create and extend distributed systems. When I mention frameworks, I mean third-party, open-source, and private suppliers of libraries for developing big data and distributed system-related applications. The term framework is already used in Mesos clusters to describe systems that are deployed onto the cluster. The frameworks described in this chapter are quite different and are used to extend and aid the development of large-scale distributed systems. I will refer to the big data stack diagram (Figure 8-1) that has been used throughout previous chapters.

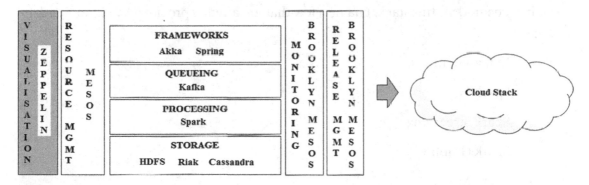

Figure 8-1. *Stack architecture*

The introduction to the Akka library illustrates many of the issues that will be faced when developing distributed applications. Actor-based programming extends the well-known object-oriented paradigm to deal with the intricacies of concurrency at scale required by distributed systems. Interactions with Kafka and Cassandra explored in earlier chapters are also mentioned. Also explored in this chapter are Netty and Spring (RabbitMQ/AMQP), which reinforces the scalability of concurrency required in distributed systems. The chapter will be very interesting to those with a Java/Scala background; and even without this, the concepts and examples are well grounded and explained.

© Michael Frampton 2018
M. Frampton, *Complete Guide to Open Source Big Data Stack*, https://doi.org/10.1007/978-1-4842-2149-5_8

Note that the stack architecture described by this diagram is almost complete. The only component missing so far is visualisation for big data, and that will be covered in the next chapter. The stack has covered the major functional big data areas, for instance

- Storage—HDFS

- Processing—Spark on DCOS/Mesos

- Queueing—Kafka with Spark on DCOS

- Release Management—Brooklyn/DCOS

- Monitoring—Brooklyn/Mesos/DCOS

- Resource Management—Mesos

Visualisation has not yet been covered, but the next chapter will examine the notebook-based Zeppelin system, which integrates well with Apache Spark. Zeppelin evolved out of the Databricks system, which was covered in my book, *Mastering Apache Spark* (Packt, 2015).

There are many frameworks that could be used to develop big data applications that could be executed on this stack. I name a few that are already provided by either Spark or Kafka:

- Kafka-client

- Spark SQL

- Spark Streaming

- Spark GraphX

- Spark MLlib

The Kafka-Client library was used in the last chapter to consume records from a Kafka-based queue. My point in mentioning the preceding list is to state that many of the big data stack components used in the preceding stack will have libraries that contain useful classes for stack manipulation. However, my aim in writing this chapter is to examine some suppliers of libraries that offer functionality that cannot be found within the stack. For this reason, this chapter will examine the Akka library from akka.io and some parts of the spring.io offering related to big data. The next section will examine Akka.

Akka

Lightbend (lightbend.com) is the company that developed Akka and open sourced it; you can see an overview of how Akka fits into their fast data platform via the URL following:

```
https://www.lightbend.com/products/fast-data-platform
```

The Akka system from akka.io is designed to make the process of building concurrent distributed systems simpler. It offers a methodology and set of supporting classes that describe an approach designed with distributed systems in mind. Before delving into the Akka system, it would be useful to describe current object-oriented programming (OOP) and some of the issues that arise when developing distributed systems.

OOP Overview

This section will examine some of the features of OOP languages (with Java in mind). The list following presents a feature list with descriptions of both OOP in general and with some Java attributes:

- Objects and Classes

  Objects are instances of classes, whereas classes encapsulate data and the methods that act on the data. A level of privacy is also maintained, with some methods and data being public while some are private to the class.

- Encapsulation

  Data and the methods that act on the data are encapsulated within a class, and data can only be accessed by public functions provided by the class. So data security is maintained because data access mechanisms have been designed and are the only access available.

- Privacy

  The privacy level controls class data and method access. For instance, Java defines the privacy levels Public, Protected, and Private. These levels in turn determine class, package, subclass, and world access.

- Inheritance

  Classes as they are defined can be created in a hierarchy so that a child class can be said to extend the functionality of the parent. Child classes "inherit" the data and classes of their parent(s). They may override parent classes and add extensions to increase functionality.

- Polymorphism

  Polymorphism is the ability of a method to take many forms. For instance, Java dynamic run time polymorphism means that methods might be overloaded at runtime using instance methods.

- Interfaces

  An interface, as used in Java, defines a set of class definitions that an implementation must instantiate. This is useful to consider when by comparison showing how Akka works in later sections. Akka uses protocols to manage actor dialogues. The next section will examine the issues that distributed systems face.

Distributed Systems Issues

There are many issues that require consideration when developing distributed systems. In this section, I want to examine some of the issues at a high level before moving on to examine the Akka system.

- Time Synchronisation

  All servers in a cluster-based or distributed system need to be time synchronized. This can be critical for event management in a distributed environment, as different event orders could have different outcomes. Synchronisation can be handled at the operating system level by services like the Network Time Protocol Daemon (ntpd).

- Locking

  Resource-based locking might work for single server-based
  systems or systems that are very minimally distributed, but this
  approach would inhibit scaling when used for large cluster-based
  systems. Resource locking information needs to be distributed
  to every node in a cluster. Consensus needs to be gained for lock
  access, and deadlocks need to be avoided. As will be shown later,
  Akka takes a completely different approach using actors and
  protocols.

- Resource Management

  When using distributed systems, a cluster-wide approach needs
  to be taken to resource management. Resources need to be
  shared across the cluster, and a cluster manager is used to allocate
  resources to tasks. Using Mesos as an example, task resource
  requirements can then be matched to the resources available
  across cluster-based agent nodes.

- Queueing

  As shown in the last chapter, the use of Apache Kafka queueing for
  big data systems needs to be approached in a distributed manner.
  Kafka uses a publish–subscribe approach to queue-based data
  stream management. Queue-based data is then distributed across
  a broker-based collection of topics.

- Message Stream Processing

  The last bullet point examined queue-based management of data
  in distributed systems. This point considers the need to be able to
  process continuous streams of data in distributed systems. Both
  Akka and Apache Spark offer stream-processing capability. Spark
  manages the distribution of data across a cluster based on data
  partitioning and control by its cluster manager.

- Configuration Management

  A distributed system needs distributed configuration management as was seen in the last chapter and when using DCOS; both DCOS and Kafka use Apache ZooKeeper. The DCOS exhibitor server is ZooKeeper-based and supports multiple systems by maintaining their configuration information. Distributed systems need distributed configuration management.

- Error Management

  Distributed systems take error management beyond the bounds of traditional OOP, for instance, as expressed in Java. It is no longer enough for an error to occur and a class-calling hierarchy to be dumped via a stack trace. In a distributed system, the flow of control in a process instance might occur across multiple server nodes and through multiple threads. Akka maintains an actor hierarchy and protocol-based system that aids distributed-system error management.

- Scaling

  Distributed systems need to scale both in terms of cluster-based agent nodes and also by the number of concurrent processes that can be run in a cluster. The issues raised in the preceding bullet points will impact the ability of distributed systems to scale, as will the design of the cluster-based processes. Akka offers actor-based functionality to aid cluster-based system development and cluster-based stream processing. The next section will examine Akka at a high level.

Akka Architecture

The Akka system is comprised of an actor hierarchy; actors are the basic functional unit of the system. Actors form hierarchies and encapsulate data, methods, state, and processing. A hierarchy of actors is formed with a predefined root guardian actor preexisting, which becomes the parent of all user- and system-created actors. A natural process of delegation is formed in which parent actors are simplified by delegating tasks to child actors.

Figure 8-2 gives an example actor hierarchy. It shows the preexisting root guardian at the top of the tree. The actorOf method is used to add actors to the tree using some context, that is, context.actorOf(). However, when first adding actors, the first actors are added using the system context, that is, system.actorOf().

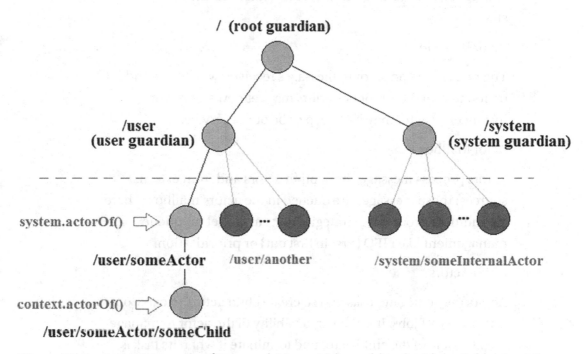

Figure 8-2. *Actor hierarchy (Source: https://doc.akka.io/docs/akka/2.5/ scala/guide/tutorial_1.html)*

As actors are created, they are assigned a context and URL within the hierarchy. For instance, the user guardian actor has a path of /user. There is also a /system URL for internally created actors that Akka uses for management purposes.

Actor Attributes

The preceding section mentions actor references or contexts that might be system or an actual context value. Each actor as it is created is assigned a unique actor reference. Each actor is a container for state, behavior, a mailbox, child actors, and a supervisor strategy. An actor is responsible for managing it's children and is also responsible for terminating them when they reach end of life.

- Actor State

  An actor's state will be implementation-dependent but must be maintained by the actor. Upon actor failure, it can either be reassigned to a starting value or recovered from the last known state.

- Actor Behavior

  The behavior of an actor to messages received will be dependent on its state, and current behaviors may set new states. For instance, an actor may be asleep or be out of service.

- Actor Mailbox

  Actors process messages from other actors and from external sources; these messages are queued in the actors mailbox. There are multiple processing strategies that can be set for queue management like FIFO (first in first out) or prioritisation.

- Child Actors

  Actors may delegate tasks and so create child actors to carry out a sequence of jobs. It is the responsibility of the actor to manage the life cycle of the child actor and terminate it when its task is complete. A child may be stopped by executing a command such as context.stop(child).

- Supervision Strategy

  An actor's fault handling strategy is static once that actor has been created. An actor's response to a subordinate fault will depend on the strategy used. The subordinate actor might suspend itself and all of its child actors and report the fault to the parent actor. The parent actor might restart the child, maintaining the previous state or stop it permanently.

- Actor Termination

  When an actor terminates itself, is stopped by a parent, or fails in a nonrecoverable manner, all of its resources are freed up. Its mailbox drains to the system dead letter box. All new messages are then sent to the system mailbox and are forwarded on the event stream as DeadLetters. This approach aids in system testing and helps with the debugging of failed tests.

Actor References

The actor reference is a subtype of type ActorRef, which is the top-level reference to an existing actor and which is created when the actor is created. This type also includes actor paths and addresses.

- Actor Path

Actors exist in hierarchies, with a guardian actor above a parent actor and a tree of subsequent child actors. Actors in separate actor trees may communicate and so need paths and addresses that uniquely identify them. A path can exist without an actor existing, whereas for a given ActorRef, an actor must exist.

Some examples of actor paths taken from the akka.io web site are given following. They include a protocol ("akka," "akka.tcp"), a hierarchical path describing the actor parent–child path in the tree ("/my-sys/user/service-a/worker1") and the fact that potentially an actor can be remote ("my-sys@host.example.com:5678").

```
"akka://my-sys/user/service-a/worker1"                    // purely local
"akka.tcp://my-sys@host.example.com:5678/user/service-b"  // remote
```

Note that in the remote example of the preceding path, the remote actor was identified by a host, port, and remote actor name ("my-sys") given that the protocol used was "tcp".

Actors

Actor classes working together can be explained by example by using the pingpong Scala code example provided on the Akka site at the following address:

```
http://doc.akka.io/docs/akka/current/scala/actors.html#creating-actors
```

The code sample starts by importing the necessary classes for actor, language, and concurrency.

```
import akka.actor.{ ActorSystem, Actor, ActorRef, Props, PoisonPill}
import language.postfixOps
import scala.concurrent.duration._
```

It then defines the two case objects that will be used to represent the actor messages; in this example, ping and pong:

```
case object Ping
case object Pong
```

The actor class Pinger is then defined by extending the class Actor. The receive method is defined to specify actions for each type of message to be received. In this case, the Pong message is acted on. A countDown value is decremented if it is above zero, and a message is output to indicate the result. If the counter hits zero, then both actors are terminated via the PoisonPill method. If a Pong message is received, then a Ping message is returned to the sender.

```
class Pinger extends Actor {
  var countDown = 100

  def receive = {
    case Pong =>
      println(s"${self.path} received pong, count down $countDown")

      if (countDown > 0) {
        countDown -= 1
        sender() ! Ping
      } else {
        sender() ! PoisonPill
        self ! PoisonPill
      }
  }
}
```

Next the Actor class Ponger is defined in the same way and acts on the message Ping. If received, a message is printed, and a Pong message is returned to the sender.

```
class Ponger(pinger: ActorRef) extends Actor {
  def receive = {
    case Ping =>
      println(s"${self.path} received ping")
      pinger ! Pong
  }
}
```

Finally, this system is activated by creating a system class called pingpong by calling the ActorSystem method. The pinger actor is then started by using the system.actorOf method. This creates the pinger actor to be a child of the pingpong actor. In the same way, the pongor actor is created. Note that the Props class has been used to define the properties of each actor.

```
val system = ActorSystem("pingpong")

val pinger = system.actorOf(Props[Pinger], "pinger")

val ponger = system.actorOf(Props(classOf[Ponger], pinger), "ponger")
```

Finally, a call to the scheduleOnce class is executed, which calls the Ponger actor and sends it a Ping message. Remember that Pinger receives a Pong message, then sends a Ping; and Ponger receives a Ping message, then sends a Pong message.

```
import system.dispatcher
system.scheduler.scheduleOnce(500 millis) {
  ponger ! Ping
}
```

This may seem like a simple example, but it explains parent and child actors, messaging, and actor control in a simple example. It can also be executed on the preceding Akka page, and some of the output in the final stages of execution are shown following:

```
akka://pingpong/user/ponger received ping
akka://pingpong/user/pinger received pong, count down 2
akka://pingpong/user/ponger received ping
akka://pingpong/user/pinger received pong, count down 1
akka://pingpong/user/ponger received ping
akka://pingpong/user/pinger received pong, count down 0
```

269

Note that the full path including default protocol used has been output for each method. For instance, the following message indicates that actor ponger received a ping message. It shows that the protocol used for the message was akka and the message system actor was pingpong, while the user actor was ponger. It also shows, due to the path, that the ponger actor is a child of the pingpong actor.

```
akka://pingpong/user/ponger received ping
```

Similarly, the message following shows the same path and protocol information. It shows that the actor pinger is a child of the actor pingpong.

```
akka://pingpong/user/pinger received pong, count down 2
```

Networking

When giving a very simple overview of actor-based networking, the best approach would be by providing a cluster-based example. Akka-based clusters are fault tolerant, peer-to-peer clusters that have no single point of failure or bottleneck. Akka uses "gossip" protocols and automatic failure detection for cluster management.

Akka clusters use seed nodes so that new cluster node members communicate with seed nodes when joining the cluster. The cluster can be deemed to have reached gossip convergence when every node in the cluster has "seen" every other node, that is, for every node, all nodes are in the seen state. After convergence, a cluster leader can be selected that can manage cluster membership.

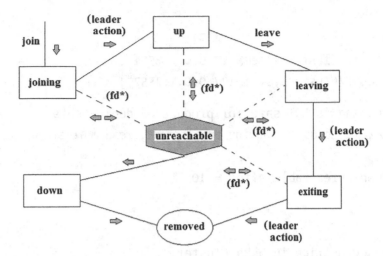

Figure 8-3. *Cluster member state diagram (Source: https://doc.akka.io/docs/ akka/2.5/scala/common/cluster.html)*

Figure 8-3 shows an example of a cluster member state life cycle. Obviously, the initial state would be joining, as perhaps the cluster or the node starts up. At any time, a node might be unreachable, for instance, due to failure or network issues. A node could be up or down and could follow a leaving/exiting process.

The following code shows an example application.conf file that defines cluster and cluster actors. It defines cluster seed nodes and cluster configuration. This example was taken from the Akka Networking page:

```
akka {
  actor {
    provider = "cluster"
  }
  remote {
    log-remote-lifecycle-events = off
    netty.tcp {
      hostname = "127.0.0.1"
      port = 0
    }
  }
}
```

```
cluster {
  seed-nodes = [
    "akka.tcp://ClusterSystem@127.0.0.1:2551",
    "akka.tcp://ClusterSystem@127.0.0.1:2552"]

  # auto downing is NOT safe for production deployments.
  # you may want to use it during development, read more about it in the docs.
  #
  # auto-down-unreachable-after = 10s
  }
}

# Disable legacy metrics in akka-cluster.
akka.cluster.metrics.enabled=off

# Enable metrics extension in akka-cluster-metrics.
akka.extensions=["akka.cluster.metrics.ClusterMetricsExtension"]

# Sigar native library extract location during tests.
# Note: use per-jvm-instance folder when running multiple jvm on one host.
akka.cluster.metrics.native-library-extract-folder=${user.dir}/target/
native
```

Note that the seed nodes have both been specified as IP address 127.0.0.1, that is, the localhost. If different nodes are to be used, then the actual IP addresses of the machines would need to be used. An example of an actor written in Scala and taken from the Akka site is as follows. First a package is defined and classes are imported:

```
package scala.docs.cluster
```

```
import akka.cluster.Cluster
import akka.cluster.ClusterEvent._
import akka.actor.ActorLogging
import akka.actor.Actor
```

Next, an actor class is defined called SimpleClusterListener, which extends the Actor class and includes logging. It creates a cluster instance using the Cluster method.

```
class SimpleClusterListener extends Actor with ActorLogging {

  val cluster = Cluster(context.system)
```

The preStart and preStop classes are overridden to carry out actions before the cluster starts and before it stops.

```
// subscribe to cluster changes, re-subscribe when restart
override def preStart(): Unit = {
  cluster.subscribe(self, initialStateMode = InitialStateAsEvents,
    classOf[MemberEvent], classOf[UnreachableMember])
}
override def postStop(): Unit = cluster.unsubscribe(self)
```

Finally, the receive method is defined to process cluster-based messages as in the previous example. It should not be a surprise to see messages such as MemberUp, UnreachableMember, and MemberRemoved here.

```
def receive = {
  case MemberUp(member) =>
    log.info("Member is Up: {}", member.address)
  case UnreachableMember(member) =>
    log.info("Member detected as unreachable: {}", member)
  case MemberRemoved(member, previousStatus) =>
    log.info(
      "Member is Removed: {} after {}",
      member.address, previousStatus)
  case _: MemberEvent => // ignore
  }
}
```

Streams

In the world of big data, many systems offer stream processing like Akka, Apache Spark, and Kafka. This allows a data set that may be too big to handle as a whole to be processed discretely as a stream of data. Given that the area of Akka streaming is a big subject, I will examine it by working through a sample of Scala code from the akka.io web site.

```
import akka.NotUsed
import akka.actor.ActorSystem
import akka.stream.ActorMaterializer
import akka.stream.scaladsl._
```

Initially, Akka-based classes are imported for actor and stream as well as a NotUsed value. Then Author, Hashtag, and Tweet values are defined as final case classes. The Author and Hashtag values are defined as strings, whereas the Tweet includes an author name, a timestamp, and a tweet body string that contains a Hashtag.

```scala
final case class Author(handle: String)

final case class Hashtag(name: String)

final case class Tweet(author: Author, timestamp: Long, body: String) {
  def hashtags: Set[Hashtag] = body.split(" ").collect {
    case t if t.startsWith("#") => Hashtag(t.replaceAll("[^#\\w]", ""))
  }.toSet
}
```

Next, an AkkaTag is defined as a Hashtag string "#akka." All streams in Akka must start with a data source; and in this case, the data source called "tweets" contains a sequence of tweets.

```scala
val akkaTag = Hashtag("#akka")

val tweets: Source[Tweet, NotUsed] = Source(
  Tweet(Author("rolandkuhn"), System.currentTimeMillis, "#akka rocks!") ::
    Tweet(Author("patriknw"), System.currentTimeMillis, "#akka !") ::
    Tweet(Author("bantonsson"), System.currentTimeMillis, "#akka !") ::
    Tweet(Author("drewhk"), System.currentTimeMillis, "#akka !") ::
    Tweet(Author("ktosopl"), System.currentTimeMillis, "#akka on the
    rocks!") ::
    Tweet(Author("mmartynas"), System.currentTimeMillis, "wow #akka !") ::
    Tweet(Author("akkateam"), System.currentTimeMillis, "#akka rocks!") ::
    Tweet(Author("bananaman"), System.currentTimeMillis, "#bananas rock!") ::
    Tweet(Author("appleman"), System.currentTimeMillis, "#apples rock!") ::
    Tweet(Author("drama"), System.currentTimeMillis, "we compared #apples
    to #oranges!") ::
    Nil)
```

The next two lines create an actor system called "reactive-tweets," while the materializer line actually creates the actor that processes the tweets.

```
implicit val system = ActorSystem("reactive-tweets")
implicit val materializer = ActorMaterializer()
```

Next, the tweets are grouped into a set with duplicates removed. The set is then converted into a stream of hashtags that are converted to uppercase.

```
tweets
  .map(_.hashtags) // Get all sets of hashtags ...
  .reduce(_ ++ _) // ... and reduce them to a single set, removing
  duplicates across all tweets
  .mapConcat(identity) // Flatten the stream of tweets to a stream of
  hashtags
  .map(_.name.toUpperCase) // Convert all hashtags to upper case
  .runWith(Sink.foreach(println)) // Attach the Flow to a Sink that will
  finally print the hashtags
```

Finally, a flow is attached to a sink in the last line to print a unique set of hashtags. It is an important point to note for Akka streams that a "source" of tweets has been connected to a "flow" of data, which has connected to a "sink," which has printed the data. The preceding Scala code produces the hashtag data result following:

```
RESULT
#AKKA
#BANANAS
#APPLES
#ORANGES
```

That was a worked example of Akka streams, which can be executed at the following URL; you can even change the Scala code:

```
http://doc.akka.io/docs/akka/current/scala/stream/stream-quickstart.html
```

Before closing this section, I wanted to mention back pressure, which is unique to Akka streams. As shown previously, an Akka stream has at a minimum a source, a flow, and a sink. There can be multiple sources and potentially multiple sinks for data in streams. So data producers act at the source to provide data, while data consumers act at the sink(s) to consume the data. What happens, however, if the consumers cannot act fast enough to consume the streamed data?

This is where the concept of Akka back pressure is used. The consumers are forced to operate at the rate of the producers implicitly in Akka streaming.

```
tweets
  .buffer(10, OverflowStrategy.dropHead)
  .map(slowComputation)
  .runWith(Sink.ignore)
```

The preceding example taken from the Akka site shows a source of tweets from the previous example and an explicit buffer size of 10 elements. The sink is defined via the runWith command. The important point here is that an overflow strategy has been defined to drop the oldest element when the buffer fills.

Other Modules

The Akka actor system, networking, and streams have been mentioned, but there are other modules available. This is a list taken from the akka.io site.

- Akka HTTP

  A full server and client-side HTTP stack on top of akka-actor and akka-stream.

- Alpakka

  Various Akka Streams connectors, integration patterns, and data transformations for integration use cases.

- Akka streams Kafka

  Akka Streams Kafka, also known as Reactive Kafka, is an Akka Streams connector for Apache Kafka.

- Cassandra Plugins for Akka Persistence

  A replicated Akka Persistence journal backed by Apache Cassandra.

- Akka Management

  Utilities for managing a running Akka Cluster.

Enterprise Offerings

Given that users will create production systems based on Akka, it is worth mentioning that Lightbend has some enterprise offerings to help Akka users. Details can be found at the Lightbend site via the following URL:

```
https://www.lightbend.com/products/enterprise-suite
```

They have offerings for application management and intelligent monitoring as well as enterprise integration. It is interesting, given the content of this book, that they offer deployment capabilities to DCOS and offer Docker support.

There is such a wide wealth of information available that needs to be consumed to gain an in-depth understanding of Akka that it is difficult to provide an overview. I have tried to provide a very high-level examination of Akka without delving too deeply into the detail available. For more information about its API and content, please consult the akka.io web site. As a starting point, look through the getting started guide at

```
http://doc.akka.io/docs/akka/current/scala/guide/index.html
```

Also work through the code-based examples (in either Java or Scala) of a simple actor-based system. This is useful, as it is builds by example in a stepwise manner with the logic behind each step explained. The next section will examine the Netty messaging system.

Netty

Having examined Akka, I have added a section on Netty because as of Apache Spark Version 1.6, Spark discontinued using Akka and instead uses Netty. This was because of upstream Akka, dependency-based issues. For instance, when writing my last book and trying to implement Spark-based Scala code to connect to the Titan graph database using Spark, I encountered Akka versioning issues.

Netty (netty.io) is an NIO (nonblocking I/O) framework for server and client network application development. It has been developed by Norman Maurer (normanmaurer. me) as an open-source system released under an Apache V2 license. A class and interface hierarchy tree can be found at the link following:

```
http://netty.io/4.0/api/io/netty/channel/package-tree.html
```

The netty.io site provides the following system architecture diagram (Figure 8-4) for Netty, which shows that Netty offers transport services, protocol support, and a multicomponent core.

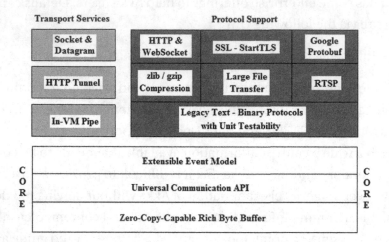

Figure 8-4. *Netty system architecture*

The best way to examine the Netty architecture is by using an example; I will use the Discard Java example from the netty.io site. The following three elements are needed to create a Netty connection:

- NioEventLoopGroup

  Creates a NIO (nonblocking I/O) selector-based channel

- Bootstrap

  Bootstraps a channel for use with clients

- Channel

  A channel for client operations, that is, read, write, bind, connect

- Channel Initializer

  Initializes channel for client access

- Decoder

  Process received messages

- Encoder

  Process sent messages

- Handler

  Determines how to handle received data

So now the preceding list can be examined in detail by listing the discard server Java example taken from the netty.io site. See the following URL for further detail:

```
http://netty.io/wiki/user-guide-for-4.x.html
```

Initially, the package name is defined, and Netty classes for bootstrap and channel are imported.

```
package io.netty.example.discard;

import io.netty.bootstrap.ServerBootstrap;

import io.netty.channel.ChannelFuture;
import io.netty.channel.ChannelInitializer;
import io.netty.channel.ChannelOption;
import io.netty.channel.EventLoopGroup;
import io.netty.channel.nio.NioEventLoopGroup;
import io.netty.channel.socket.SocketChannel;
import io.netty.channel.socket.nio.NioServerSocketChannel;
```

Next, the DiscardServer class is defined along with a port value data item that will be the communications port for server data.

```
public class DiscardServer {

    private int port;

    public DiscardServer(int port) {
        this.port = port;
    }
```

The public run method is defined, and two NioEventLoopGroups are created. The boss value accepts the incoming connection, while the worker value handles the traffic on the connection.

```
public void run() throws Exception {
    EventLoopGroup bossGroup = new NioEventLoopGroup();
    EventLoopGroup workerGroup = new NioEventLoopGroup();
```

The bootstrap sets up the server.

```
try {
    ServerBootstrap b = new ServerBootstrap();
    b.group(bossGroup, workerGroup)
```

NioServerSocketChannel instantiates a new channel to accept incoming connections.

```
.channel(NioServerSocketChannel.class)
```

The ChannelInitializer class helps a user configure a new channel. Note the handler DiscardServerHandler has been added to the channel data pipeline. This class will be defined later.

```
.childHandler(new ChannelInitializer<SocketChannel>() {
    @Override
    public void initChannel(SocketChannel ch) throws Exception {
        ch.pipeline().addLast(new DiscardServerHandler());
    }
})
```

Options are now set to determine the number of connections queued and to specify keep alive packets that can be used to determine the status of the channel.

```
.option(ChannelOption.SO_BACKLOG, 128)
.childOption(ChannelOption.SO_KEEPALIVE, true);
```

Now the port is bound to the channel and the server is started to accept incoming connections.

```
ChannelFuture f = b.bind(port).sync();
```

Now wait until the server socket is closed; in this example, this does not happen, but you can do that to gracefully terminate.

```
        // shut down your server.
        f.channel().closeFuture().sync();
    } finally {
        workerGroup.shutdownGracefully();
        bossGroup.shutdownGracefully();
    }
}
```

Finally, the main method is defined to set the port value to a parameter or a default value of 8080. An instance of the preceding DiscardServer class is then created.

```
public static void main(String[] args) throws Exception {
    int port;
    if (args.length > 0) {
        port = Integer.parseInt(args[0]);
    } else {
        port = 8080;
    }
    new DiscardServer(port).run();
}
```
```
} // end class DiscardServer
```

That completes the definition of the Discard server. But what about the discard message handler? The following code taken from the same example receives and discards each message received. Initially, the package name is defined and Netty buffer and channel classes are imported.

```
package io.netty.example.discard;
```
```
import io.netty.buffer.ByteBuf;
```
```
import io.netty.channel.ChannelHandlerContext;
import io.netty.channel.ChannelInboundHandlerAdapter;
```

Next, the DiscardServerHandler class is defined, which extends the ChannelInboundHandlerAdapter class. This class provides a series of message event handlers.

```
public class DiscardServerHandler extends ChannelInboundHandlerAdapter {
```

The channelRead method is overridden to discard the received message, which is of type ByteBuf.

```
@Override
public void channelRead(ChannelHandlerContext ctx, Object msg) {
    ((ByteBuf) msg).release();
}
```

The exceptionCaught method is overridden to print a stack trace of an exception and close the connection after the stack trace has been printed.

```
@Override
public void exceptionCaught(ChannelHandlerContext ctx, Throwable cause)
{
    cause.printStackTrace();
    ctx.close();
}
}
```

This gives a simple Netty server example that can be compared to the previous Akka examples. It can be seen that the Netty implementation is simpler than Akka.

The next section will discuss some of the big data functionality of the spring.io system.

Spring

The RabbitMQ system (rabbitmq.com) is a messaging system that is open source and was originally developed by Rabbit Technologies Ltd. but is now owned by Pivotal (pivotal.io). It was developed in the Erlang language and has been open sourced under a variety of licenses. The RabbitMQ system is released by Pivotal under an MPL (Mozilla Public License), whereas the code for the rabbitmq.com web site on GitHub at

```
https://github.com/rabbitmq/rabbitmq-website
```

is released under an Apache V2 license. Pivotal also maintain trademarks. I have named this section Spring after the Spring framework because RabbitMQ is also implemented via Spring AMQP (Advanced Message Queueing Protocol). The Spring framework contains an extensive range of projects, and I cannot cover it all here. (Check the spring. io web site for details.) I thought that a combination of RabbitMQ and AMQP would be informative and fit well with the other topics covered in this chapter.

RabbitMQ Overview

Figure 8-5 gives a simple, high-level overview of the RabbitMQ broker architecture. It describes RabbitMQ in terms of the producer, broker, and consumer.

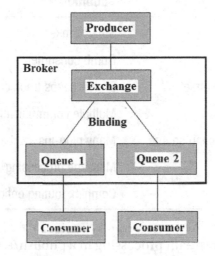

Figure 8-5. *RabbitMQ architecture*

Figure 8-5 further describes the messaging broker in terms of the exchange, message queues, and the binding between exchanges and message queues. A message producer publishes a message to an exchange. The exchange must route that message to a given queue. So the message is bound from the exchange to a given queue. The message is then read from the queue by a consumer. There might be many types of binding or messaging protocol. For instance, the message might be peer to peer, from a single producer to a given consumer. It might use publish/subscribe, that is, it might be from a given producer to multiple consumers. Otherwise the message might use complex routing, or the contents of the message might dictate its routing.

Kafka or RabbitMQ?

The last chapter showed how Apache Kafka could be deployed on DCOS; it showed how queues could be populated and data consumed. However, what is the difference between Kafka and RabbitMQ, and when should each be used? This section seeks to compare the two messaging options (Table 8-1).

Table 8-1. *Kafka vs. RabbitMQ*

Kafka	RabbitMQ
Dumb broker	Smart broker
Smart consumer	Dumb consumer
Consumer tracks queue offset	Broker keeps track of consumer state
Publish/Subscribe only	Multiple communications patterns
Fewer plug-ins; mainly open source	Many plug-ins available
Stream processing	Message processing
No complex routing	Complex routing options

So Kafka can be used for stream processing in a publish/subscribe manner where each consumer tracks its queue consumption position. The logic of consumption is maintained by the client consumer. Conversely, RabbitMQ uses a complex broker system and simple consumer. The broker offers support for multiple protocols and routing methods. RabbitMQ can also route messages by message content.

Messaging Protocols

RabbitMQ supports a number of messaging protocols, which are described following:

- AMQP < 1.0 (Advanced Messaging Queueing Protocol)

  AMQP is a binary protocol; RabbitMQ was originally designed to support this protocol.

- AMQP 1.0

  This version of AMQP for RabbitMQ differs from earlier versions in that the protocol is more complex.

- HTTP (Hypertext Transfer Protocol)

  RabbitMQ can transmit messages over HTTP via a management plug-in, a web STOMP (see definition following) plug-in, or a JSON RPC (remote procedure call) channel plug-in.

- MQTT (Message Queue Telemetry Transport)

  A lightweight binary protocol supported via a plug-in for publish/subscribe messaging.

- STOMP (Simple Text Oriented Messaging Protocol)

  A simple, text-based messaging protocol supporting via a plug-in.

Languages

For a full list of the RabbitMQ languages, operating systems, and clients supported, please see the RabbitMQ web site at

```
https://www.rabbitmq.com/devtools.html
```

To give an idea of the languages supported, the preceding URL lists the following languages as supporting or integrating with the RabbiotMQ system:

- C/C++
- Clojure
- Erlang
- Go
- Groovy
- Java
- JavaScript
- JRuby
- .NET
- Objective-C

- Perl

- PHP

- Python

- Ruby

- Scala

- Unity3D

Clustering

Clustered nodes must have the same versions of RabbitMQ and Erlang, as they use Erlang message passing. These nodes form a single logical broker, with all nodes able to see all queues.

When examining clustering for RabbitMQ, a distinction must be made for clustering across the LAN and WAN. For instance, are all cluster nodes on the same intranet, or are they dispersed across different geographic locations? For local LAN nodes, RabbitMQ supports clustering; and for WAN dispersed nodes, RabbitMQ supports Federation and the Shovel:

Federation allows an exchange or queue on one broker to connect to an exchange or queue on another broker. The connection is a point to point AMQP link.

The Shovel is a low-level, queue-based system for forwarding queue messages one way from one broker to another.

The clustering comparison table (Table 8-2) best describes the different clustering options for RabbitMQ and the differences between them. I have reproduced it here for clarity.

Table 8-2. Clustering Comparison (Source: RabbitMQ, `https://www.rabbitmq.com/distributed.html`)

Federation/Shovel	Clustering
Brokers are logically separate and may have different owners.	A cluster forms a single logical broker.
Brokers can run different versions of RabbitMQ and Erlang.	Nodes must run the same version of RabbitMQ, and frequently Erlang.
Brokers can be connected via unreliable WAN links. Communication is via AMQP (optionally secured by SSL [Secure Sockets Layer]), requiring appropriate users and permissions to be set up.	Brokers must be connected via reliable LAN links. Communication is via Erlang internode messaging, requiring a shared Erlang cookie.
Brokers can be connected in whatever topology you arrange. Links can be one- or two-way.	All nodes connect to all other nodes in both directions.
Chooses Availability and Partition Tolerance (AP) from the CAP theorem.	Chooses Consistency and Partition Tolerance (CP) from the CAP theorem.
Some exchanges in a broker may be federated, while some may be local.	Clustering is all-or-nothing.
A client connecting to any broker can only see queues in that broker.	A client connecting to any node can see queues on all nodes.

Enterprise Support

Although much of my work and research in recent years has evolved around open source and apache.org, enterprise support may make sense especially in support of production systems and services. Enterprise support may be needed in terms of level-three backup and technical advice when things go wrong. Extensions may be needed for user authentication and authorisation.

Hosting of RabbitMQ may be the preferred choice so that a third party either takes care of the service itself or the nodes that it resides on. RabbitMQ can run on AWS and Azure as well. Companies such as Pivotal, CloudAMQP, and Google Cloud Platform also provide support for cloud hosting for this messaging system.

Routing

It has already been mentioned in the preceding comparison that one of the main differences between Kafka and RabbitMQ is RabbitMQ's ability to provide complex message routing options. In this section, I will concentrate on the four exchange types available for RabbitMQ brokers—direct, fanout, headers, and topic. These routing types will be explained with the aid of adjusted diagrams from the RabbitMQ (rabbitmq.com) site.

In all of the example diagrams used in this section, messages are created by producers (P) and consumed by consumers (C, C1, C2). Exchanges (X) receive producer messages and through binding route the messages to queues. Consumers retrieve the messages from queues.

Direct Exchange

Messages go to the queue whose binding exactly matches the routing key of the message for direct routing (Figure 8-6).

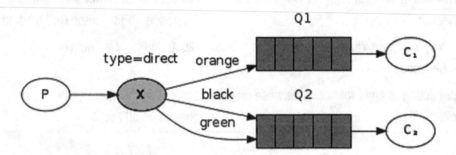

Figure 8-6. *Direct exchange (Source: `https://www.rabbitmq.com/tutorials/tutorial-four-python.html`)*

Fanout Exchange

The fanout exchange type is essentially a publish/subscribe method of routing (Figure 8-7).

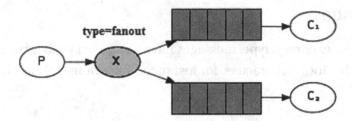

Figure 8-7. *Fanout exchange (Source:* `https://www.rabbitmq.com/tutorials/tutorial-four-python.html`*)*

This method of routing publishes all messages received to all queues.

Headers Exchange

When using a headers exchange type, messages are routed using the contents of the message header. A header may have a series of fields, and routing will depend on binding. The special field below "x-match" can have two values: "any" and "all." The "any" value means at least one field must match. The "all" value means that all values must match.

The routing in Figure 8-8 shows that messages with header field "key1" matching "value1" go to the consumer1 queue. Headers with field "key2" matching "value2" go to the consumer2 queue.

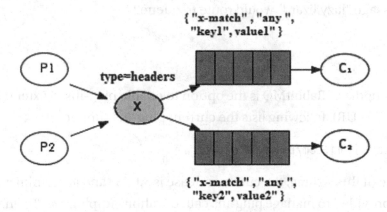

Figure 8-8. *Headers exchange (Source:* `https://www.rabbitmq.com/tutorials/tutorial-four-python.html`*)*

Topic Exchange

When using a topic exchange type, messages have a routing key that contains a series of words delimited by dot ". " characters, for instance, "big.orange.rabbit" in Figure 8-9.

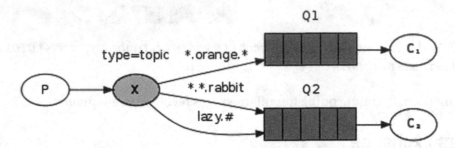

Figure 8-9. *Topic exchange (https://www.rabbitmq.com/tutorials/tutorial-five-php.html)*

The binding key is then generated in the same way with the addition of special characters. The "#" and "*" characters can be used instead of words in a string to replace exactly one word and zero or more words, respectively. So using the diagram in Figure 8-9

- Message "big.orange.lizard" would route to queue1.

- Message "big.blue.rabbit" would route to queue2.

- Message "lazy.lizard" would route to queue2.

Plug-ins

One of the strengths of RabbitMQ is the option to enable plug-ins to extend its functionality. The URL following lists the current plug-ins supported.

```
http://www.rabbitmq.com/plugins.html
```

At the time of this writing, the current release is 3.6.11, and an administration command is provided to manage plug-ins called "rabbitmq-plugins." To enable a plug-in, use the "enable" option with the <plugin-name>.

```
rabbitmq-plugins enable <plugin-name>
```

To disable a plug-in, use the "disable" option with the <plugin-name>.

```
rabbitmq-plugins disable <plugin-name>
```

Finally, to retrieve a list of enabled RabbitMQ plug-ins, use the "list" option.

```
rabbitmq-plugins list
```

It may be that the list of plug-ins available from the preceding RabbitMQ URL does not meet your needs. The RabbitMQ site offers a development guide for plug-ins at the URL following to allow you to develop your own:

```
https://www.rabbitmq.com/plugin-development.html
```

Finally, I would say that the RabbitMQ site plug-ins page offers a list of supported and experimental plug-ins. Obviously the experimental offerings may not be as robust as the supported offerings. It may also be worth searching for third-party offerings; for instance, I found the following delayed message plug-in:

```
https://github.com/rabbitmq/rabbitmq-delayed-message-exchange
```

Administration

The RabbitMQ management plug-in allows the system user to manage a RabbitMQ server. Check the RabbitMQ URL following for the latest management plug-in updates:

```
http://www.rabbitmq.com/management.html
```

This plug-in is released as a part of the RabbitMQ distribution.

Management Plug-in

Given that management functionality on a RabbitMQ server is released as a plug-in, it must be enabled before it can be used, that is

```
rabbitmq-plugins enable rabbitmq_management.
```

This allows the user to access a management user interface at the URL

```
http://<server-name>:15672/,
```

where "15672" is the port number to use, and <server-name> is the name of the node on which you installed RabbitMQ. The web-based user interface uses an HTTP API to execute commands. This will be described in the next section. You can also execute the same functionality using this API.

HTTP API

At the time of this writing, the latest version of RabbitMQ is 3.6.11. The RabbitMQ URL supplied at the start of this section specifies an HTTP API URL, which defines the full HTTP API.

```
https://rawcdn.githack.com/rabbitmq/rabbitmq-management/rabbitmq_v3_6_11/
priv/www/api/index.html
```

I have listed the current 3.6.11 API URL; note that by the time you read this, a new version may be available. Most of the API commands will return a JSON string containing the returned information. Some examples of API HTTP commands would be the following:

```
/api/overview
/api/nodes
/api/connections
```

So for instance, to get a server overview, you might use

```
http://<server-name>:15672/api/overview.
```

Statistics Database

Each RabbitMQ server has an in-memory statistics database. Although the management user interface can be used to access management statistics from this database, the HTTP API can also be used to access it directly. The URLs supplied in this section will allow you to access the latest API commands list as well as details on how to restart server databases if you need to.

Monitoring

The preceding sections describe the RabbitMQ server management plug-in, user interface, and HTTP API. The standard installation then gives you a number of monitoring options for a RabbitMQ server:

- The user interface

    Use the following URL as described previously to access the user interface for a single server:

    ```
    http://<server-name>:15672/
    ```

- The HTTP API

  Use commands from the HTTP API (URL example preceding this) to access JSON-based RabbitMQ server information. The command following gives an overview:

  ```
  http://<server-name>:15672/api/overview
  ```

- The `rabbitmqctl` command

  Use the "`rabbitmqctl`" control command to obtain the RabbitMQ server status, that is,

  ```
  rabbitmqctl status.
  ```

  I generally attempt to remain within the open-source world, but I think it is also worth noting that there are some third-party suppliers of administration and monitoring tools for RabbitMQ. You will need to carry out your own search (and research), but some examples are the following:

- DataDog (`https://www.datadoghq.com/`)

- NewRelic (`https://newrelic.com/`) via a plug-in

Conclusion

The aim of this chapter has been to introduce some frameworks for big data, stack application development. Akka and Netty were introduced due to the fact that both Apache Hadoop and Spark have used them in historic releases. Anyone who has previously investigated Hadoop logs will be familiar with Akka log messages.

Although Netty, Akka, and RabbitMQ have been investigated as examples of potential frameworks, there may be many more both now and in the future that may be available. Obviously try to match your requirements to those frameworks that you find when searching. Also, try to keep integration in mind when choosing a framework. Will the framework that you choose integrate with, for instance, Apache Spark?

Might there also be wider integration issues when trying to connect systems together? For instance, as I previously mentioned, I had tried to connect the Titan graph database to an earlier version of Apache Spark using Scala. This failed because at the time, both Titan and Spark were using different versions of Akka.

The next chapter will examine visualisation when using a big data stack. Management loves graphs, and it is often easier to understand a graph than pages of data.

CHAPTER 9

Visualisation

In this chapter, I will examine the visualisation options available for Mesos-based clusters. As you will see from the stack architecture diagram (Figure 9-1) that has been used throughout this book, data visualisation is the last element to be considered before the final chapter is used to consider the stack as a whole.

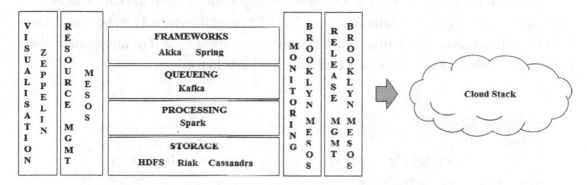

Figure 9-1. *Stack architecture*

Given that big data systems will contain a wide variety of structured and nonstructured data in large volumes, a method of visualisation is needed that integrates with the preceding stack and allows data to be visualized in a variety of ways. The data might form a stream or a relational table; it might be necessary to allow group collaboration or send visualisation results to remote parties.

The data visualisation options offered by the Apache Mesos-based system DCOS will be examined in this chapter. I concentrate on DCOS because it offers a robust Mesos-based environment and has large community support. This ensures that it will continue to evolve in the years to come.

This chapter will initially examine data visualisation options using Apache Zeppelin, the Notebook-based visualisation tool.

© Michael Frampton 2018
M. Frampton, *Complete Guide to Open Source Big Data Stack*, https://doi.org/10.1007/978-1-4842-2149-5_9

Apache Zeppelin

Apache Zeppelin is a notebook-based, collaborative, data visualisation tool that is released under an Apache V2 license. It offers a wide variety of scripting and integration options by supporting many interpreters, which I will examine later. The Zeppelin web site is at the following URL:

```
https://zeppelin.apache.org/
```

I have installed Zeppelin from within the DCOS Version 1.9.1 environment, and so I am using Version 0.5.6-2. The current version of Zeppelin available from the Zeppelin web site at the time of this writing (September 2017) is 0.7.3. This will be shown to be important later, as Version 0.7.x has extra functionality, which I will discuss.

Zeppelin is installed, as with all DCOS-based applications, from the Universe ➤ Packages option on the left-hand menu on the DCOS user interface. I just accepted the default configuration, which installed Zeppelin onto a single node. For information, the default Zeppelin DCOS JSON-based configuration looks like this:

```
{
  "service": {
    "name": "zeppelin",
    "zeppelin_java_opts": "-Dspark.mesos.coarse=true -Dspark.mesos.
executor.home=/opt/spark/dist"
  },
  "spark": {}
}
```

You can see that the service name and Java options are set, as well as a couple of Spark Mesos variables. You could add extra variables to this string as needed. There is also an empty placeholder for spark configuration. Once installed on DCOS, the Zeppelin user interface can be accessed from the DCOS Service/Services menu. Select the Zeppelin service, then select the running service ID. (Mine was named zeppelin.00ad09c0-a0be-11e7-91a2-f6d02ba4c4a5.) Then select one of the active "ENDPOINT" values. For instance, my DCOS assigned Zeppelin user interface URL is the following:

```
http://192.168.1.109:26225/#/
```

This gives the Zeppelin user interface shown in Figure 9-2. I have modified this image to make it fit the page.

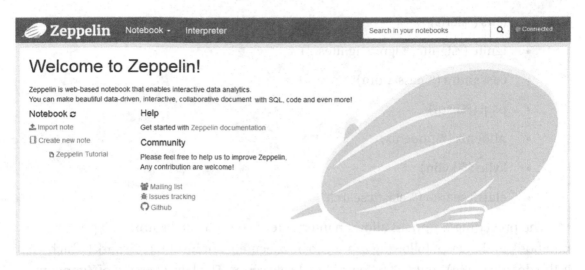

Figure 9-2. Zeppelin user interface

Note that the interface is very simple; there are notebook and interpreter menus. The interpreter menu allows you to configure the environment for each interpreter available. Each interpreter allows you to use a different processing engine when running scripts within a notebook. That will be examined later.

The Notebook menu option allows you to create a new notebook or examine an example notebook called "Zeppelin Tutorial." The tutorial is useful, as it shows how to run Spark scripts in Zeppelin and create tables. You can see also from Figure 9-2 that it is possible to save and import notebooks. Let **us** look at interpreter options first.

Interpreters

This version of Zeppelin (0.5.6-2) offers the following interpreters:

- Spark (%spark (default), %pyspark, %sql, %dep)
- md (%md)
- angular (%angular)
- sh (%sh)
- hive (%hive)
- tajo (%tajo)
- flink (%flink)

- lens (%lens)

- ignite (%ignite, %ignite.ignitesql)

- cassandra (%cassandra)

- psql (%psql)

- phoenix (%phoenix)

- kylin (%kylin)

- elasticsearch (%elasticsearch)

The preceding % options allow an interpreter to be activated within a Zeppelin notebook and a script following this tag to be executed. For instance, %spark (which is the default value) could be followed by a Scala script. The latest version of Zeppelin (0.7.3) now uses an interpreter plug-in, which offers more options and allows you to define your own interpreters to be used within Zeppelin.

Figure 9-3 shows the latest Zeppelin interpreters; Apache Beam, Scio, and Apache Pig are also available for notebook-based scripting. It can be seen that in Zeppelin interpreter terms, things have changed dramatically as of Version 0.7.x. So it is worth taking note of the version of Zeppelin that you are using.

Figure 9-3. *Latest Zeppelin interpreters*

It is time to examine Zeppelin using a worked example; to do this, a new notebook must be created. This is simple: choose the Notebook/"Create new note" menu option. Specify a name for the new notebook; I called mine "example1." Then click the "create note" button. This new notebook can then be accessed from the notebook menu option.

Worked Example

Having selected the preceding "example1" notebook, a notebook session user interface opens as shown in Figure 9-4. This allows you to interactively and collaboratively create multiple interpreter-based scripts and run them. You will see by examining the user interface that the notebook session contains a series of source and output cells.

Figure 9-4. *Example notebook*

Note the green connected icon in the top right corner of the interface to indicate that this session is connected to the interpreter (in this case Spark) and not offline. There are a number of notebook-based menu options here that need to be examined before moving on to a worked example and some graphs. The first block of menu options is shown in Figure 9-5.

Figure 9-5. *Notebook menu icons (1)*

The first option allows all code within the notebook to be run, while the second option allows all code to be hidden. The third icon allows all output to be hidden, while the fourth clears all output. The last three icons allow the notebook to be removed, cloned, and exported. The export option allows the notebook to be saved and imported to a later DCOS Zeppelin session. The notebook is exported as a JSON file with a file name that matches the notebook name. The remaining notebook menu icons are shown in Figure 9-6.

Figure 9-6. *Notebook menu icons (2)*

These options allow you to list short cuts, examine notebook-based interpreter binding, and change the layout of the notebook—the options are default, simple, and report. It is worth mentioning the bound interpreters at this point because these are the interpreters that can be used in this notebook session. For instance, Figure 9-7 shows the interpreter options that can be used in this notebook.

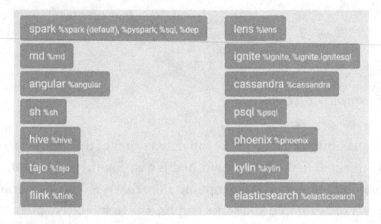

Figure 9-7. *Notebook bound interpreters*

These options should be familiar from your previous big data experience (i.e., spark, hive, cassandra). There are also options here for adding notebook text (md) and connecting to a Postgresql database (psql). Having explained the notebook user interface, it is time for a worked example. I will use the default option Apache Spark for processing. I have Spark running on DCOS as well as Zeppelin. I have sourced some csv (comma-separated values) data related to assault crimes from the following NZ government web site:

http://www.stats.govt.nz

Any data would be fine; this will just be used to process, create a table, and create graphs from the data. I have created the following Spark Scala script, which is based on the Zeppelin tutorial provided with Zeppelin. First, I import Java and Apache commons libraries.

```
import org.apache.commons.io.IOUtils
import java.net.URL
import java.nio.charset.Charset
```

Next, I load the assault csv data from a Spark subdirectory on my web site semtech-solutions.co.nz. This data is split by line and placed into a variable assaultText.

```
val assaultText = sc.parallelize(
    IOUtils.toString(
        new URL("http://www.semtech-solutions.co.nz/spark/assaults-2015-
        csv.csv"),
        Charset.forName("utf8")).split("\n"))
```

A case class called Assault is then created to represent the csv-based data line.

```
case class Assault(
  Index: Integer,
  Area unit_2013_code: Integer,
  Area_unit_2013_label: String,
  Victimisations_calendar_year_2015: Integer,
  Population_mid_point_2015: Integer,
  Rate_per_10000_population: Integer,
  Rate_ratio_NZ_average_rate: Double,
  Urban_area_2013_code: Integer,
  Urban_area_2013_label: String,
  Urban_area_type: String,
  Territorial_authority_area_2013_code: Integer,
  Territorial_authority_area_2013_label: String,
  Region_2013_code: Integer,
  Region_2013_label: String
)
```

The columns in the csv data are then split into a variable called assault. Data values are converted to integer, string, and double as needed. Also the csv header row (starting with "Index") is ignored. This is then converted to a Spark Scala data frame.

```scala
val assault = assaultText.map(s => s.split(",")).filter(s => s(0) !=
"Index").map(
    s => Assault(
            s(0).toInt,
            s(1).toInt,
            s(2).toString,
            s(3).toInt,
            s(4).toInt,
            s(5).replaceAll("-", "").replaceAll(" ", "").toInt,
            s(6).replaceAll("-", "").replaceAll(" ", "").toDouble,
            s(7).toInt,
            s(8).toString,
            s(9).toString,
            s(10).toInt,
            s(11).toString,
            s(12).toInt,
            s(13).toString
        )
).toDF()
```

Finally, the data in the assault variable is converted to a Spark-based table called assault. This can then be used in Spark-based SQL.

```scala
assault.registerTempTable("assault")
```

Note that the %spark value was not used in this script; but because it is the default value, it was inferred. Most of the notebook session menu options as shown in Figure 9-8 will be familiar. However, the last option (the cogged wheel) controls the notebook session.

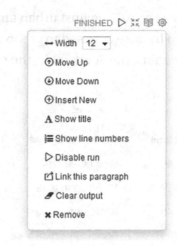

Figure 9-8. *Notebook session options*

The options available can be seen in Figure 9-8 to move the session, insert new, clear, run, and remove. Note also the state of the session shown previously ("Finished"). This might also be "Pending" or "Running." Note also that the width of the session can be changed; it is currently 12. By running the following Spark SQL-based script, I can now access the Spark SQL-based table assault created previously.

```
%sql select  sum(Victimisations_calendar_year_2015) as victims, Urban_area_
type

from assault

group by Urban_area_type

order by Urban_area_type
```

This just sums victims for the year 2015 against urban area type; an order by clause is used to sort the data, and a group by clause is used to group the summed values by area. When the preceding SQL is run against the Spark table, the output is shown in Figure 9-9.

victims	Urban_area_type
18,991	Main urban area
1,989	Minor urban area
1,349	Rural area
1,706	Secondary urban area

Figure 9-9. *Notebook session output*

Note that there are a number of graphing option icons shown in Figure 9-9. They will be explained in the next section.

Graph Options

By selecting the Zeppelin notebook session display icons, the data from the SQL statement can be presented in a number of ways. By selecting the second display icon "bar chart," the data can be presented as shown in Figure 9-10.

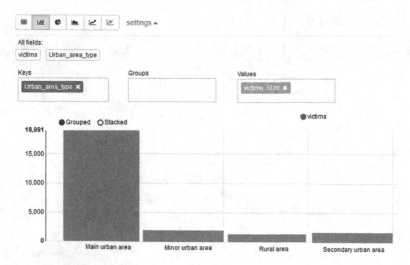

Figure 9-10. *Notebook session bar chart*

Note that the data value on the y axis has been defined to be the numeric sum "victims," while the key is defined as the "Urban_area_type." Selecting the next icon displays the data as a pie chart, as shown in Figure 9-11.

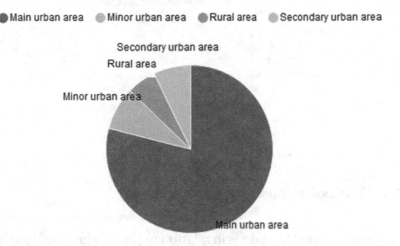

Figure 9-11. *Notebook session pie chart*

Choosing the solid graph icon changes the graph format to Figure 9-12.

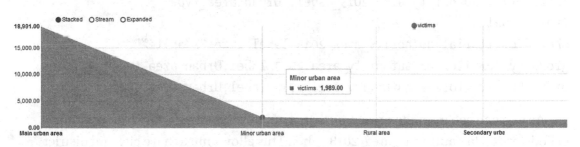

Figure 9-12. *Notebook session solid graph*

Choosing the line graph option creates a similar graph to the solid option (Figure 9-13). It is perhaps a little clearer, neater, and easier to comprehend.

Figure 9-13. *Notebook session line graph*

The next option creates a scatter graph of points; this would be useful if you wanted perhaps to determine clustering in the data (Figure 9-14).

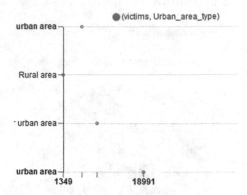

Figure 9-14. *Notebook session scatter graph*

The final point I wanted to make is in relation to pivot or grouped graphs. To create this example, I need to change the SQL used to access the assault table.

```
%sql select  sum(Victimisations_calendar_year_2015) as victims,
Territorial_authority_area_2013_label, Urban_area_type
from assault
where Territorial_authority_area_2013_label like "%Kapiti%"
group by Territorial_authority_area_2013_label,Urban_area_type
order by Territorial_authority_area_2013_label,Urban_area_type
```

As you can see from the preceding SQL, I am now selecting a third data column called Territorial_authority_area_2013_label. This allows me to have city and district area names as well as area types. I can now pivot or group the data by area type. I have also used a where clause to limit the data to the Kapiti region.

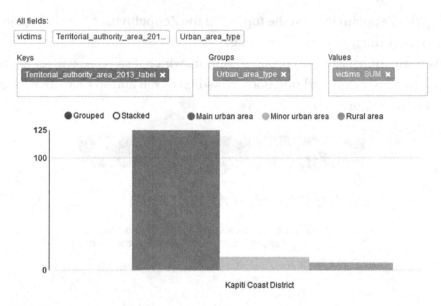

Figure 9-15. *Notebook session pivot graph*

The example output shown in Figure 9-15 has the same data value victims and a key of Territorial_authority_area_2013_label. The data has now been grouped by the urban area type.

Notebook Import

Previously, I showed how a notebook could be exported to a JSON-based file so that the notebook's information could be saved between Zeppelin sessions. In this section, I will show how the saved JSON file can be imported. In this case, I will import the file example1.json to recreate the notebook example1. Note that if the notebook already exists, then Zeppelin will recreate a new notebook with the same name.

Figure 9-16. *Zeppelin icon*

Clicking the Zeppelin icon on the top left of the Zeppelin user interface (shown in Figure 9-16) takes the user to the home page.

On this page, there is an "import note" option, which if selected will let the user choose the previously exported notebook-based JSON file and so recreate a saved notebook session (Figure 9-17).

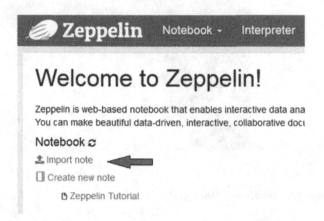

Figure 9-17. *Import notebook*

Dynamic Forms

Having examined the many forms of graphs that Zeppelin has to offer, I thought that it would also be useful to examine dynamic graphs. These are graphs that can be changed by the user entering form data. For instance, the graph can contain an input field or menu where the user can either make a selection or add data to change the graph's appearance. Making a selection or data change forces the graph to refresh and so the underlying SQL script to rerun.

The following SQL creates a menu that allows me to choose area data for Auckland, Kapiti, and Wellington dynamically. This menu is acting on the data from the select statement that is already in memory:

```
%sql select  sum(Victimisations_calendar_year_2015) as victims,
Territorial_authority_area_2013_label, Urban_area_type
from assault
where Territorial_authority_area_2013_label="${item=Auckland,Auckland|Kapi
ti Coast District|Wellington City}"
group by Territorial_authority_area_2013_label,Urban_area_type
order by Territorial_authority_area_2013_label,Urban_area_type
```

Figure 9-18 shows the menu that has been created, which resides between the SQL statement and the SQL results. It can be seen that the resulting data table matches the menu option. The menu options are formed as a bar ("|") separated list in the preceding SQL statement with the term "Auckland," forming an initial menu option.

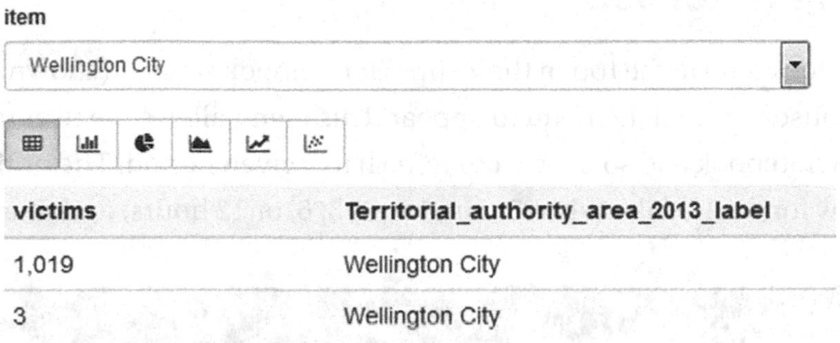

item

| Wellington City | ▾ |

| ⊞ | ᴫ | ● | ▲ | ⤳ | ⋉ |

victims	Territorial_authority_area_2013_label
1,019	Wellington City
3	Wellington City

Figure 9-18. *Dynamic menu*

I can change the preceding SQL so that a form field is created instead of a menu so that I can now filter the data by entering a search string. The SQL line is now changed to

```
where Territorial_authority_area_2013_label="${item=Auckland}"
```

This creates a form with a text field shown in Figure 9-19. Of course, if the string value entered does not match data values, then no data will be returned.

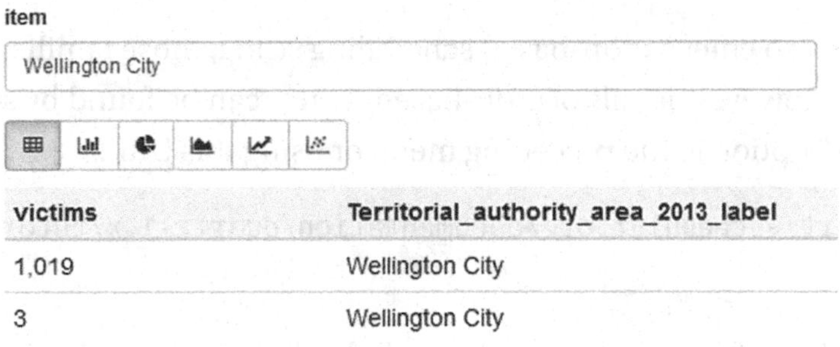

item

| Wellington City |

| ⊞ | ᴫ | ● | ▲ | ⤳ | ⋉ |

victims	Territorial_authority_area_2013_label
1,019	Wellington City
3	Wellington City

Figure 9-19. *Dynamic form field*

It is also possible to separate the display values from data values in a dynamic menu. The sample code following creates a dynamic menu with options A, B, and C, where A is the default value. However, the actual data items used in the SQL would be 1, 2, and 3.

```
value="${item=A,1(A)|2(B)|3(C)}"
```

This would be useful when dealing with numeric dimension values where the dimension has a logical meaning, that is, 1=Wellington, 2=Auckland. It would make the menu more meaningful for the user.

Scheduling Notebook

Selecting the clock icon at the top of the Zeppelin notebook session (shown grayed in Figure 9-20) causes a schedule menu to appear. This menu allows the user to specify a schedule for a notebook and so cause it to refresh to a given period. The options shown following allow for a schedule of 1 or 5 minutes; 1, 3, 6, or 12 hours; and finally daily.

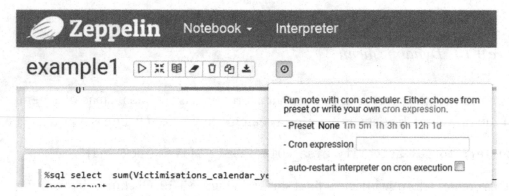

Figure 9-20. *Notebook scheduling*

The user can also enter a cron-based scheduling string; those familiar with Linux will understand this. However, details of cron-based strings can be found by selecting the "cron expression" option in the preceding menu or using this URL:

```
http://www.quartz-scheduler.org/documentation/quartz-1.x/tutorials/
crontrigger
```

Scheduling allows for a notebook to be periodically refreshed without user intervention, which makes the notebook more realistically represent the current data state. This is useful from a reporting point of view when sharing a notebook. This will be examined in the next section.

Sharing Session Output

Each paragraph within a notebook can be linked externally by using the rightmost menu icon option in the paragraph and choosing "Link this paragraph" (Figure 9-21). This creates a new window that shows the output of the paragraph only. This is useful for providing for instance management reports.

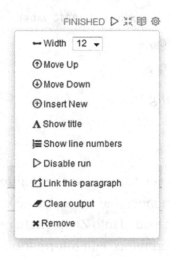

Figure 9-21. Paragraph linking menu

This does assume that the remote user has access to the intranet within which Zeppelin resides. For instance, linking one of the notebook example1 paragraphs from the last section provided this URL:

```
http://192.168.1.113:7055/#/notebook/2CV44QMXU/paragraph/20170925-
021044_2089430645?asIframe
```

This provides access to the following data-only, paragraph-based report in Figure 9-22. This URL could then be embedded into a separate web site or sent via an html-based email. If the notebook were scheduled, then the data would be periodically refreshed.

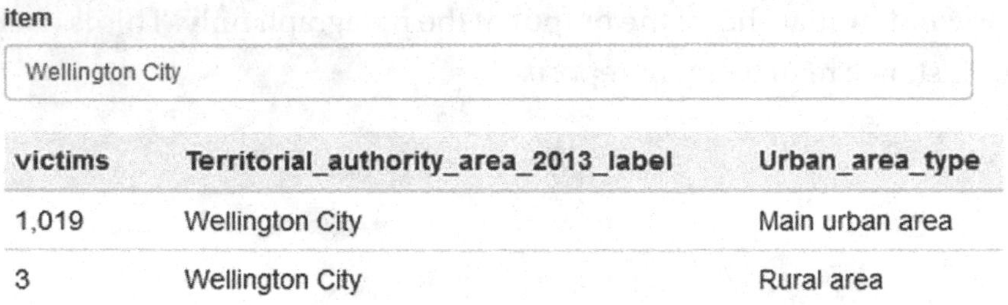

item

Wellington City

victims	Territorial_authority_area_2013_label	Urban_area_type
1,019	Wellington City	Main urban area
3	Wellington City	Rural area

Figure 9-22. *Paragraph linking*

Helium

Before closing this section, I wanted to mention the Helium framework that has been introduced in Zeppelin 0.7 (remember that we are using Version 0.5.6-2). The Helium framework allows plug-ins to be loaded into Zeppelin to provide extra functionality, for instance, for visualisation or interpreters. Full information can be found at the Zeppelin web site using the following URL:

```
https://zeppelin.apache.org/helium_packages.html
```

As Helium-based visualisation plug-ins are added to Zeppelin, they are added to the list of visualisation options that were examined in previous sections. This is a very powerful framework, as it extends Zeppelin's functionality and is only limited by what the community can conceive and develop. A new plug-in is developed and enabled in Zeppelin using npm (node package manager) repository at npmjs.com. The next sections will explain how this is accomplished.

Enable Plug-in

To be aware of a plug-in, Zeppelin 7.x searches for Helium package files in the local registry, by default the helium directory within the Zeppelin installation. It searches for JSON files such as helium/zeppelin-example-horizontalbar.json, an example file found at the preceding Helium URL. It looks like this:

```
{
  "type" : "VISUALIZATION",
  "name" : "zeppelin_horizontalbar",
  "description" : "Horizontal Bar chart (example)",
  "artifact" : "./zeppelin-examples/zeppelin-example-horizontalbar",
  "license" : "Apache-2.0",
  "icon" : "<i class='fa fa-bar-chart rotate90flipX'></i>"
}
```

It specifies the plug-in type, name, description, location, license, and icon type. When found, it allows the plug-in to be visible in the Zeppelin Helium plug-ins list, from where it can be enabled via a toggled button. When enabled, an extra visualisation icon button appears in the Zeppelin data visualisation. An example is shown in Figure 9-23 for the horizontal bar chart (grayed icon).

Figure 9-23. *Helium icons*

Develop Plug-in

To create a new Helium plug-in, you need to create a new Helium npm package. This is started by creating a package.json file. An example is shown following taken from the Zeppelin Helium web site:

```
{
  "name": "zeppelin_horizontalbar",
  "description" : "Horizontal Bar chart",
  "version": "1.0.0",
  "main": "horizontalbar",
  "author": "",
  "license": "Apache-2.0",
  "dependencies": {
    "zeppelin-tabledata": "*",
    "zeppelin-vis": "*"
  }
}
```

You can see that there are some extensions in the preceding JSON compared to the last example. A version and license value have been added, as well as a main function call reference. There are also two dependencies specified: zeppelin-vis for visualisation and zeppelin-tabledata for data management.

Next, the actual visualisation file needs to be created in Javascript. Some example URLs to provide sample code are the following:

- github.com/apache/zeppelin/blob/master/zeppelin-web/src/app/ visualisation/visualisation.js

- github.com/apache/zeppelin/tree/master/zeppelin-examples/ zeppelin-example-horizontalbar

- github.com/apache/zeppelin/tree/master/zeppelin-web/src/app/ visualisation/builtins

Then you need to create a Helium package file, an example of which was provided in the last section. This tells Helium where to find the plug-in, what the icon is, and what to call the plug-in. Finally, place this file in the helium registry directory. I think it would be useful to examine some example plug-ins to show what Helium in Zeppelin can offer. The next section will provide this detail.

Example Plug-ins

Be careful to check the licensing for Helium Zeppelin plug-ins, as not all plug-ins are released under an Apache 2 license. Also, many plug-ins have different licensing options depending on commercial or private use. The zeppelin-bubblechart graph shown in Figure 9-24 allows data to be presented as a series of colored bubbles.

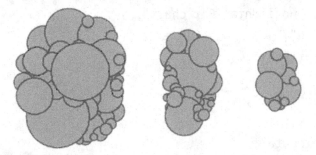

Figure 9-24. Bubble graph

The ultimate heat map option allows data to be presented as a color-coded heat map (Figure 9-25). Data values can be added to the graph or hidden.

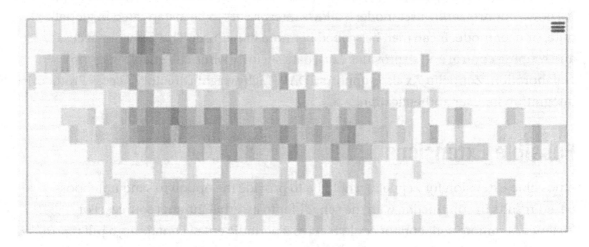

Figure 9-25. *Ultimate heat map*

The ultimate-pie-chart plug-in takes pie chart data visualisation to a new level, allowing for standard pie charts, chart cutout sections, and ring charts as shown in Figure 9-26.

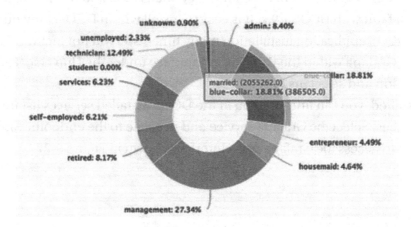

Figure 9-26. *Ultimate pie chart*

Multi-user Support

One weakness of Zeppelin in the past has been user access and access control. Zeppelin 7.x now supports multi-user mode; it allows interpreters to be instantiated in global, note, or user mode. It can then be scoped per note or per user. This provides access and scoping control and so provides extra data security while still enabling group collaboration. Zeppelin 7.x also supports LDAP (Lightweight Directory Access Protocol) integration for user authentication.

Possible Extensions

A possible extension for Zeppelin would be to provide the option to send notebook-based results in conjunction with the scheduler to external intranet sources. For instance, a remote collaborator could receive a periodic email containing a pdf report containing a snapshot of the notebook's data content.

The next section will examine Grafana-based visualisation.

Grafana

Grafana is an open-source system used for data visualisation and monitoring. It is provided by default with DCOS 1.9.x. It is easy to install within DCOS. Previous chapters have shown DCOS application installation many times, so I will not include details again here. Just find Grafana within the DCOS user interface under the Universe/Packages left-side menu option and select install.

Once installed, you can find Grafana in the DCOS installed services list under Services/Services. Select the Grafana service and navigate to the endpoint value, which you can select to access the Grafana login interface shown in Figure 9-27.

Figure 9-27. *Grafana login*

The default login account and password is admin/admin, which gives access to the Grafana (Version 4.5.2-03) user interface shown in Figure 9-28. Under the Grafana menu option Admin/Preferences, it is possible to change the "UI Theme." I have changed the value from "Dark" to "Light" for the rest of this section in the hope that the Grafana-based screenshots will be more legible.

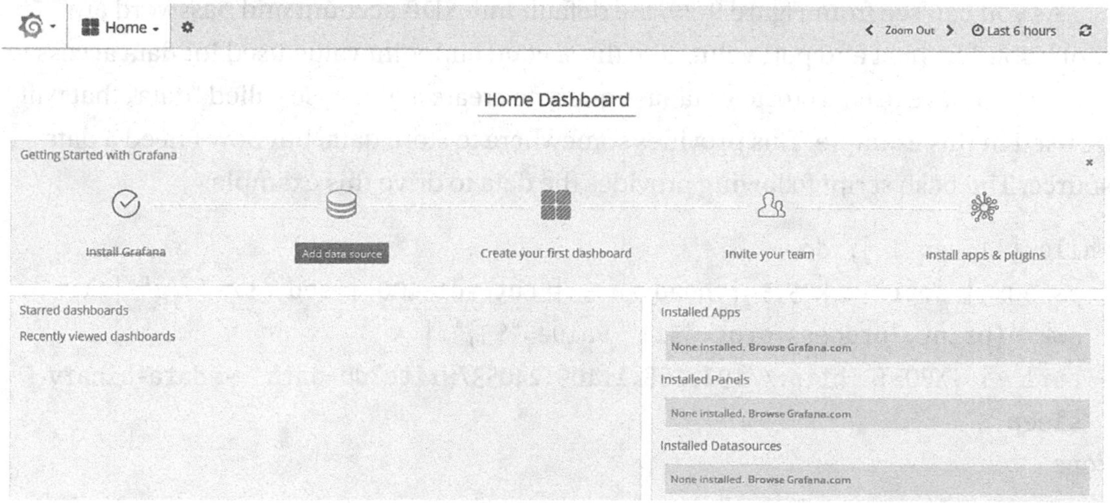

Figure 9-28. *Grafana user interface*

It is my intention to create a simple interface within Grafana and show how data can be streamed into panel-based graphs within a dashboard. The useful thing about Grafana is that it can be used to monitor data streams in real time. So in this section, I will create a data stream, feed that data into a database, and then use a data source within Grafana to consume and graph that data.

I have also installed InfluxDB (Version 0.13-0.1) to use as a data source. Once installed onto DCOS, two InfluxDB endpoints are created: the first provides access to the InfluxDB user interface, while the second provides the means by which data can be written to InfluxDB.

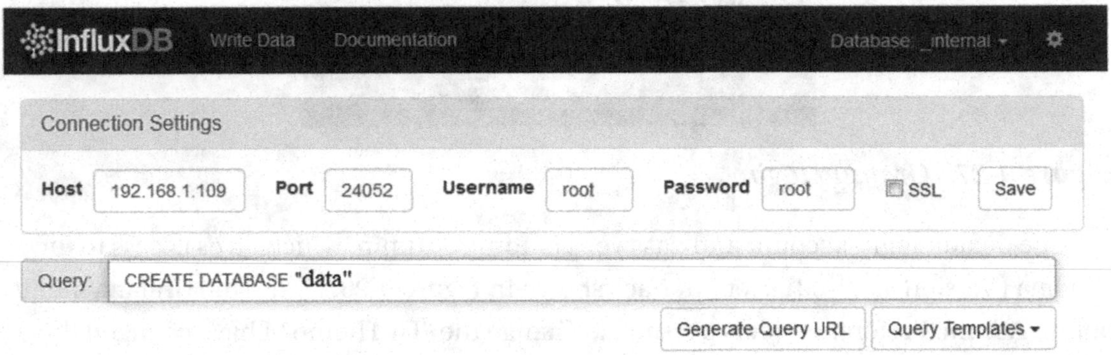

Figure 9-29. *InfluxDB user interface*

As you can see from Figure 9-29, the default InfluxDB account and password are root/root. The host and port values are the second endpoint value used for data access to InfluxDB. I have used a create database query to create a database called "data" that will be used in this example. This provides somewhere to store data, but now I need a data source. The bash script following provides the data to drive this example:

```
while [ 1 -eq 1 ]; do
  ps aux | sort -nrk 5,5 | head -n 5 | cut -c1-100 | sed 's/-/ /g' | \
  awk '{print "process,proc="$11" value="$5}' | \
  curl -i -XPOST 'http://192.168.1.109:24053/write?db=data' --data-binary @-
  sleep 5
done
```

318

It runs continuously on any machine in the cluster and uses the Linux ps command to list processes running on that server. The data is sorted by the fifth column (VSZ) Virtual Size. The top five values are then selected. The data is cleaned to remove unwanted characters and limit data width, and then the process name (column 11) and the size value (column 5) are selected. This data is then written to InfluxDB using the host and port value shown in Figure 9-29. The preceding script creates a table called "process" in the data database with columns proc and value.

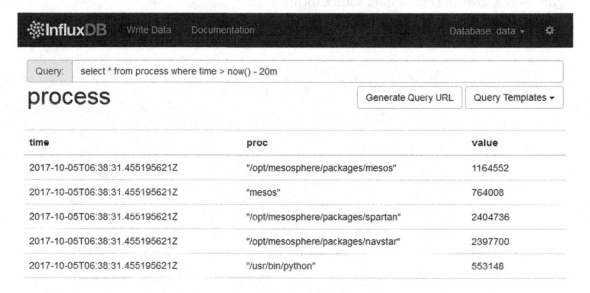

Figure 9-30. *InfluxDB data*

Figure 9-30 shows the InfluxDB user interface with the data database selected. A query has been used to select the data that was created by the preceding script. Note that InfluxDB automatically assigns a time value to each record. The preceding query lists all of the data available in the process table for the last 20 minutes. Now that data is available, a data source can be created within Grafana.

By selecting the "Add Data Source" option, I can now create a Grafana data source to connect to the InfluxDB table process in the database data that was just created. Figure 9-31 shows the create data source form.

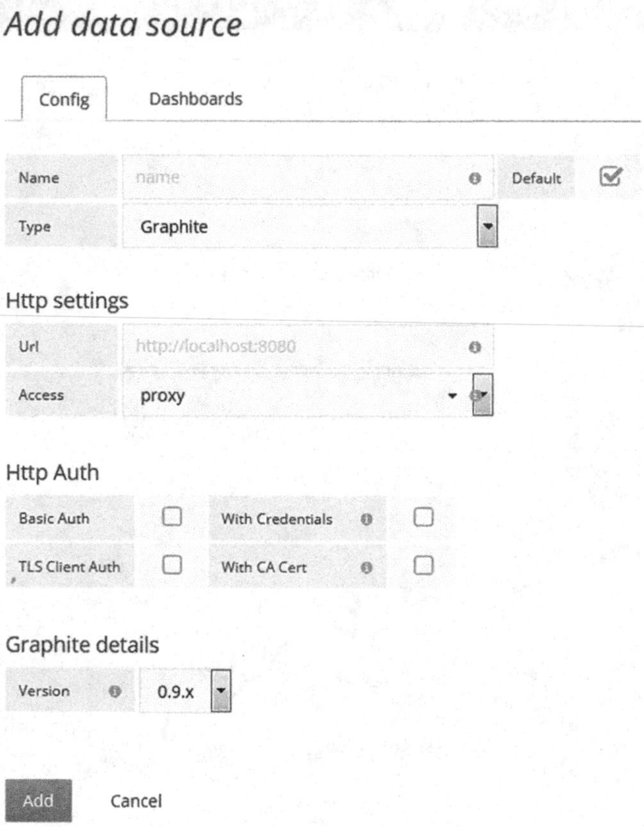

Figure 9-31. *Grafana data source*

A name and type must be assigned to the data source as well as http settings. I will not use a proxy to access InfluxDB and so will set the "Access" value to "Direct" and the "URL" value to the http string used in the bash script previously, that is, "http://192.168.1.109:24053." It is worth noting at this point that the "Type" menu on this form lists the data source types that can be used with this version of Grafana. There are also a range of official and community-built data source plug-ins available at

`https://grafana.com/plugins?type=datasource`

I will set it to "influxdb," but Figure 9-32 shows all possibilities.

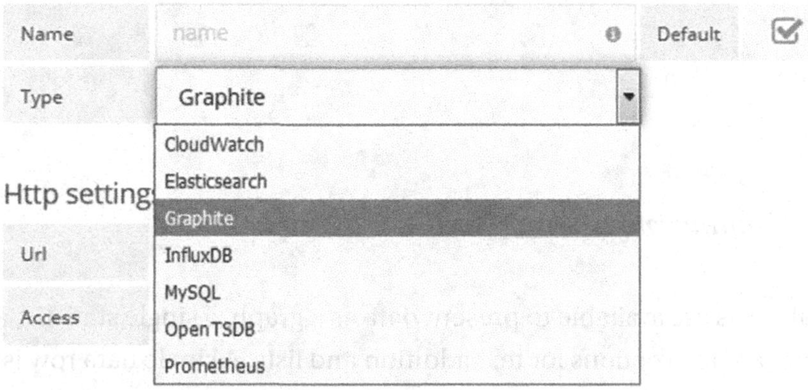

Figure 9-32. *Grafana data source options*

Selecting "Add" then saves the changes and provides a new set of options as shown in Figure 9-33. There is now an option to delete or save and test the data source.

Figure 9-33. *Grafana data source test*

Having selected "Save & Test," if all goes well, a green banner should appear as shown in Figure 9-34 If this is not the case, then return to the data source form and check your details. Ensure that your endpoint matches the value from InfluxDB. Also ensure that your database is running.

Figure 9-34. *Grafana data source test results*

Now that a working data source exists, a Grafana dashboard can be created to display the data. Selecting the "Create your first dashboard" option from the main Grafana menu opens an empty dashboard. Figure 9-35 shows the empty dashboard as well as the functional options available.

Figure 9-35. *Grafana empty dashboard*

Functional icons are available to present data as a graph, a single statistic, a table, or heat map. There are also options for text addition and lists. A single data row is shown in Figure 9-35 into which these icons can be dragged. Extra display rows can be created using the "Add Row" button at the bottom of the form. A panel menu is available on the left-hand side of the panel display denoted by three vertical dots. Figure 9-36 shows the panel menu options.

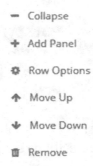

Figure 9-36. *Grafana dashboard panel menu*

You can see that there are options to move a panel within a dashboard, add a new panel, collapse the display, and examine panel options. Having dragged a graph into a panel row, it can be edited by clicking on the panel title and selecting edit as shown in Figure 9-37. This allows the data source for the graph to be defined.

Figure 9-37. *Grafana dashboard graph edit*

This displays a series of panel options that can be used to define the data source for the panel as well as the graph appearance. Figure 9-38 shows the Metrics tab from those edit options. It shows that I have defined InfluxDB as my data source. Also, the process table has been selected in the FROM clause. The value field has been chosen in the SELECT clause, so it is the numeric data item that will be displayed in these graphs.

Figure 9-38. *Grafana dashboard panel definition*

The data is grouped by time and formatted as time series data, that is, a stream of data items over time. I added a graph, a table, and a heat map to my dashboard using the same data source and refreshed the data using the refresh icon in the top right of the form. The result is shown in Figure 9-39.

Figure 9-39.   *Grafana dashboard*

I think that Grafana has a powerful way to monitor a data stream in real time, providing multiple ways to view facets of the data at the same time. This section has only examined a small sample of the functional capabilities of Grafana. However, I hope that I have given you some idea of the possibilities that it offers for data analysis. For more information, check the Grafana site at grafana.com. The next section will examine the Datadog application.

Datadog

In this section, I will examine the Datadog (datadoghq.com) application. Normally, I concentrate on open-source and distributed systems. However, Datadog is not an open-source product. I have included it in this chapter because it ships with DCOS as an application, and as you will see provides very effective cluster monitoring and visualisation. To write this section, I used the free, 14-day trial offered on the Datadog web site. On accepting the terms, I was asked to provide my email address, name, company name, a password, and my phone number. The setup process leads to the choice of platform used, in my case Centos, followed by instructions to install Datadog agents on cluster nodes. Figure 9-40 shows the install instructions along with a wide range of supported platforms.

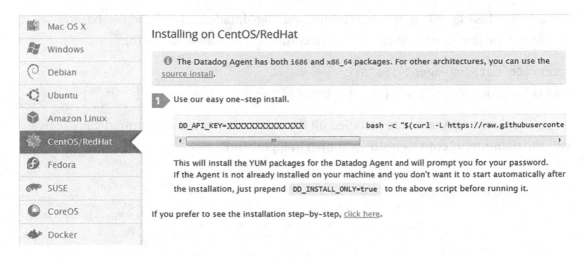

Figure 9-40. *Datadog Agent setup*

The install instructions, shown following, for the Datadog Agent on Centos use the Linux curl command to download the agent and a bash shell to execute the install. The variable DD_API_KEY specifies the key needed for the session to enable the Datadog Agent to run.

```
DD_API_KEY=xxxxxxxxxxxxx bash -c "$(curl -L https://raw.githubusercontent.
com/DataDog/dd-agent/master/packaging/datadog-agent/source/install_agent.sh)"
```

The install creates a Datadog Centos service called datadog-agent as shown in the listing following:

```
$ cd /etc/init.d ; ls
datadog-agent  functions  netconsole  network  README
```

For some reason, the agent install was not set up to auto start on cluster server reboot, but that is easily fixed. Use the Linux chkconfig command as shown following with the service name and "on" as parameters:

```
$ chkconfig datadog-agent on

Note: Forwarding request to 'systemctl enable datadog-agent.service'.
Created symlink from /etc/systemd/system/multi-user.target.wants/datadog-
agent.service to /usr/lib/systemd/system/datadog-agent.service.
```

Logs for this agent can be found under /var/log/datadog, and the agent-based service can be restarted using the `service` command as shown following:

```
$ service datadog-agent restart
Restarting datadog-agent (via systemctl):                    [  OK  ]
```

As the Datadog Agents are installed on the cluster servers, they automatically register with the datadoghq.com web site as shown in Figure 9-41.

Figure 9-41. *Datadog Agent registration*

Much of this section was then driven by the "Get Started" menu provided at the top of the datadoghq.com user interface. It provides a suggested order of actions as shown in Figure 9-42.

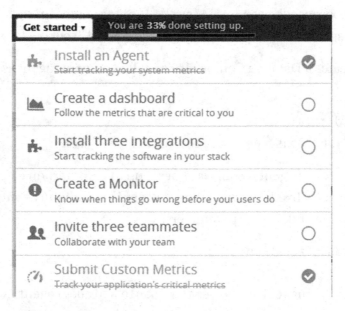

Figure 9-42. *Datadog get started menu*

So having installed agents and proved that they have all registered with the Datadog user interface, the next suggested step is to create a dashboard. Selecting this option from the preceding menu presents the user with a form that allows a dashboard to be named and its type chosen. A dashboard can be a "TimeBoard" or a "ScreenBoard." The first offers time-synchronized metrics and event graphs with an automatic layout. The second allows the user to create a custom layout and mix widgets and timeframe graphs.

Figure 9-43 shows the empty dashboard that has been created; I called my dashboard "dash1." I have elected to create a "TimeBoard" dashboard so I don't have to worry about layout. I just drag the available icons, that is, Timeseries, onto the dashboard editing pane denoted by a dotted line. Note that the left-hand menu also has a Dashboards option.

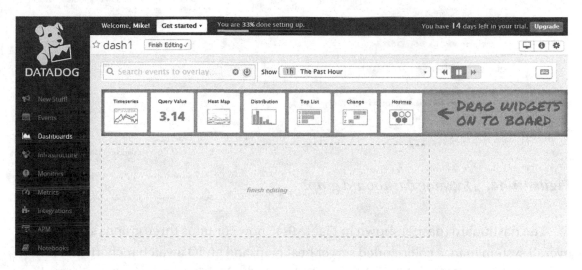

Figure 9-43. Datadog empty dashboard

Dragging a timeseries icon onto the dashboard creates a form that allows the visualisation type, metrics, and title to be chosen for the graph.

For instance, Figure 9-44 shows a sample graph indicating potential appearance, timeseries visualisation, and system load as the metric. Use the Save button to add this graph to the dashboard, and repeat this process for other graphs. With these options, it is possible to quickly create a meaningful dashboard.

Figure 9-44. *Datadog dashboard graph*

The dashboard (dash1) shown in Figure 9-45 now contains three graphs showing overall system load, a color-coded server heat map, and an IO await bar chart. The time period covered by the dashboard can easily be changed by using the show menu; and historical data can be displayed using forward, reverse, and pause buttons.

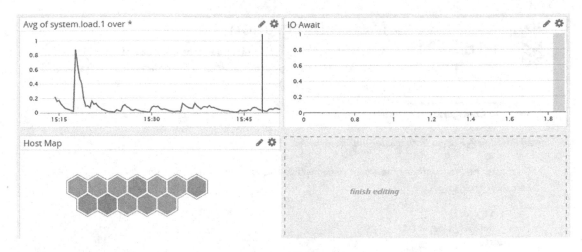

Figure 9-45. *Datadog dashboard multiple graphs*

The leftmost Integrations menu option shows the standard application integration available using Datadog. This means that Datadog can monitor applications running on the cluster as well as the cluster itself. I counted well over one hundred application integration icons available, many of which relate to apache.com software. Given that this book is based on Apache Mesos-based big data stacks, I will elect to install the Mesos integration. (A Marathon application integration is also available.)

Selecting the Mesos integration application and choosing the Configuration option shows how the application can be installed. It involves creating a configuration file that the Datadog Agent uses to monitor Mesos. There is an option for the Mesos master servers and a different option for the Mesos slaves, as shown in Figure 9-46.

Mesos Integration

Apache Mesos is a cluster manager that provides efficient resource isolation and sharing across distributed applications, or frameworks.

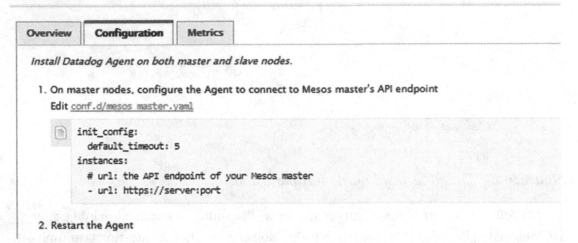

Overview   **Configuration**   **Metrics**

Install Datadog Agent on both master and slave nodes.

1. On master nodes, configure the Agent to connect to Mesos master's API endpoint
   Edit conf.d/mesos_master.yaml

```
init_config:
    default_timeout: 5
instances:
    # url: the API endpoint of your Mesos master
    - url: https://server:port
```

2. Restart the Agent

Figure 9-46. *Datadog Mesos application*

There are example files already provided with the Mesos agent under the directory /etc/dd-agent/conf.d as shown following:

```
$ cd  /etc/dd-agent/conf.d
$ ls *mesos*

mesos_master.yaml.example   mesos_slave.yaml.example   mesos.yaml.example
```

I used the example file on my Mesos master server and specified my servers IP address to monitor Mesos. I copied the mesos_master file from its example file name to an active .yaml-based file name. I then changed the localhost value in the file to use my server's IP address, that is

```
$ cp mesos_master.yaml.example   mesos_master.yaml
$ cat     mesos_master.yaml

init_config:
  default_timeout: 10
instances:
  - url: http://192.168.1.112:5050
```

The port number 5050 shown in the preceding refers to the port number used by the Mesos master service. Once this change has been made, the Datadog Agent on each server needs to be restarted.

```
$ service datadog-agent   restart
```

If you now use the leftmost Datadog menu option Infrastructure/Infrastructure List, you will see an infrastructure status. This will include icons that show a color-coded status for the Mesos application across nodes as well.

Note that in the infrastructure list in Figure 9-47, the server hc4r1m0 is my Mesos master server, while all others are slave Mesos servers, with the exception of hc4r2m1, which is an install server. Note that as well as system application icons like ntp and system, there are also Mesos-based icons as well.

Hostname ↑	Status ↓	CPU ↓	IOWait	Load 15	Apps
hc4r1m5.semtech-solutions.co.nz	⬧ ✦ - UP	2%	0%	0.025	mesos ntp system
hc4r2m2.semtech-solutions.co.nz	⬧ ✦ - UP	2%	0.8%	0.025	mesos ntp system
hc4r2m3.semtech-solutions.co.nz	⬧ ✦ - UP	2%	0%	0.025	mesos ntp system
hc4nn.semtech-solutions.co.nz	⬧ ✦ - UP	1%	0.2%	0.025	mesos ntp system
hc4r2m4.semtech-solutions.co.nz	⬧ ✦ - UP	1%	0.2%	0.025	mesos ntp system
hc4r2m5.semtech-solutions.co.nz	⬧ ✦ - UP	1%	0.2%	0.025	mesos ntp system
hc4r1m3.semtech-solutions.co.nz	⬧ ✦ - UP	1%	0%	0.025	mesos ntp system
hc4r1m4.semtech-solutions.co.nz	⬧ ✦ - UP	0.7%	0%	0.035	mesos ntp system
hc4r1m0.semtech-solutions.co.nz	⬧ ✦ - UP	0.7%	0.2%	0.012	mesos ntp system
hc4r1m2.semtech-solutions.co.nz	⬧ ✦ - UP	0.7%	0%	0.025	mesos ntp system
hc4r1m1.semtech-solutions.co.nz	⬧ ✦ - UP	0.6%	0%	0.025	mesos ntp system
hc4r2m1.semtech-solutions.co.nz	⬧ ✦ - UP	0.5%	0.4%	0.025	ntp system

Figure 9-47. *Datadog infrastructure status*

The menu option Infrastructure/Host Map provides a color-coded heat map of your cluster, which provides an instant visual reference for potential problems. Figure 9-48 shows a status "green" cluster due to the fact that it is idle, but it could have been orange due to a CPU utilisation problem.

Each element in the grid represents a cluster server. Although it may be hard to see in Figure 9-48, the server name is overlaid on each element. The applications being monitored on each server (mesos, ntpd, system) are shown as status green blocks within each server.

It is also possible to change the appearance of the hosts heat map by using the menu options above the heat map display. For instance, the item being displayed (i.e., CPU) in Figure 9-48 can be changed using the "Fill By" menu.

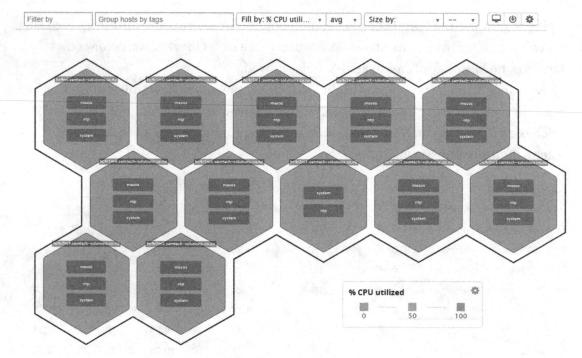

Figure 9-48. *Datadog infrastructure host map*

Dashboards can be created in an ad hoc manner using the Dashboards menu option. For instance, in Figure 9-49, a dashboard has been created for the master server hc4r1m0.

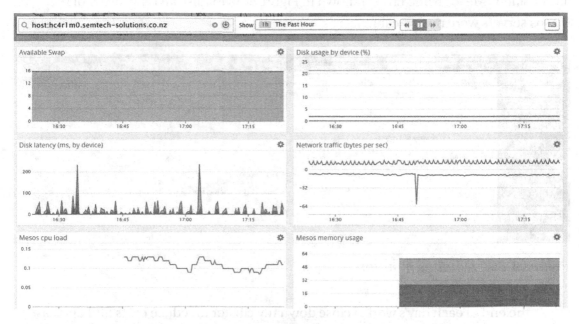

Figure 9-49. *Datadog master server dashboard*

Figure 9-49 automatically shows a myriad of color-coded time series information. The graphs cover CPU, disk, and memory usage, as well as swap. There is a process memory usage map as well as Mesos-related graphs. Dashboards like this can quickly be created and adjusted using the menu options at the top of the form. The dashboard display can also scroll through historic data using the forward and reverse icons.

The next thing that I wanted to cover that Datadog handles well is monitors. It is not enough to have a dashboard that will display an issue, because there might not be a person available to see that event. An alert is needed when an event occurs to contact people and make them aware.

The Datadog Monitors menu option allows a monitor to be created by selecting a hostname, specifying the alert conditions, specifying a message to explain the issue, and finally, to specify who should receive the alert. I created the Mesos server monitoring alert (called "Mesos Node Error") shown in Figure 9-50 to raise an issue if any of my Mesos servers were not available.

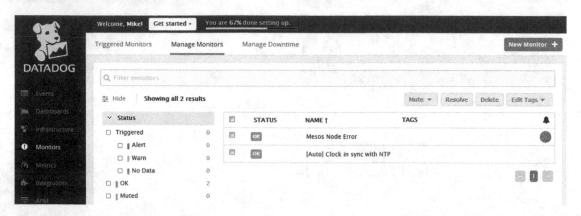

Figure 9-50. *Datadog monitors*

At the end of each day's work, I close down my cluster to reduce costs and decrease the heat, noise, and vibration caused by all of these servers. Because Datadog is a service in the cloud, the monitor I created previously is still operating, even when my cluster goes down. Given that the Mesos servers were down, I received a series of Datadog alert messages generated by the monitor. A sample message is shown in Figure 9-51.

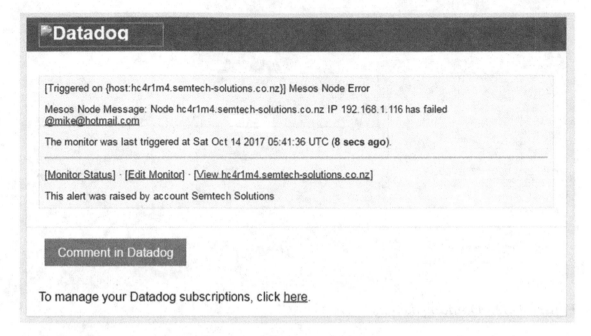

Figure 9-51. *Datadog monitor alert*

The last thing that I wanted to cover in this section is the Datadog Metrics menu option. This allows you to monitor a vast variety of provided metrics for the cluster or individual servers. You can specify the type of aggregation to be used on the data, and you also have menu options to scroll through data and show preset time periods. Figure 9-52 shows cluster system memory used over the last hour. There are also options to save the graph to a timeboard.

Figure 9-52. *Datadog metrics*

I hope that this gives a flavor of the functionality available within Datadog. It offers cluster and server-based monitoring and visualisation as well as alerting in the case of cluster-based issues. It has a wide range of integrations available, including some notable Apache offerings like Mesos, Hadoop, Cassandra, and Kafka. It is an impressive product that seems to fill a much-needed function. I hope that this section has given some idea of Datadog's functionality. More information can be found at datadoghq.com.

Conclusion

This chapter has examined some of the visualisation and monitoring options available within the DCOS system. As data volumes grow, the problem of data comprehension increases. Visualisation and monitoring methods are needed to examine data trends over time. Dashboards are needed to offer a snapshot in time of related data items.

Rich functionality is needed to present data in a variety of forms: for instance, line graphs, heat maps, and bar and pie charts. Methods are needed to send reports in a scheduled manner to remote parties in a variety of formats.

Three visualisation and monitoring applications were examined in this chapter: Zeppelin, Grafana, and Datadog. Whereas the first two are open-source applications, the third is a commercial offering. This is offset by the fact that it is an excellent product offering much needed cluster/application monitoring and alerting. The collaborative notebook development approach of Zeppelin was interesting, along with the Helium plug-in technology that it is now using.

By the time that you read this chapter, there may be more visualisation options available within DCOS. I selected those available at the time of this writing (October 2017). I hope that this chapter has provided enough interest that you will carry out your own research into the options available.

The next chapter will sum the Mesos-based big data stack as a whole. It will examine the interfaces between stack elements and bring the information presented in previous chapters together to form a whole.

CHAPTER 10

The Big Data Stack

Chapter 10 provides a summary of each of the components explored in detail in earlier chapters as well as raising deeper issues for consideration and looking at potential further work that has not yet been explored. Reading this final chapter reminds one of the tremendous amount that has been achieved on this journey, from starting with a physical bare metal cluster; to setting up a private cloud; and then methodically building a complete functional, manageable, and scalable big data stack able to handle large batch loads as well as real-time stream processing.

This chapter will cover all of the subjects examined in the previous chapters and discuss the interfaces in the stack architecture diagram (Figure 10-1). It will bring the topics described in previous chapters together to form a whole.

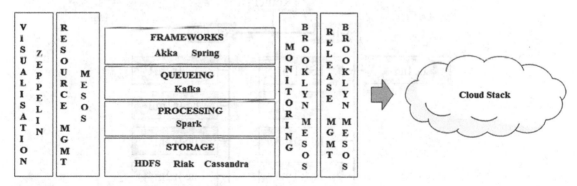

Figure 10-1. *Stack architecture*

© Michael Frampton 2018

M. Frampton, *Complete Guide to Open Source Big Data Stack*, https://doi.org/10.1007/978-1-4842-2149-5_10

I feel that the Data Center Operating System (DCOS) created by mesosphere.com provides a much more robust and functional environment than Mesos alone. I think that the Mesos-based chapters covered so far in this book show this. DCOS is robust in that it is self-healing: there is an excellent user interface to manage the system and track problems. There are also a wide range of applications that are provided that are easy to install and configure. Before moving on to the topics covered by Chapters 2 to 9, I wanted to examine the hardware architectures that were used during the development of this book. The next section will cover this.

Hardware Architecture

In Chapter 1, the introduction, I specified the server architecture that I would use in this book. This is shown in Figure 10-2, and this is the architecture that was used in Chapters 2 and 3 when creating a cloud and release management systems using Apache Brooklyn. However, this architecture did not meet the needs of DCOS, the Mesos-based cluster control system.

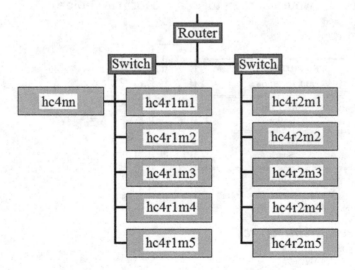

Figure 10-2. *Server architecture*

As is the case with all authors, the work presented in a developed book represents a fraction of the work carried out. When creating a hardware architecture for Mesos and DCOS, I tried many configurations of hardware and software. I used architectures with multiple Mesos masters and single Mesos masters. I tried systems with an install server and without. The architecture that you see in Figure 10-3 worked well and allowed me to install multiple frameworks onto Mesos at the same time.

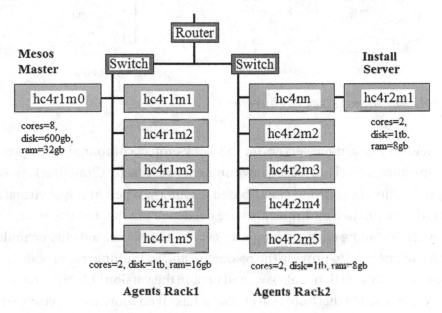

Figure 10-3. *Stack architecture Mesos*

Note that I used a Dell PowerEdge 2950 blade as a master server to provide extra master-based resources and core-based power. As I stated in previous chapters, I am limited in what I can try and research by a lack of funding. Having worked through the previous chapters, you may have noticed that I did not use Mesos or DCOS in combination with a cloud. I would have liked to have tried this, but I did not have the necessary servers. If I wanted to create a Mesos-based cluster with a suitable number of slaves or agents, I did not have any spare servers for a cloud.

I am also limited by running these servers in a home-based environment. Apart from the cost of running them, they also generate a lot of heat, noise, and vibration. My optimum architecture is shown in the Figure 10-4 with extra racks for a low-cost cloud. Perhaps at some future time when the funds are available or I find a corporate sponsor, this might be possible.

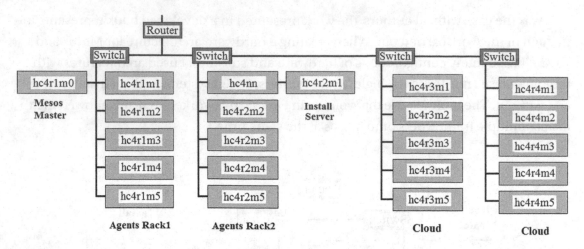

Figure 10-4. *Optimum stack architecture*

I have needed to use more servers for this book project compared to my previous books. For instance, in a cloud-based environment like Apache CloudStack, hosts are added to the cloud to provide cloud-based resources. When multiple virtual host instances are created, then multiple hosts are needed to provide the necessary resources. Similarly, when installing multiple frameworks onto a Mesos-based cluster, multiple Mesos slaves are needed to provide the resources, and so multiple servers are required.

Before closing this section, I also wanted to note the versions of the CentOS operating system used in this book. Given that it has taken more than a year to write, I started by using CentOS 6.5 and ended Chapter 9 with CentOS 7.3 server installs. Having covered hardware architectures, I will now move on to examine the topics raised in the previous chapters of this book and provide an overview.

Chapter Topics

Each of the following sections will examine the content of Chapters 2 to 9 and provide an overview in terms of the big data stack.

Chapter 2 Cloud

As I stated in Chapter 2, the only reason that I did not use a cloud-based service like AWS for this project was due to the financial costs involved. I preferred to use what resources I have to purchase physical servers rather than pay for cloud-based services. Local servers can be reused for multiple projects. Also, given that this book has taken more than a year to write, the cloud-based costs would have been considerable. I think that the compromise of using Apache Cloudstack to create a local cloud was a good one. Cloudstack is an enterprise standard system. As Chapter 2 showed, the functionality that it introduced could be scaled to cover multiple data centers. The cloud that was created in Chapter 2 was then used as a target release location for Chapter 3 on Apache Brooklyn, which I will cover in the next section.

Chapter 3 Brooklyn

In Chapter 3, Apache Brooklyn was installed and examined as a release management and system monitoring component of the stack. It was shown to support an internal catalogue of applications, entities, policies, and locations. So external applications like Mule ESB, the ETL tool, could be modelled as an entity within the catalog. It was shown that YAML-based scripts could then be created to have Brooklyn release entities to generic locations.

Brooklyn would then treat a server or a cloud location as a generic location and use them as a generic install site. This is interesting because it suggests that hybrid systems could be created using multiple clouds and on-site servers. Scale into the cloud as demand increases or contracts. In fact, Brooklyn has policies for scaling released applications. As you spend time investigating Brooklyn, you might develop your own policies to support your systems.

I showed by example the release of a Mule-based system using Brooklyn in Chapter 3. If you examine the code that was used for this, you might consider doing something similar to have Brooklyn release to DCOS. The DCOS CLI allows command line release of frameworks. These simple commands could be embedded into a Brooklyn entity.

As I stated previously, Brooklyn has not been used in this book beyond Chapter 3. I either had to use my limited servers for a cloud or a Mesos cluster. Also, this book has taken more than a year to write, and I need to finish it. The Brooklyn to DCOS interface will have to form a later project once this book has been released.

It should be noted that if Brooklyn treats cloud-based servers as just another generic location, then the dependence on any given cloud provider is diminished. Cloud providers could be chosen where there is perhaps a price advantage. It might be possible to build systems using multiple providers and move data between providers as the cost landscape changes. This approach would negate or perhaps mitigate against using higher level cloud-based services like databases. Vendor lock in would not seem to be desirable.

The next section will examine resource management using Mesos and DCOS.

Chapter 4 Resource Management

Chapter 4 examined resource management in a big data stack in terms of a stand-alone Mesos install followed by a DCOS install. In Mesos terms, this chapter, and I hope later chapters, show you that the DCOS environment is more functionally rich and more robust. It offers a wide range of standard applications that can be installed with a few mouse clicks. It also offers the ability to define new frameworks using JSON to install your own applications.

As I said previously, it is more robust than Mesos alone, which will become apparent if you need to restart your servers. It is also self-healing and offers some very good user interfaces for the ZooKeeper-based exhibitor and DCOS itself. It is possible to examine cluster server state and errors.

I also briefly examined the Myriad project, which intends to enable the Hadoop-based Yarn scheduler to work within a Mesos-based environment. A Myriad executor would allow Yarn to interface with the Mesos slave. I examined this project to make you aware of potential future changes.

Also, it is worth noting that in Apache Spark terms, Mesos and ZooKeeper in combination are one of the main cluster management options for Apache Spark; the others being Yarn Client, Yarn cluster, and stand-alone. For more information, see my previous books:

```
https://www.amazon.com/Michael-Frampton/e/BOONIQDOOM
```

The next section will examine storage in a big data stack.

Chapter 5 Storage

Chapter 5 and other chapters provided examples of Mesos-based storage frameworks for Riak, Cassandra, and HDFS. It should be noted that in Mesos and DCOS terms, the components of a Hadoop stack are installed separately. So for instance, HDFS is offered as a framework, and the Apache Myriad project will offer Yarn.

It should also be noted that Mesos clusters are not persistent; for instance, if a cluster is restarted, a framework might be redeployed. This is different from say a Hadoop stack, which if restarted, should not lose data.

In this case, it is possible and perhaps probable that a redeploy will cause a loss of data that was previously stored. In enterprise terms, the use of multiple masters and a large number of Mesos slaves minimizes this risk. However, it is worth noting this point and being aware to incorporate it when considering system design and processes.

The storage options used here are all for distributed systems; however, DCOS offers many more. For instance, the visualisation chapter used InfluxDB as a time series data store, and Postgresql is also available. You might need a big data cluster as well as a relational business intelligence server to receive aggregated data from your stack. You might then need to create reports from smaller data pools as your big data stack grows.

The next section will give an overview of the processing chapter for the Mesos-based big data stack.

Chapter 6 Processing

Chapter 6 showed how Apache Spark-based applications can be run against Mesos and DCOS clusters. Chapter 7 also includes a Spark-based example and shows how Scala sbt assembly can be used to create a fat jar file to run a Spark-based application. At the time of this writing, DCOS 1.9.x does not support the Spark submit --jars option, so all jar files needed for an application need to be packaged into a single fat jar file.

I hope that this chapter and previous chapters show an integration trend. I mean that in my first Hadoop book, I started by building and installing Hadoop from source and ended with integrated stacks from Cloudera and Hortonworks. In my second Spark-based book, I started with raw Spark builds and ended with databricks.com, the notebook-based online system that supports Spark.

I think that it is always better to use integrated systems and think about wider integration options. Integrated stacks are more robust than single components brought together to create a system. They have been designed to work together and tested to prove that they do.

You might ask "why Apache Spark": why not an alternative big data system like perhaps Storm? I'm always interested in integration possibilities for the big data components that I use. I know that a system like Storm has a large community and a strong following. However, I like Spark for the range of functionality that it offers and the systems that it will work with. It is widely supported and has a strong future.

The next section will examine big data queueing in a big data stack.

Chapter 7 Queueing

For this section of the big data stack, I decided to use Apache Kafka: when people think of big data queueing, it is Kafka that comes to mind. It is designed to scale and integrates well with components like Spark and storage mechanisms like HDFS. It works with multiple producers and consumers as well as now being designed to access databases and act as a stream processor as well. Check the kafka.apache.org web site for the latest Kafka details.

I showed the use of Kafka with DCOS as well as the DCOS CLI and showed how Kafka-based data could be accessed via the CLI as well as Spark. Chapter 8 examined the Spring RabbitMQ framework. Kafka is a publish/subscribe messaging system that is able to store data. RabbitMQ offers many ways to route data based on header, content, or publish/subscribe. This offers the interesting possibility of using RabbitMQ and Kafka together if needed. RabbitMQ does not store data but uses a broker to just forward it.

Using RabbitMQ and Kafka together would allow for data to be routed by content and then published to various topics based on content waiting for various endpoints to consume. If that was of interest, the question would be this: can RabbitMQ scale as well as Kafka? It is an interesting possibility though!

The next section will examine the frameworks chapter.

Chapter 8 Frameworks

Although I did not have the time or resources to implement application frameworks during this project, I used Chapter 8 to investigate some of the possibilities. I examined Akka and Netty frameworks because they both have or are being used by Apache Spark. I then examined the Spring RabbitMQ framework because it is related to the previous chapter. It may well be used in big data systems for time series processing or to route data based on content.

It is interesting to examine both Akka and Netty to understand how they allow distributed systems to be developed and how they support messaging within those systems. If you create an app or multiple big data applications for say stream processing, you might need to use these frameworks.

The next section will examine the final chapter, visualisation.

Chapter 9 Visualisation

I used this chapter to examine data visualisation possibilities available within a standard DCOS-based install. (I'm currently using DCOS Version 1.9.1.) Given that big data offers vast data sizes, variety and velocity, and possibly reduced veracity, the ability to visualize data and data streams becomes ever more important.

I show within this chapter practical examples of graph- and dashboard-based visualisation as well as the use of Spark within Zeppelin as a notebook-based processing engine for preparing data to visualize. The ability of Grafana to create real-time dashboards was examined along with its ability to present the data in a range of forms. It was apparent that Grafana is supported by a large community and offers a wide range of plug-ins.

I normally concentrate on open source distributed systems, but system and cluster monitoring in enterprise systems is critical. Datadog is offered as a default option within DCOS; and as this chapter shows, it is an impressive offering. It easily monitors cluster servers and the applications running on them like Mesos. It provides graphs and dashboards and handles streamed data. It also offers monitoring and alerting to make team members aware of problems. From an enterprise perspective, it is easily capable of monitoring a big data stack.

Application Architecture

Figure 10-5, taken from Chapter 6, the processing chapter, shows a possible big data stack application structure. It shows how big data stack applications built to run against Apache Spark will incorporate the use of multiple resources to access each layer of the big data stack.

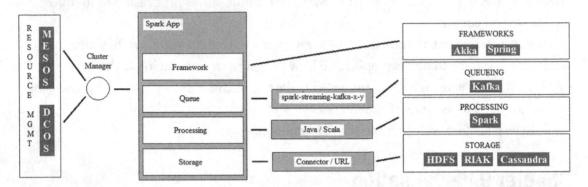

Figure 10-5. *Application architecture*

For instance, to access Cassandra, an application would use a connector library; whereas access to the HDFS framework would be possible using an HDFS-based URL. The actual data processing to be carried out would be possible in either Java or Scala using Spark, although if you have followed my books, you will see that I favor Scala and sbt (I use sbt assembly as well in this book).

The application could then be monitored as a Spark framework task in the Mesos user interface. The task could be executed using the DCOS CLI as shown in Chapter 7. That will be examined in the next section.

Application Submission

This example code taken from Chapter 7, the queueing chapter, shows how an application built as a fat jar file using sbt assembly can be submitted to the DCOS-based Apache Spark framework. The PATH value is updated to include the location of the DCOS CLI command. The auth login option is used with the CLI to authorize the session to access DCOS. Then the DCOS CLI Spark run option is used to execute the application class within the jar file. The fat jar file that is used will not be distributed by a DCOS framework-based Apache Spark. The jar file is placed in a web-based location that all Spark servers can access.

```
$ export PATH=$PATH:/opt/dcos/bin/

$ dcos auth login

$ dcos spark run --verbose \
--submit-args=' --driver-cores 1 --driver-memory 1024M --class KafCom1
http://www.semtechsolutions.co.nz/spark/kafcom1-assembly-1.0.jar'
```

The diagram following (Figure 10-6) gives a visual interpretation of this control flow. In Step (1), the login authorisation is obtained via a DCOS CLI "auth login" call. The jar file needs to be within a location that Spark can access, in this case, a web URL. Also, the submit-args string can be extended with extra command options for Spark; this is a simple example.

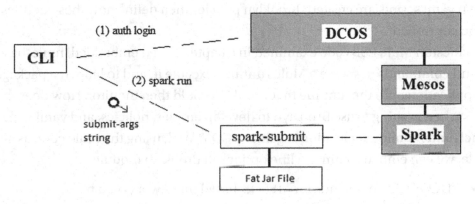

Figure 10-6. *Application architecture*

This describes how Apache Spark-based application code developed for the big data stack can be launched against a Spark framework running on Mesos. How does Brooklyn, examined in Chapter 3, and also Brooklyn-based locations, relate to a DCOS environment? Remember that a Brooklyn location can either be a physical server or a cloud-based server. The next section will examine this topic.

Brooklyn and DCOS

Due to a lack of time, the necessary servers, and funding issues, it was not possible to extend this work to integrate Apache Brooklyn with DCOS and cloud-based locations. It was also not possible to consider application- or Mesos-based framework scaling from a Brooklyn point of view. However, this section can be used to examine these topics and perhaps a later version of this book can expand on these areas.

Remember that when creating a Mesos or DCOS cluster, master and agent locations are specified. It would be quite possible to have Mesos or DCOS agents in the cloud registering with cloud-or server-based masters. So a Mesos-based cluster could scale into the cloud.

When creating Brooklyn-based components, DCOS CLI authorisation (auth login) could be a problem. How would Brooklyn know what the authorisation string would be? This problem could be solved by having the DCOS CLI installed on the same server as Apache Brooklyn and authorizing the session manually. This would be a long-running session valid for as long as DCOS is up.

If you examine the Ricston Mule code for a Brooklyn entity from Chapter 3, you will see it as a good blueprint and example for future development of Brooklyn-based entities and policies. Remember that entities model the unit elements from which Brooklyn yaml scripts are created. Brooklyn policies then define how these entities will act or be controlled.

The Ricston Mule ESB code examined in Chapter 3 used embedded, mule-based paths and commands to source a Mule runtime, execute it, and to launch a packaged Mule application onto the runtime that Brooklyn could then monitor. How does that assist us when wishing to use Brooklyn to develop entities, policies, and yaml code to launch and monitor applications against DCOS? Well, using the Mule code as an example, we can embed command line options in Brooklyn modules.

- DCOS CLI commands for MESOS-based frameworks can be embedded in Brooklyn code. If the DCOS CLI session is already authorized, this simplifies the process.

- Mesos frameworks need to be well designed and enabled via the CLI: not just for install but also for status. Brooklyn can then use CLI commands like `status` to provide framework monitoring.

- Chapter 3 showed how an application could be launched from Brooklyn onto a Mule runtime running via Brooklyn. It is not a stretch of the imagination to extend this analogy to launching Spark-based applications via Brooklyn onto a Spark framework.

- In Brooklyn policy terms, scaling needs to be considered. How can a framework or an application (if it is distributed) be scaled via Brooklyn? Well the DCOS CLI Marathon command offers group scaling, and there is also a Marathon REST API available. For instance, Version 1.9 is available at

  `https://dcos.io/docs/1.9/deploying-services/marathon-api/#.`

This is an area of work that needs further time and effort spent on it to create some real-world practical examples. It will have to wait for a future project though.

Figure 10-7 shows visually what was discussed in the preceding section. The units developed within the Brooklyn catalogue, that is, entities and policies, can access both the DCOS CLI and the Marathon REST API. By doing this, they can manage both Mesos frameworks and tasks within those frameworks.

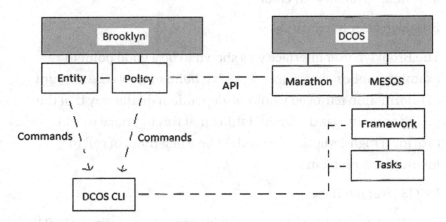

Figure 10-7. *Brooklyn DCOS*

The next section will examine big data stack monitoring.

Stack Monitoring

The previous chapters have shown many ways to monitor Mesos-based servers, frameworks, and tasks. I think at this point a recap is needed to list all of the options and see how they compare.

- CloudStack User Interface

  If you remember in Chapter 2, it was shown that within an Apache CloudStack user interface it was possible to obtain cloud server metrics. This showed the resource usage and load on cloud-based servers. It was a useful place to examine the load on the cloud when troubleshooting. You probably won't use CloudStack, but your cloud user interface would be a useful place to seek information about your cloud.

- Brooklyn User Interface

  The Brooklyn user interface was shown to be a good point to examine applications from a Brooklyn point of view. The amount of information retrieved would be dependent on the way that the policy or entity was designed. I think that this interface would provide a high-level view and might be a first point of call to investigate a problem.

- DCOS User Interface

  The DCOS user interface is a useful interface for examining DCOS node status, DCOS processes, and accessing Mesos framework-related interfaces from a single point. Log files can be accessed from here as well as the Marathon scheduler. This might be the second place you look to track a problem.

- Mesos User Interface

  Mesos is the resource manager used for this big data stack. From here, we can examine what frameworks are running and what tasks exist within those frameworks. It is possible to see whether a task or framework has had multiple failures and to check its log files. This might be the third location to check. You can see that we are moving down the stack layers to investigate a problem.

- Marathon User Interface

  From the Marathon user interface, running under DCOS, we can
  see the DCOS-based applications that Marathon has scheduled.
  Their configuration, state, and logs can be checked from this
  point. Applications can also be paused, scaled, and restarted from
  within Marathon. Be careful though to think about persistence, as
  restarting or scaling an application might cause data loss.

- Spark User Interface

  From the Spark application, both the Spark executors and Spark-
  based tasks can be examined. Their log files can be checked for
  process flow and errors.

- Log Files

  At the lowest level, file system-based log files can be checked.
  Many times during the previous chapters, it was shown that
  Mesos-based task stdout and stderr log files could be checked to
  determine information about the task at the lowest level.

- Datadog

  The last monitoring system that I will mention in this section is
  Datadog. It is not an open source system, but it is impressive. It
  offers cluster-based monitoring, dashboard creation, and the
  ability to graph real-time data. It offers something that all of the
  other monitoring methods do not. It is able to create alerts and
  raise awareness of issues. This applies to both the cluster servers
  as well as the applications, like Mesos, running on the cluster. It
  will need significant configuration, but it will be a very useful tool.

I hope you can see a trend in the monitoring described in this section; while tracking
a problem, you will probably access all levels of the stack to find information sources.
Apart from Datadog, you might start at the Brooklyn or Cloud level and work your way
through the stack layers to raw data files or error logs.

The next section will examine visualisation.

Visualisation

In Chapter 9, I presented three visualisation options: Zeppelin, Grafana, and Datadog. I generally try to stay in the open source domain, but Datadog was impressive, and it was offered within DCOS. It provides a function that none of the other applications do: cluster-based monitoring and alerting.

The visualisation that you choose will depend on the type of data that you have and where it resides. For instance, Grafana has a limited number of integration data source options. Will you require real-time graphs and dashboards?

Last, how will you get your graphs and dashboards to your customers and management? Will you expect them to log into your cluster and application, or will they reside in a remote country and expect e-mailed pdf files?

Will the tool that you use need the ability to periodically refresh your graphs and dashboards, and will it be expandable by plug-ins? The Helium plug-in system offered by Zeppelin seems to be an interesting area to watch in the future.

You may use one of these tools or a future DCOS offering. I hope that the ideas raised in Chapter 9 will assist you in your choice of visualisation application and your creation of graphs.

The next section will briefly examine the choice of platform architecture.

Cloud or Cluster

I briefly raised the issue of how to choose the platform on which to build your distributed systems. I think that this is an area that requires much more investigation and metrics gathering. Perhaps it is a future project.

As I had previously mentioned, I think that the criteria for your choice of platform, be it cloud or physical cluster, needs to be considered at an early stage. Should it be price or some other criteria like security or perhaps reliability?

Remember that with big data systems, the data pool is going to grow over time and be substantial. It is likely that corporations will want to retain data for the future and build future service offerings against it. It would therefore be wise to consider what will happen to that data pool at system end of life. Many cloud-based service providers allow free deposit of data but charge to move data off of the service. These charges need to be considered when planning. They may impact the choice that this section describes.

Also, when creating cost models to compare a multiyear costing of a cloud-based system against a physical cluster, you are examining a multidimensional problem. No two examples will be the same due to different costs associated with hardware, personnel, taxes, location, and architecture. These are just a few attributes; there are many more.

I think that this subject needs to be examined at an early stage and thoroughly so that architectural platform choices are logical and can be defended metrically.

Conclusion

As I have already explained, there are many areas that could be examined in greater depth in relation to Mesos-based big data stacks: for instance, the use of Brooklyn with DCOS and cloud; the development of Brooklyn-based components to use both the DCOS CLI and the Marathon REST API; and the development of frameworks for Mesos that are designed to scale, provide status, and work with Brooklyn.

I have attempted to examine each element and layer within a Mesos-based big data stack and provide worked examples where possible. As with many of my books, I start with the least integrated solution and work toward integrated solutions. So, for instance, I have shown the use of Mesos on its own followed by DCOS. I hope that you can see that the more integrated solutions like DCOS are more functional, robust, and reliable.

Depending on your project needs, you may have to integrate systems outside of DCOS to create your wider systems. You would need to consider these areas at the outset of your project planning. Examine integration options, create new frameworks, use the Marathon API, or create a new Marathon application using JSON.

I hope that you find the building blocks and examples presented in these chapters useful. You should be able to expand on the work carried out here to create full-scale systems.

Having examined all of the Spark-based, cluster management, architectural options in this and my previous two books, I plan to tackle an AI (artificial intelligence) based book in the future. It will use the systems and architectures described in these books as well as visual ETL tools to source data as streams. It will then use AI techniques to examine the data. Given the scale of this project, the funding required, and the size of the cluster needed, I think I would need corporate sponsorship and group involvement.

However, this is a task for another year. I hope that you have enjoyed reading this book and found the examples useful. I find that as each book progresses, the projects that I undertake require more time, greater effort, and larger clusters. As ever I am happy to connect with people on LinkedIn at

nz.linkedin.com/pub/mike-frampton/20/630/385

Details of my books can be found on my author page on Amazon:

amazon.com/Michael-Frampton/e/B00NIQDOOM

And I can be contacted via e-mail at the following address:

info@semtech-solutions.co.nz

I may not have the time to tackle every problem, but it is interesting to hear about reader projects. Remember, try to solve your own problems and come up with a few suggestions as to the source of problems. If you just keep at it, anyone, given enough time, can solve any problem. Best Wishes.

Mike Frampton
November 2017

Index

© Michael Frampton 2018
M. Frampton, *Complete Guide to Open Source Big Data Stack*, https://doi.org/10.1007/978-1-4842-2149-5

C

Get the eBook for only $5!

Why limit yourself?

With most of our titles available in both PDF and ePUB format, you can access your content wherever and however you wish—on your PC, phone, tablet, or reader.

Since you've purchased this print book, we are happy to offer you the eBook for just $5.

To learn more, go to http://www.apress.com/companion or contact support@apress.com.

Apress®

Printed in the United States
By Bookmasters